If prophecies have any useful function at all, it is to reveal a glimpse of the future for examination now. In the case of a particularly fearful augury, we can ignore it or try to understand its practical implications. These would be: a) to warn, b) to prepare, and c) to provide an opportunity in the present for changing the future. The destiny of a nation can be modified by the collective free will of its people, and the fate of a planet can be changed by the collective free will of its nations. That is what the following prophecies all have in common …

Each of these of these prophecies originated in different times from a variety of diverse, respected, cultural traditions. Together they constitute a coherent, solid body of world prophecy relevant to our times. Different descriptions of the same picture are presented, but what emerges is a single prophecy, a single theme. Its message is clear and the conclusion unmistakable.

Let us then be warned. Let us also be prepared, and above all, let us realize this opportunity now to work together and influence destiny.

D1393244

PROPHECIES TO TAKE YOU
INTO THE 21ST CENTURY

Moira Timms

Thorsons
An Imprint of HarperCollins*Publishers*

Thorsons
An Imprint of HarperCollins*Publishers*
77–85 Fulham Palace Road,
Hammersmith, London W6 8JB

First published as *The Six O'Clock Bus*
Revised edition published as *Prophecies and Predictions*
by Unity Press 1980
Published by Ballantine Books, New York 1994
This edition published by Thorsons 1996
10 9 8 7 6 5 4 3 2

A catalogue record for this book
is available from the British Library

ISBN 0 7225 3337 3

Printed in Great Britain by
Caledonian International Book Manufacturing, Glasgow

DEDICATION

To Alan

Acknowledgements

It is with deep gratitude and love that I acknowledge my husband, Alan Stein, whose unconditional love, support, nurturance, patience and positive energy during a prolonged and difficult period have made this work possible.

Special acknowledgement and thanks to Ron Polsky for his generous role as computer guru and troubleshooter; to Graeme Jones for his sage insights, reflective wisdom, humour, and political astrology expertise; to Joel Brodksy for help with polar motion tracings and for composing the map of the ancient Middle East; to Keith Simons for the stimulating conversations that prompted me to research Babylonian prophecies, and for allowing me to access his research and international relations expertise in interpreting Nostradamus's prophecies relative to Middle Eastern events; to dear friend Christine Payne-Towler for generous assistance in fine-tuning points of scholarship, and for opening her library to me.

Heartfelt appreciation to my agent David Morgan for his faith in the book; to my editor Cheryl Woodruff for her sisterhood and flexibility; to Kristine Sohnrey for her early encouragement by transcribing the original book onto computer; to pyramidologist Michael Mooney for sharing his vision of the 'great step'; to Tom Tarbet for clarity and insight into the Hopi Way; to Douglas Robertson of the Geodetic Research and Development Laboratory of the

National Geodetic Research Survey for information on polar motion; to John Elvert, Director of the Lane Education Service District Planetarium; to Pam Rasmussen and Lorna McMurray for information about Meishu Sama's teachings; to Mayaist Barbara Master; to astrologer Dean Price; and to the staff of the Eugene Public Library's Reference Department for their helpfulness and cooperation.

Deep feelings of gratitude in memory of my dog Kit, who kept my heart open and my spirit attuned to the natural world; and to dear catmeister Zabionne for purrrrsonal assistance.

Contents

Introduction

In surfing circles, there's a term that relates to the towering megawaves unique to certain beaches in Hawaii and Australia. This term evokes adrenaline rush and Zenlike respect. It represents the ultimate challenge and demands the utmost skill. It's called 'the impact zone'.

What is the impact zone? How does one prepare for it? The impact zone is that instant in time and space when the wave crests at its climax. For the surfer, it is the space between synapses, the freeze-frame between neurons firing, when everything – stops. Thinking and the rational mind cease to exist. Body wisdom, impeccable reflexes, and raw instinct take over. One simply *acts*. In that transcendent instant is the seed of success or failure.

As surfers of the ultimate 'Big One' (what I really want to say is, THE BIG ONE) we are riding this wave together. I use the present tense, because we are already *on* this wave, rising to the occasion, fully engaged in an accelerating flood of change, an eschatological heave of epic proportions. As the substructure of our reality shifts, slipping away beneath us, we register the swell, the roar, the undertow that pulls us out to the deep. We are moving fast on a rising tide. Now dark below. Now bright above. Alert, together and tensing, we share its power, know its force. As the roaring wall of water rises before us and the wind-ripped foam tears white and deep beneath us, our collective instinct tells us – for we know it deeply – it's ... 'that time'.

When our moment of truth comes, in the impact zone, we must be in full resonance and synchronicity with the power of nature. The evolutionary force is always moving through us, embracing and transforming us within itself. It wants us to have a good time, play in the sun, respect the Earth, go surf a little. The ultimate wave, the 'Big One', is an inevitable, cyclical event within the natural evolutionary scheme. It is for those who, upon hearing the call, are ready to ride the wave to the next level.

When *Prophecies & Predictions* first appeared in 1980, its main purpose was to let people know that 'something's up'. Since then, important aspects of the prophecies of the Hopi, Nostradamus, Edgar Cayce, astrology, the Great Pyramid of Egypt, the Bible, among others presented here, have already come to pass. There is more on the way. What used to be the background hiss of denied crises now features loudly in the foreground – screaming for attention. Now we *can't* tune it out and it won't go away. We *must* deal with it. So, this revised edition will not need to send out those hundred monkeys again with all that information for the wake-up call – we know something's up; we've all *got* it now.'

But now that we've got it, what do we do with it? That is the challenge of the 1990s. And that is the challenge of *Prophecies and Predictions* this time around. How we respond to this challenge will determine the fate of humanity, and of the world itself. The 1990s *are our impact zone* – the most momentous decade in the history of the world.

Therefore, it is important to understand that current planetary crisis is a transitional aspect of an immense evolutionary turning point. The cosmological context within which world prophecy unfolds provides a coherent framework for understanding current world events and trends, and where they are leading. The synthesized prophecies in this book provide a timetable for the events agenda – which began in 1945 AD and is predicted to climax around 2012 AD.

In accordance with Maya calendric prophecy, this introduction is being written at the exact midpoint of a crucial
five-year period that will set the rudder and determine our
course as we move toward 2012 AD and humankind's apotheosis or nemesis. Unexpectedly, a synchronous confirma-
tion occurs as I write this – I have the experience of getting
up to review my source of Maya prophecy dates and am
taken aback to see the author of the 'Mayan Factor' José
Argüelles's words jump out at me: 'During this era
[1987–92] – the storm of transformation – the entire wave of
history crests. Maximum acceleration and random entropy
give way to ever-widening circles of synchronization.'

Therefore, the point needs to be clearly and forcefully
made that from this time on, the call is to *action*. It is the
Earth who calls. We ignore Her at our peril. We must recognize our common unity, stop participating in destructive
and defoliational lifestyles, and create a world that works
for everyone. We must speak for the Earth. We *are* the
Earth.

This book is my privileged opportunity to relay 'the call'.
'Surf's up!'
Pass it on ...

Moira Timms
Eugene, Oregon
October, 1993

PART ONE

Tools for the Journey

1

Cosmic Primer

Science is still divided in its opinion of how the universe originated, but on one thing there is agreement – that there is order in the universe. Webster defines 'order' as 'conformity to law,' and 'orderly' as 'well managed.' Just what is the order of the universe? We know that it does conform to law and that it certainly is well managed. What is the meaning of life? What is the nature of WoMan, of the universe? What's for dinner?

Ever since we became intelligent enough to ask these questions, they have intrigued each generation, and the answers are still unclear. One thing we can know, however, is that all manifestations of nature are governed by cosmic laws which are simple and immutable. Cosmic law is the common denominator of the shifting spectrum of physics versus metaphysics. Reality, as we understand it, is only what the majority (influenced by the whims of fashion and the growing edge of science) agrees upon at any given time. In perpetual motion, it changes from generation to generation. But set apart from all of that are seven first cause principles, or laws, which form the dynamic matrix of all existence.

We shall describe them a little as preface to the rest of the book so that we may share a common understanding of the elements upon which the subject is based. Individual belief systems, especially those pertaining to established theisms, are particularly difficult to reconcile, because each stubbornly stakes its claim to the ultimate truth. Therefore, if we can find common ground upon which to work collectively toward a more complete understanding of ourselves and our universe, we shall come much closer to the truth. The laws have always existed but somewhere along the way we decided to play by our own rules. Our free will has been allowed to weave the fabric of our present circumstances and it is the violation of these laws and indifference to their importance that has caused most of the trouble in the world today. It's time to get back on track. A new respect for and adherence to the laws, combined with a new responsibility for the way in which we exercise our free will, is what will determine our future.

Because the Christian tradition is familiar to Westerners, and readers may relate to that source more easily than to those of other cultures, biblical references have been drawn upon in many instances. However, it definitely is not the author's intention to promote any one religion's point of view, but rather to emphasize the similarity of many religious belief systems where truth is concerned, and to show that the divergence of the material world can be reconciled to the subtler world of spirit. A continuum exists. Physics and metaphysics are different stages of the one science.

Each of the following Laws is an aspect of that primal energy in which absolutely everything we can name (and even those things we cannot) evolves and has its being. Just as Deity can only be interpreted in terms of attributes, these laws defy exclusive definition and must be described by arbitrary illustration, as they mix and merge with each other.

The Law of Mentalism

In a nutshell: 'All is mind.'

The universe is a manifestation of divine consciousness, infinite mind, say the cosmologies of the world's major cultures. Hinduism describes the mind of the Creator as the ultimate reality, and the physical universe as only relatively real – a dream within the Creator's mind. In order to explain an infinite process with a finite example, hermetic teachings compare Creator and creation to the process of an artist who becomes so wrapped/rapt up in the mental process of creating that the separative sense of self temporarily dissolves and becomes absorbed into and identified with the creation.

The Law of Mentalism describes the creative force of thought, from which all things, events, and words first take seed. Thoughts are the underlying, causative principle and resource from which humans create reality. The popular notion that 'you create your own reality,' although true in the ultimate sense, is generally interpreted as if it were simply a matter of putting one's mind to it, or as if we had complete conscious mastery over the process. (If we actually had that, it is doubtful that we would even need to be here on the physical plane.) However, a fundamentalist version exists for literalists. A video technology called 'virtual reality' allows users the illusion of whole-body participation in three-dimensional reality simulations of their own creation. One can't help but wonder if this is how God started out as a teenager.

'You are *responsible* for, or *affect* your own reality' is more accurate, because at the average level of consciousness, things tend to happen more by default than by design, and more from reaction than action. The reason you don't get to vote on the way life is, is because – at the personal preconscious level, or that of the collective unconscious – you already did! While 'awakened' (i.e., enlightened) consciousness permits one to consciously create one's reality, the average state of 'waking' consciousness is actually more like a danger zone where the creative process is unconscious and out of control. Freight cars of the mind, cargo-laden with emotionally charged thoughts and feelings, careen subliminally through the stations of our mind. The stream of consciousness gushes forth unceasingly in what the meditation masters call 'chatter in the skull'. Meditation is a way to still the mind, tame the thoughts, relax the emotions, heal the body, and change the world.

So, you're waiting for an incentive? Along the path to the mastery that empowers us to *effectively* create our own reality, other abilities of the mind unfold, which, although they may seem miraculous, are but the budding of a much greater mental potential – a potential that, by all accounts, is infinite.

Years ago, Uri Geller, the Israeli psychic, astounded audiences and scientific researchers by using mental energy to bend metal, to stop or start timepieces, and so on. One would like to believe there are more creative ways of using this energy, but, in the meantime, he demonstrated extended capabilities of the mind. After one television appearance, the station's lines were flooded by calls from parents whose children were suddenly able to duplicate the phenomenon they had just seen. This led to the theory that children between the ages of seven and ten are psychically receptive and have not yet developed the screening mechanism of self-imposed limits about what is, or is not, possible. The Universities of London and South Africa recognized a new frontier for academia, and subsequently began programmes to study such children.

We have all experienced mind over matter to some extent; and, one hopes to a lesser degree, its opposite, in the form of psychosomatic illness. Not so long ago, only advanced yogis knew how to control bodily functions with the mind. To do so was considered a 'siddhi' (miraculous power). Today, ordinary people are learning similar mental techniques. Biofeedback, which electronically monitors the body's responses in relation to altered states of consciousness, has shown that as thoughts decrease, the mind becomes calmer, and remarkable success has been experienced in 'uncreating' symptoms and stress. It is even scientifically verified that creatively visualizing desired results can measurably enhance success in business, athletics, learning ability, recovery from surgery, and healing in general.

Eastern philosophy teaches that our thoughts are influenced and our minds shaped by the impressions we receive from the outside world through our five senses. It is these impressions that create seed patterns for thought. Our thoughts give rise to our words. The words we speak are connected to what we then do. And the things we do become the actions that define who we are, and that shape our world. On all levels, in every facet of life, the battle for a fair market share of your mind is raging. As my old guru used to say, 'Junk in, junk out! Master your mind. The future is mental. Deal with it!'

The continuously negotiable contract of reality that we call the 'Big Picture' has been painted by numbers – changing numbers composed of group agreements. Like the intricate sand paintings painstakingly constructed by Navajo shamans to focus healing energies, or the Buddhist sand mandalas of the cosmos meditatively created for ritual empowerments only to be obliterated when their purpose has been served, the Big Picture, as we know it, will either be transformed or self-destruct – soon.

Indigenous native peoples speak of 'the mind within nature' who is being and becoming, meaning and possibility. They strive, in the face of Western encroachment, to heed the rhythms of the Earth and the ways of the wild that weave them into the network of life and the threads of the web. They see how we are tearing the web, and tell us that 'the changing of the worlds' is close. And they exhort us, urgently, to revise our conception of reality before it is too late.

Whatever the future holds, you can be sure that it lies not within the domain of science or technology (which, according to interpretation of the Maya calendar, climaxed in 1987), but within the rapidly expanding dimensions of the mind – universal mind, Gaian mind, and our mind. It's all mind, and we're it.

Understanding the Law of Mentalism helps us to see the Big Picture, to claim and own it. Doing this, we enter psychological space within the luminosity of our highest collective consciousness. This is the place from which conscious and responsible transformation of the Big Picture is happening, the place from which the resacralization of the planet and a world that works for everyone is being cocreated. We're not sure what the transformed Big Picture will look like, but we know how it will feel.

It will feel like Home.

'Be not conformed to this world; but be ye transformed by the renewing of your mind ...'
(Romans 12:2)

The Law of Vibration

This Law states that nothing rests; that the universe, and every thing else that exists, is in motion.

After the Creator conceived the idea of the universe, he willed and spoke it into existence. 'In the beginning was the Word ...' (John 1:1). Sound is vibration. Vibration is sound. Words are the prime organizing vibration/sound of consciously directed thought. 'And God said, "Let there be light." And there was light.' (Genesis 1:3).

The spoken word is a vehicle of power, giving form and expression to thought. If you do not want something to become a reality, don't verbalize it; for, by so doing, you set in motion the vibrations, the forces, that create circumstances. Words clothe a thought with a matrix of vibration, amplifying and easing it out into the physical world of matter and action. Floating there like a tangible echo, this bubble of spoken thought has an inherent creative and magnetic quality.

Many people creating and sharing the same vibrations generate a force field of energy. This is the power of music, singing and chanting to unify hearts and minds, to heal, inspire, and celebrate. And we are told that a *kiai* (a fighting cry used in Japanese martial arts) uttered in a minor key can effect partial paralysis of one's opponent by abruptly lowering the arterial blood pressure.

Vibration, however, is more than just the narrow sound band audible to the human ear. From *A* for 'alternate' to Z for 'zigzag' and all the shake, rattle, and roll in between, everything vibrates as frequency, sound, and temperature. Rocks, insects, plants, and people differ from each other, and everything else, because of their unique vibrational frequency and energy pattern.

We know that subtle matter, once believed to be composed of finite particles, is now identified as a wave-form process. British scientist Michael Faraday first conceived the electromagnetic field as the lowest element of physical reality, and now this invisible principle of nonlinear bonding is recognized by science as 'resonance'. Each molecule of the body is held in place, keeping its relationship to all the others, because of its programmed resonant frequency. A tuning fork, pitched to a certain note – just like a smile, a yawn, or anger – will cause other objects of the same frequency, with which it comes in contact, to resonate. In this sense, like attracts like, and objects of disparate vibration gravitate to their own frequency as they are held in orbit around their common principle, the resonance factor. On a human level, it is love that is the creative force and cohesive element. Without it, we become isolated and out of harmony with others. Using this model, it is easy to see how individuals, held together by a common positive goal and rightly motivated, can, like the wave-form, transform others around them. A wave of dissonance can generate destructive force to the same power.

I CHING:Pi/Holding Together

Water flows to unite with water because all parts of it are subject … to the same laws. So too should human society hold together through a community of interests that allows each individual to feel him/herself a part of the whole.

The molecules of an ice cube vibrate faster when it is heated, and transform it into water, and then vapour. It changes form as a result of melting and then evaporation, which is simply the excitation of its molecules to a faster dance. None of us questions this, and yet some people cannot understand that matter itself is a condensation of an energy which is usually referred to as spirit; a state to which it eventually returns by way of evolution.

Expanding one's consciousness (like increasing the light in a dark room) and raising one's vibration are synonymous. Yoga, meditation, breathing exercises, pure diet, body work, and so on, help cleanse mind and body of the impurities that keep it gross. Likewise, dealing with one's inner issues, past trauma, and old habit patterns is part of what it takes to unload the ballast of the past, and prepares one to receive more light and function at a higher vibratory rate (frequency).

The link between particle physics, relativity, and human consciousness is now within the purview of science. According to physicist David Finkelstein of New York's Yeshiva University, 'The way has been prepared to turn over the structure of present physics to consider space, time and mass as illusions in the same way that temperature is only a sensory illusion.' The wisdom traditions agree. Meanwhile, Dr Timothy Leary, in his work of inner research, *Neurologic,* declares, 'The neurological transformation [of these formulae] substitutes number of neurons firing per second as the velocity factor in the relativity formula.' Similarly, the Carlos Castaneda books on becoming a 'person of knowledge' speak of increasing one's 'speed'. The message seems to be that in order to attain the breakthrough from ordinary consciousness as we know it to that of direct perception of reality, or self-realization, one must cultivate within one's self the microcosmic equivalent of the macrocosmic speed of light! That's the complex version! The simple one is that the more focused the attention, the calmer the mind, and the slower the brain waves (all very stress-reducing and achievable by meditation), the closer one's approach to higher spiritual vibration and ultimate transcendence is likely to be. In other words, the higher the vibration of human consciousness, the more time and space condense.

Get it? We are living in a time period when the vibration of human consciousness is increasing. This means that our innate knowingness and intelligence of the heart are coming to the fore. And, since inner and outer worlds are reflections of each other, this means that the rate at which matter (i.e., the physical plane) vibrates is also changing. And, as the following chapters explain, this phenomenon is intricately involved with the changes the world is now experiencing – changes that are the stuff of prophecy.

Understanding the Law of Vibration opens up the lens of perception. Zooming-in to the vibrating 'print dots' of the Big Picture magnifies our worldview and sense of common unity. Every picture (reality construct) may look different, but beneath it all, they each comprise the same print dots. The Big Picture is created by Divine Mind extruding itself, as spirit, into the grosser energy vibration of matter. So, the 'truth of the matter' is that we are spirit having a human experience, rather than humans trying to have a spiritual one.

'If you're Spirit and you know it, clap your hands …'

The Law of Polarity

This Law expresses the dual nature of things. As the Creator spoke the universe into existence, the Law of Polarity came with the territory and piggybacked in on the vibrations – because vibration creates polarity (i.e., opposite movement).

The physical world comes packaged in pairs of polar opposites to ensure that we recognize reality when it shows up. The stuff of the physical world is defined by, and takes identity from, that which it is not – its antipode. Only then can it be apprehended or wrapped in language.

The universal flow and interplay of opposing yet complementary extremes is known to Asian cultures as 'Yin and Yang'. We tend to describe the 'either/or,' 'this-and-that' ness of the world in terms of positive/negative, male/ female, etc. All of creation – its forces, energies, and matter – animate and inanimate, is based upon this principle of gender and opposites.

At the personal level, however, we often are confused or judgmental about the polarities we encounter. Polarities are so named because they *appear* finite, like the opposite ends of a pole. But viewed from a broader perspective, one finds that opposites are identical in nature but different in degree; that extremes meet; that all truths are but half truths.

Consciousness of reality is something like a small night light in a huge, dark room. As the wattage of the light bulb is increased, more of the room can be seen in detail. The room itself never changes, only the observable reality, according to the intensity of the light. Things are seldom as simple as they seem when they appear in stark contradiction.

Unless something is experienced first, its opposite is not recognizable. The 'good' in life depends for its very existence upon its polar opposite, 'evil'. (Interestingly, evil is 'live' spelled backwards.) It is the depth that determines the height; if the valleys filled up, the mountains would disappear! Without darkness there would be no light – or colour. Since there is no order without chaos, joy without sorrow, success without failure, wisdom without ignorance, and so forth, these extremes are the illusions that facilitate our experiential existence. They provide us with a necessary frame of reference, without which we literally 'would not know which end is up'. But as each of us moves toward greater wholeness, we begin to understand this Law without letting it limit or hem us in.

No two ways about it – all opposites are poles of the *same thing,* with many degrees between the two extremes. There is no ceiling or absolute degree of sad, low, cold, or soft, and no ultimate measure of their opposite extremes, happy, high, hot, or hard; it's all relative. The balance between extremes is somewhere around the midpoint, where the difference is comfortable or imperceptible. The hard knocks we receive from bouncing like a pinball between life's extremes, beyond the outer limits of our comfort zone, are our greatest teachers. They let us know when we're off course, teach us discrimination, stretch our abilities and capacities. All antagonisms are complementary and ultimately serve life's purpose.

The separation and fragmentation of life into aspects of good and bad varies between individuals and cultures and changes with historical perspective. Judgments like 'good' and 'bad' may be resolved in the wise and compassionate light of greater understanding. There are no fixed polar extremes, only reality, which changes according to natural rhythms and the fallible nature of human perception. If life is approached with flexibility and sensitive awareness, rather than rigidity and blind faith, it becomes apparent that fear and ignorance incline us toward suffering, while love

and awareness draw us toward wholeness, i.e., happiness, or the 'good'. By increasing the light of our awareness and understanding we can dissolve ignorance and penetrate the illusions that bind us.

Let us be mindful that even Truth has two poles – the absolute and the relative. The two often are confused, which is why so many half truths obscure the Big Picture. Understanding the Law of Polarity, we learn the ways of harmony and the paths between extremes. This fosters our spiritual growth, saving us from myopia and the onesided view. It reminds us to keep both eyes open so we can see more of the Big Picture.

The Law of Karma

'What goes around comes around' describes the Law of Karma. 'Karma' is the Sanskrit (ancient language of India) word for action. This Law refers to action and the effects of action, cause and effect, which bring about cosmic justice.

The word 'karma' usually carries a negative connotation, because when we violate the natural order of things, some form of distortion or confusion is always the result. Good karma passes unnoticed most of the time, or disguised as good luck, because it is a continuation of the harmony in our lives. 'Luck' never hits a random target, but we would certainly experience more of it if we understood natural law better, and how to integrate it into our lives.

Several kinds of karma are common to everyone: personal, family, national and planetary, and each of us is responsible for all of them in varying degrees. Dues have to be paid when a lesson of life remains unlearned. There are three ways to pay off karma – through grace, service, or pain and suffering. The prime historical example of all of this is that, as a gift of grace, Jesus as avatar (divine incarnation who comes to serve humanity) redeemed the negative karma of humanity through His death.

Grace is divine dispensation that waives the payment of karmic debts. It is earned by committing one's life to truth, love, and integrity, no matter what. And it is earned by service; not by going through the motions, but rendered from the heart, through true empathy and compassion. The old adage, 'Now is the time for all good people to come to the aid of the party' – *in service,* we would add – has never been more true. The fate of our planet depends upon it. The years remaining to the end of the century represent the climax of the prophecy cycle. The immediate future is the time frame recognized by the world's major spiritual traditions as the culmination of planetary karma.

Edgar Cayce, the American prophet, had some interesting things to say about this Law: 'In the last analysis, it must be realized that all karma is mind-created. An error of conduct arises from an error of consciousness. Hence, unless a person can understand his own mental relationship to creative energy, he can not hope to redeem his negative karma. Man constantly meets himself. 'Do good' then, as He said, 'to those who have despitefully used you' and you overcome then in yourself what you have done to your fellow-man.'

Understanding the Law of Karma puts you in the driver's seat. 'Keeping your karma clean' means being responsible for the effects you create, honouring agreements, keeping commitments, not cutting corners or compromising your integrity. Above all, it is through service and action that we reduce karma and restore resolution to the Big Picture.

The Law of Rhythm

Rhythm is the measured motion that occurs between the two poles established by the Law of Polarity. The universe, and everything in it, is rhythmic. Life itself is a rhythmic process, full of periodicities, repetition and recurrent cycles.

Rhythm is organized vibration. Rhythm is to melody what vibration is to musical notes. Similarly, as the atoms and molecules within our cells vibrate in harmony with the larger rhythms of the body, so, too, the rhythms of the body harmonically mirror the cycles of the cosmos and celestial spheres. All too often, however, our natural rhythms are disturbed by the unnatural effects of technology or lifestyle.

Electromagnetic fields disrupt normal body rhythms. The psychophysical effects on people from power lines, ceiling heat, computers, office machines, fluorescent lights, colour TV, etc., is the subject of growing concern and research. And if you've ever experienced jet lag, you know how long distance travel can disrupt your eating and sleeping cycles. When the natural rhythms of our bodies or those of the planet are disturbed or out of phase, we begin to lose our patterns of meaning, and chaos sets in. When this happens to growing cells, cancer results. In growing cities, you get Los Angeles, Benares, or Rio. Globally, it becomes what the Hopi call 'Koyaanisqatsi' – 'world out of balance.' Rhythm is the very pulse of life. In the healing rituals of many indigenous peoples, drumbeats are paced to the sick body's rhythms. By gradually adjusting the beat to that of the optimum life force, the 'dis-ease' or imbalance can be normalized. Sickness can also be avoided by adjusting lifestyles to honour the rhythms of our bodies and the natural world.

Our daily biological timing mechanisms (circadian rhythms) are entrained by the rotational light/darkness cycles of the Sun. Other biorhythms are apparent in our twenty-three-day physical energy cycle; the twenty-eight-day cycle governing emotions; and a thirty-three-day cycle related to intellect and mental ability. The natural female menstrual event is synchronized to the monthly lunar cycle. And the major life change experienced by most people around age thirty is astrologically significant of Saturn's orbital return to the position it occupied at one's time of birth.

An infinite combination of natural rhythms and cosmic timing frequencies influence life on Earth – day/night, lunar phases, sunspot cycles, planetary movements, the monthly influences of the zodiac and the great astrological ages. The seasons of our solar year, and the seasons of the Great Year are represented by the 26,000-year cycle known as the pre-cession of the equinoxes. The seasons of this Great Year

IT'S PLAYING ITSELF AGAIN, SAM!

Brahma,
in breathing world conceiving.
  Brahma exhales and the world
    issues out in a shower of ...
      stars.
    and when the Great One sleeps
   our world becomes
  quiescent
translucently suspended within the
  void,
    within the cosmic bubble of
    consciousness.
      circadian rhythms um-
       bilically tie
      pulsating flesh to time
    tables of the sky.
    expanding and contracting,
liquid life-force
  around the freeways of our free
   form flowing ...
    ebb and flow
     in breath
     reflecting
    tide rhythms and

    small rockpools
    awash.
   new cells: regeneration
every seven years.
  the cycles of celestial spheres
  needlepoint the heaven.
   changing faces of the
    moon and
   sunspots each eleven.
   precession of the equinoxes.,
  a tilting wheel
of twenty six thousand
earth years.
 around its mighty centre
  slowly turning ...
  like galaxy yawns
  silently digesting
   eons
   within its centre point.
  two hundred million years
  round trip
 repeating itself
eternally ...
and again

                Moira Timms

bring recurring, predictable kinds of evolutionary change to our planet. These changes are the surges upon which civilizations rise and fall. The Great Year is the prophecy wheel, the monitor of time, the central core of world mythology – and the backbone of this book.

According to philosopher Alan Watts, 'whatever we experience as existing, as continuing in time, is not so much persistent stuff as repetitive rhythm or vibration.' The still frames of a film reel are accelerated to form the illusion of movement. In the same sense, light is both particle and wave ('wavicle'). The entire universe can be defined in terms of vibrations, rhythms and waves; a sequence of structured phases implicit in every process.

The oneness of creation, in its continual expansion, is always manifesting perfectly in divisions of itself, and this creates two basic forces – expansion (centrifugality) and contraction (centripetality). This echoes again the Law of Polarity, Yin and Yang, which describes the shifting forces that complement yet repel each other, that merge and transmute in continual spirals of power and inertia. Likewise, on/off, in/out, hot/cold, day/night, etc., are not really pulsating contradictions, but aspects of the time-space continuum we call reality. It is cyclical, like a wave, but periodic in its separation from the whole. Time is the moving face of eternity, and you are right in the centre of it.

Part of what it means to be in the final phase of the prophecy cycle is that the way in which we perceive and experience time is changing. Time is the holding pattern of the Big Picture. Like chaos theory, which indicates that maximum chaos synchronizes into order, the wavelike rhythm of time's cyclicality and the periodicity of its separation are also in the process of synchronizing. This means that time is about to do something rare, epochal, and incredibly special – like *CREST*...

Understanding the Law of Rhythm helps one hear the base rhythm of harmony amidst increasing dissonance. It lets you know when a chord change is coming up, or when the Big Picture is about to be radically transformed.

The Law of 'As Above, So Below'

That which is above is like that which is below
– Hermes Trismegistus

The same systems and organizing principles govern both macrocosm and microcosm. In the miniature solar system of the atom, for example, we see electrons spiralling the nucleus like planets around the sun.

The world's wisdom traditions teach that everything is within us, that universe and self reflect each other. Inner and outer, above and below, converge within the individual. The centre of the universe is everywhere; as well as within you. This model of human as transformer, human as traffic monitor at the universal crossroads of eternity, we call the holographic model.

Hebraic, Greek and biblical texts tell us that human beings are made in the 'image and similitude' of the divine, and that the body is the temple of the spirit. To historic cultures, the temple was also the body of the spirit. In the sacred architecture of ancient Egypt and India, as well as medieval Europe and Italy, temples and churches were constructed in the proportions of the human body (the inner sanctum representing the centre of the forehead) to provide, not just a house for the deity, but a physical body within which the deity literally could dwell. Rituals and observances matched the movement of the stars and the turning of the seasons. Thus were planting, harvests, fertility cycles, and human affairs paced within the year. Astronomy and astrology were closely linked in fact and function. Through their religious science and architecture, the ancients sought to unite themselves, literally as well as symbolically, with the forces of heaven and Earth.

Many neolithic burial mounds were stone-lined, womb-shaped chambers, constructed half above and half below ground. Several of the mounds in southwest England were built directly over a ley line (subterranean energy channel), energizing the space from below. (Some of Britain's mysterious 'crop circles' are located close to these burial mounds and aligned on the same ley lines that run through the mounds.) The top covering was of earth and alternating layers of organic material, generating orgone energy (life force) from above. The positioning of these mounts was such that at equinoxes or solstices, the rays of the sun penetrated directly into the tomb. Father Sun thus fertilized Mother Earth, and the spirit of the deceased within the tomb could be revivified. Whether or not these mounds, like the Great Pyramid, functioned as burial *and* initiation chambers, or as root cellars, we do not know. But it is very clear that the builders were sophisticated in their knowledge and ability to integrate the energies of heaven and Earth, and that they not only understood the Law of 'As Above, So Below,' but made it work for them in ways that we are only beginning to appreciate.

In ancient Greece, human psychological archetypes were embodied by the planets and constellations as gods and goddesses, heroes and heroines, and incorporated into stories and complex celestial mythology. In the Eastern philosophies of Taoism and Confucianism, the five-element theory correlates the planets with the organs of the body. Astrology deals with the positions and aspects of celestial bodies and their influence on human affairs. The twelve signs of the zodiac are a blueprint of the universe, as well as of the individual, containing in essence the totality of all possible experience. Each zodiacal sign represents the external and internal part of the human body, and its function. (Aries, for example, as first sign of the zodiac, governs the head and brain and the function of ideation. Libra, sign of balance and sixth of the twelve signs, represents the lower back, the kidneys and harmonization. Pisces, the last sign, deals with the feet, the liver, and lymphatics, and the function of dissolution.)

At this time when science and prophecy are basically in agreement about many geophysical, environmental, and economic aspects of the future, science has risen to the occasion and acknowledged that our planet meets basic criteria that establish it as a living system. Our self-regulating, self-maintaining, self-repairing planet has been reacknowledged as a living being, and named, appropriately, after the Greek Earth goddess – Gaia. To indigenous peoples, this was not news. The planet had always been Mother Earth, and the natural world, suffused with a sense of the sacred, was her living body. Native people say, 'When the flesh grows old, it begins to resemble the Earth.'

The Law of 'As Above, So Below' shows us that the Big Picture is but a reflection of the small picture – the one we see when we look in the mirror.

The Law of Correspondence

This Law says that everything is interdependent and participates in the integrity of the whole.

In relation to nature, we speak of this concept as ecology: the study of the interrelationships between organisms and environment. The web of life sustains all things in its fragile balance. The violation of natural law leads to imbalances that create more and still more imbalances in an attempt to maintain a working harmony. Disruption or extinction of one form calls for adjustment and compensation by all forms.

Relating the Law of Correspondence to the experiences of life means cultivating the facility of overview. This way we can understand the wholeness of things and fill in the details later. Predicating life entirely upon the demand for facts, scientific proof and economic value has brought our culture to its present predicament. And, individually, we find ourselves perplexed, confused, seriously insecure and surrounded by failing systems.

The cultural paradigm of the last few centuries has been one of separation, analysis and fragmentation. We experienced ourselves as separate from each other and nature, and have not understood whole-systems thinking. But we are now beginning to recognize that nothing stands alone; that every apparent separation is like a semipermeable membrane capable of osmosis; an interface. Within our bodies, osmosis maintains equilibrium through the free flow and exchange of excess and inadequate energies, nourishment and waste. This mechanism is consistent on every level of life. Socially, blocked or congested energies become the symptoms of hate, separation, unrest, scarcity, etc., which touch our lives daily. Blocked impurities on the cellular scale create organ malfunction and sickness of the body. The most subtle energies are the first to become congested, beginning within ourselves and radiating like pool ripples, to the external environment. The state of the world is both wonderful and terrible – a very real magnification of our collective inner state.

Even at the outermost reaches of space, osmosis seems to occur. If our universe is expanding, what are the ones next to us doing? Are galaxies separated by the osmotic membranes of space? Black holes in deep space are invisible, but, like cosmic vacuum cleaners, they suck up any stellar material in their vicinity. Where does this material go? And what about the inevitable white holes? Intense amounts of energy and radiation emanate from distant quasars centred in other galaxies and our own Milky Way. Their energy output versus distance from the Earth is something of a paradox, greater than can be accounted for by any known methodology of science. To astronomers, this indicates white hole phenomena where energy sweeps in ... presumably, from other universes. Our black holes would be their white holes, and vice versa. Thus, the flow of starstuff between universes is kept in balance.

The quality of daily life cannot be removed from the arena of nature, although for the past 150 years (specifically, since the advent of the industrial revolution), we've been trying hard to do just that. Our impact upon the planet has irrevocably tilted the dynamic balance of nature in our favour, and now we must deal with the consequences. In the very beginning, God apparently said, 'Be fruitful, and multiply, and replenish the earth, and subdue it: and have dominion over the fish of the sea, and over the fowl of the air, and over every living thing that moveth upon the earth' (Genesis 1:28) and, sure enough, we did! The problem is, we just haven't wanted to stop.

The Law of Correspondence is well illustrated by indigenous native cultures whose consciousness, although centred in their head, is not confined to it. It extends into the environment, psychically blending inner and outer worlds as aspects of whole consciousness. Such diffusion of consciousness seems to render competition and individuality less important than the interdependence that makes the community a healthy unit. And the safety and well-being of seven future generations is factored into all decision-making. Owing to our reality construct, Western consciousness is 'confined to quarters' *within* the head – a limited view of reality through

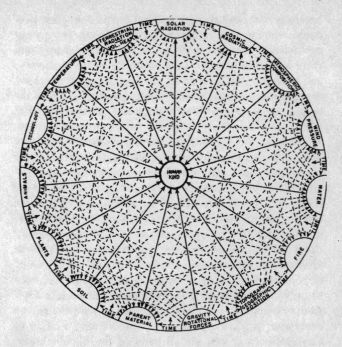

A holocoenotic environmental complex. Solid lines show factor-humankind relationships. Dashed lines show relations between factors. Arrowheads show the general direction of the effect. If the effect is reciprocal, arrowheads are placed at both ends of the line. [Adapted from W. D. Billings, 'The Environmental Complex in Relation to Plant Growth and Distribution', Quarterly Review of Biology, 27:251–264 (1952).]

very small windows. Consequently, the boundaries between self and other, self and environment, are pronounced. By objectifying, controlling and demystifying the external world, the dominant scientific paradigm has reinforced the ancient barricade between order and chaos – in this case, quantifiable versus unquantifiable reality. This modern version of the primordial human fear that order must be fortified against the ever-present threat of annihilation by chaos is why bombs are stockpiled; why political regimes suppress freedoms; why our shadow gets projected onto others; why our ego defences alienate others; and why we resist change. But there was a Big Bang (or loud 'Word'?), and the universe is still expanding. So, in spite of, and because of, all the chaos, we continue to evolve and grow, gradually dilating the boundaries of the ego self into the greater collective Self of all life.

The Law of Correspondence accommodates the paradox of both separation and unity. It allows us to move in the surety that 'both and' is a better formula than 'either/or,' and that we are all connected and more similar than we are different. The Native American affirmation, 'Mitakuye Ouasin,' which means 'To all our relations,' the Maya greeting 'In Lak'ech,' which translates as 'I am another yourself,' the Asian salutation 'Namaste,' which means 'I bow to the God within you,' and the Egyptian 'Ua Hua,' 'We are One,' all convey a sense of what it means to exchange the currency of unified consciousness. The American 'Have a nice day!' sounds more like a greeting card, but is, nevertheless, an expression of good will. When you understand the Law of Correspondence, you see all parts of the Big Picture as equally valid because they are all part of yourSelf.

And Spirals

Being great, it passes on;
Passing on, it becomes remote;
Having become remote, it returns.

＿ Lao Tsu, describing the Tao

A spiral is a symbol of eternity – a spherical vortex or vortical funnel, the centre and circumference of which are perpetually alternating. While all manifestations are governed by the ordering principles of the seven Laws described above, they move within time in spiral patterns. Spiral forms are the shape of energy in motion as it evolves order from chaos. This occurs in harmonically repeating cycles of creation, expansion, and growth; decline, contraction and destruction.

According to philosopher Michio Kushi, 'Because the laws of change are the order of the universe, electrons may slowly spiral towards the nuclei of their atoms and change into protons. In a like manner, we may imagine our sun to be the melting point of a solar spiral in which comets change into planets and planets eventually refuel the sun.'

Some galaxies are spirals, as are cloud formations and weather patterns photographed from high altitudes. The wind itself, cyclones, hurricanes and tornadoes are also spirals. Even water, as it flows down a drain, swirls away spirally. Crystals are formed from molecular spirals. And then there are the biological spirals of fingerprints and hair growth patterns, in addition to those of living cells, protein molecules, and that tiniest seed of intelligence, the helix of the DNA.

The centrifugal spiral (counterclockwise, expansive) creates disbursement and separation. The centripetal (clockwise, contractive) spiral of natural things has the cohesive force of uniting and drawing together – holding from the centre. The One that became the many is again becoming the One. This is the gathering of the sparks. The latter part of the twentieth century is identified as a particular turning point of history emphasized by the Maya calendar, prophecied by the world's major cultural traditions, articulated by the visionaries of science, and strongly felt within the inner knowingness of vast numbers of ordinary people.

It is the progressive, repetitious nature of cycles that creates spirals – different each time around, but with the same patterns of meaning. Not understanding the cyclical nature of time, we have thought of history as a linear progression, the 'march of time'. Owing to its patriarchal nature, Western culture has unfolded along very yang lines (the positive, masculine principal of nature characterized by direct energy and straight lines), monopolized by intellect, science, technology and materialistic focus – all of which are yang attributes.

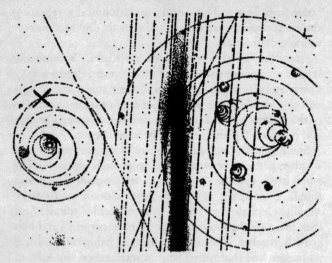

Electron tracks in a bubble chamber.

Within this male dominator model of culture, 'national defence' has supported the phallacy that draining a nation's budget to erect as many warheads as possible meant security. A feminized definition of culture is one of relationship and interdependence, and a redefinition of 'national defence' would broaden it to include defence of Mother Earth – her resources, species and biosphere, and social programmes for the true needs of her people. In the United States, the early stages of the Clinton/Gore administration have held this promise of healthy change and inspired vision; a drive to 'get back on track' with right action and appropriate priorities.

Philosophically speaking, masculine energy is like the sun, which appears to move across the sky in a linear direction. Yin, or feminine, energy is cyclical like the moon, and revolves around the sun. And perhaps this model was, historically, partly responsible for women's passive 'satellite' role. On a global level, the women's movement is vital because its ultimate function is to yin up the planet sufficiently to create the necessary pro-evolutionary synergy of balanced male and female energies.

The picture of electron tracks in a bubble chamber shows a direct analogy of this dynamic and integrative process. Male particles, seen as linear, positive energy tracks, collide with female, negative particles moving in circular paths. From this conjugation a spiral is born inheriting the forward thrust of the line while maintaining the conserving principle of the circle. Clearly, such a union in human affairs is desirable. Balance and harmony begin with our concepts.

We are challenged by a rite of passage into the twenty-first century as our world approaches the centre of an evolutionary spiral, one that will culminate in a new direction for human development. 'Forward march!' is being replaced by 'Onward flow …'

The Big Picture is about to change … It's show time!

Please stand by …

PART TWO

Outward Bound

2

A Different Theory of Evolution

> But the natural man receiveth not the things of the spirit
> of God, for they are foolishness to him; neither can he
> know them because they are spiritually discerned.
>
> (1 Corinthians 2:14)

A different theory … isn't that what has prefaced all major
scientific breakthroughs and inventions throughout history? We discover a set of rules, formulae, or theories that
apply and serve a purpose, and then discover that they must
be modified or changed in order for us to progress further.
It would seem that laws of logic are inviolate, yet they can,
on occasion, be eclipsed by others that supersede them. The
higher principles govern the lower ones and foster the progression of human knowledge. One thing is certain, however: understanding the higher laws makes the lesser ones
easier to deal with.

For instance, simple arithmetic formulas work fine until
the need for more complex computations poses a problem.
Then one can turn to calculus, or computers. The flat-world
theory was OK, too, until men's curiosity drew them to the
known edges of the world. They must have thought it
incredible that the world gradually became round to accommodate their quest for new lands. Later, it seemed impossible for a plane to fly faster than the speed of sound, because
as the craft approached the necessary speed it would dive

out of control. Finally, contrary to the logic of such an emergency, one test pilot accidentally reversed the 'joy stick' while in the spin, and found that it brought the plane out of its dive and penetrated the sound barrier in the process.

A synopsis of the alternative theory of evolution is presented here in brief outline as just such a case. Because of evolutionary dictates and the momentum of human energy patterns like politics, technology, economics and the material needs of civilization today, the progression of world events cannot be altogether avoided. However, positive changes in the mass consciousness and constructive actions can lessen or modify the intensity of the planetary karma and avert much catastrophe.

If the chapters that follow are disturbing, they also show that taking full responsibility for one's individual life and actions will enable us collectively to 'pull out of our spin'.

At this time in the twentieth century, humankind approaches the end of a minor cycle: the passing from the Age of Pisces to the Age of Aquarius. Events between now and the early part of the next century will be most transformational and prepare us all for the culmination of a major cycle, which is the precession of the equinoxes. These two cycles happen to coincide with the repolarization point of a final cycle of human history, the end of the *Yuga*. So, with three cosmic cycles (explained later) about to be completed, you can be sure we are in for a period of heavy changes. In order to be clearer about what all this means, let us go back to the beginning (an arbitrary definition) and see how it all started.

The evolution of cosmic time is divided into world Ages known in the Hindu tradition as *Yugas*. At the end of each *Yuga*, there occurs a phenomenon known as 'the progression of the life waves', or the graduation from the Earth plane of all human souls in existence during a given *Yuga*. All of us here now are at varying stages of our own personal unfoldment, but we're all part of the same life wave.

This, the *Kali Yuga, is* the most negative of all the cycles. There is very little perception of the true nature of reality, and chronic ignorance of the Law (i.e., cosmic, natural, or divine law) seems to be humanity's natural state. However, because all things eventually come full circle (or, more correctly, full spiral), and we now approach the closing phase of the *Yuga,* a human and planetary transition between the old age of darkness and the new upswing of consciousness toward the New Age of light is coming about. It is sometimes called the Golden Age. With this passage, the wisdom tradition indicates that the sun will be influenced by changing cosmic energies that will project radiations of transformed energy to the entire solar system. This will be a period of great positive influence and understanding, because it represents the high point and culmination of civilization this time around.

The human race will be fully equipped to complete the remainder of this Earth sojourn in a state of perfection: harmony with each other, nature and the Creator. By gaining mastery over the physical plane, this life-wave will then be ready to progress to a higher sphere of existence on its evolutionary journey.

These cycles parallel the model of history in parts of the Western world. According to Christian theory, a long time ago, coexisting blissfully with the Creator, we were really very happy. But, after the 'Fall' from that idyllic state, we descended into physical form here on planet Earth in order to exercise our free will between the ways set out by Lucifer and those of the Creator. (Lucifer apparently had challenged Him, and in the ensuing power struggle was vanquished and cast out of the celestial realms into the grosser vibration of the physical plane, accompanied by his followers.) In His infinite wisdom, the Creator indulged the willful departure from divine harmony and leased out the Earth 'reservation' until humanity came to the realization that the only way to go, while allowing negativity to control, was down. Naturally, returning home to the source is the brighter alternative, and we now find it necessary to free ourselves from all the tricks and illusions of matter (*maya*) before we can graduate back to that original state of perfection with full co-creative God power. That old black magic has mesmerized the Earth for so long that it is no longer so easy to just pack up and go back home to the Father. With the passing of each Age, it has become progressively more difficult to master the task of the return. However, for reasons that will become clearer as you read on, now is the time when the evolutionary forces are such that we can catch the tide and make the change together as a planet of unified consciousness.

Life on Earth is a school for God's co-creators, and the souls who fail to learn their karmic lessons before the coming 'graduation' will be left behind to populate yet another *Yuga*, where they will 'do it again and again until they get it right.' In fact, it's pretty certain that most folks are laggards held up from the last cycle.

Before the change to the new harmonious state can happen, though, some very drastic events are in store.

International chaos, distress of nations, famine, natural and humanly generated catastrophes, geophysical and celestial anomalies, are the outward appearance of these events, which are prophesied by many cultures and many religions. However, they can more accurately be described as a healing crisis and cleansing of the Earth, the karma that is due and payable before the new phase can become operable. Only the purest water can become vapour, and this is how it will be with us humans caught up in this evolutionary process. Chances of survival are related to the state of one's inner being and its relative purity. If a person wishes to explore more of his or her divine potential, there must first be an attunement with that higher frequency, which is spiritual in nature. This divine radiation comes from universal life energy, and can be personally contacted by a number of disciplines and paths. Everyone needs most urgently to purify – physically, mentally, and spiritually. Techniques for purification and service to humanity (*karma yoga*) will help one work off negative karma. (Negative karma represents unlearned lessons.) Therefore, progressing to a more elevated condition is only possible when the backlog can be processed, providing us with new understanding and insights of past mistakes as we go.

The planet itself has been badly abused, because we are out of harmony with the universe. We have created a dysfunctional planet! Production and technology have desecrated and polluted the Earth in the process of sustaining our culture. These conditions, in particular, will be karmically rectified. The planet kept a pretty low profile in the past, quietly sustaining, gently nurturing and getting ripped off in the bargain. But all that is about to change: diverse disturbances of nature, geographical shiftings, eruptions and earthquakes will be but symptoms of the planet's reaction to man-made ecological imbalances. Like a sick body, the Earth will rebel in its attempt to regain equilibrium. The Hopi refer to this phenomenon as the time of the great purification.

We know from Kirlian photography that there is a body of energy surrounding living forms. This is a significant step in understanding that all natural forms have a refined energy form or spiritual counterpart. The Western Mystery tradition, Theosophical writings, and some channellings say that our own planet and the others of this solar system also have a spiritual body, that our sun receives its radiant energy from a larger, more powerful sun in deep space. It radiates beyond the ultraviolet end of the spectrum, and, because its light is scientifically undetectable at this time and its emanations so refined, we refer to it as the Central Sun or Spiritual Sun.[1] Its light is referred to as spiritual light or energy. This Central Sun is energized by yet another interdimensional sun, which emits an unimaginable radiance from another level, and so on through a series of supraphysical suns.

The elliptical revolution of our solar system around the undetected Central Sun produces spiritual seasons on Earth and within ourselves, just as revolution around our solar system's sun causes the familiar seasons of spring, summer, autumn and winter. We are now entering the invisible aura of the Central Sun, the influence of which is responsible for the new consciousness that everyone is experiencing to some degree. As the light becomes stronger, it affects our spiritual bodies, displacing the accumulated clouds of negative karma and thus purifying our planet and our beings.

Hard times, sickness, and adversity in many forms on mental, physical and emotional levels, are the physical way these clouds are dissipated. None of us can do anything to avoid or prevent the process. Through grace and the right kind of aspirations, though, it can be lessened both individually and collectively. And that's why understanding the significance of the coming changes and flowing along with them will enable us to enter into greater acceptance of them, knowing that purification is the positive side of hardship.

The Bible speaks of 'signs and wonders in the heavens' in the last days. Whatever form they take, they undoubtedly will be related to many other phenomena taking place within and around the Earth and affecting its stability. The globe's axial spin is slowing down and contributing to weather changes right now, prior to a reversal of the poles. This particular phenomenon has occurred before, and can be expected to happen again – conceivably in the relatively near future. This is because pole reversal represents a principal phase of cosmic evolution for our solar system and all its life forms. Subsequent to the events culminating in the Earth's polar shift (magnetic and/or terrestrial), a new sun and moon will govern our planetary system. You'll be relieved to know that this heavy change does not represent the 'end of the world', but the end of the present world system and the beginning of the New Age (i.e., the 'New Order of the Ages'). 'And I saw a new heaven and a new earth: for the first heaven and the first earth were passed away …' (Revelation 21:1). With a change in the positions of the poles, the map of the heavens viewed from Earth certainly would appear as a 'new heaven', and the Earth changes accompanying an event of such magnitude assuredly would create the geography of a 'new Earth'.

Although what has been described might sound like science fiction, this book is committed to presenting its reality to readers in a practical way. Each of the following chapters represents a piece of the total picture, fleshing out the various aspects of this synopsis. Cosmic and astrological cycles, the context within which this drama unfolds, are explained, in addition to the significance of weather changes and Earth anomalies related to polar shift. Prophecies are also explored as important clues to the future, together with insights into environmental, food and financial crises. It is important to keep in mind that the promise and aspirations of the New Age are scheduled to stabilize the planet within our own lifetime and bring to a close the errors of the past.

Physical preparation has its place in terms of surviving the future transitional phase, but it is the change of consciousness and spiritual attitude that is the real challenge. It cannot be emphasized too strongly that attunement to the higher principles and the One/God will be the ultimate protection, and that forming supportive groups of good, close, loving friends will generate much creative energy and offset despair and fear. This is a time for the members of the planetary family to get to know each other.

3

Cosmic Cycles

The legends, histories, and religious folklore of almost all ancient peoples contain some reference to previous world ages or civilizations that flourished for millennia and ended in cataclysm.

Here in the Western world, we are both sceptical and intrigued about the biblical Flood and the lands of Atlantis and Lemuria, which disappeared in the big splash. Did these events really occur; and, if so, why? Since our own civilization is destined to face the same kind of changes experienced by many past 'mythical' cultures, it seems wise to search history for an overview of just what went on, and see whether it provides any clues to our own situation today, and the one we must face tomorrow.

According to the Hindu tradition of cosmology mentioned-earlier, we are now nearing the end of the *Kali Yuga* (the Age of Iron), which is the final and most negative of four evolutionary Yugic cycles. Each *Yuga is* like the season of a super-cosmic year, even greater than the cosmic year of the precession of the equinoxes. When the Earth came into its current phase of manifestation, the first *Yuga* began *(Sathya Yuga,* meaning 'Purity'), symbolized by gold – hence the term 'Golden Age'. During this historic period, humanity was barely removed from its original state of god-like innocence. As time progressed, the planet underwent the influence of a negative descending spiral, and the quality of life in each successive *Yuga* became increasingly removed from the knowledge of truth and natural law (in other words, 'Reality'). In the second, *Treta Yuga* (Silver Age), spiritual awareness decreased by one fourth, and by the time of *Dvapara Yuga* (Copper Age), negativity had a fifty percent holding. In this, the *Kali Yuga* (Iron Age), the vibration has become pretty murky, and humanity is labouring against heavy odds. Kali is the female counterpart of Shiva in the Hindu trinity. She is the goddess of the dissolution of time (we are living in what the Hindus call 'the dregs of time') and the destroyer of illusion. During this *Yuga*, righteousness has shrunk, like income after taxes, to a scant one fourth of its original strength. Throughout our current history, we have created and been assailed by all the evils of Pandora's box. No wonder the human race is having such a difficult time. But the turning point has now arrived, and the dawn once more sheds its light on a confused and ignorant planet.

Division of Time

18 Nimeshas (Twinkling of an eye)	= 1 Kashtha (3⅓ sec.)	3600 Years of the Gods	= 1 Treta Yuga
30 Kashthas	= 1 Kala (1⅓ min.)	2400 Years of the Gods	= 1 Dvapara Yuga
30 Kalas	= 1 Muhurta (48 min.)	1200 Years of the Gods	= 1 Kali Yuga
30 Muhurtas	= 1 Day and Night	12000 Years of the Gods	= 1 Mahayuga (4 Yugas) or an Age of the Gods
30 Days and Nights and odd Hours	= 1 Month		
12 Months	= 1 Year (Human)	1 Age of the Gods multiplied by 71	= 1 Manvantra
1 Year (Human) or 365 Days and Nights	= 1 Day and Night of the Gods	4380 Millions of Human Years or 1000 Divine Ages	= 1 Kalpa or Day of Brahma (the night of Brahma is of equal duration)
365 Human Years or 365 Divine Days and Nights	= 1 Year of the Gods		
4800 Years of the Gods	= 1 Satya Yuga	36000 Kalpas	= Maha Pralaya

(According to the Hindu tradition, this is the 28th Yuga under the laws of Manu Vyvaswata, seventh Manu, who reigns over this Manvantara)

The *Vishnu Purana*, one of the oldest sacred texts of India, says about the *Kali Yuga*:

The leaders who rule over the Earth will be violent and seize the goods of their subjects ... Those with possessions will abandon agriculture and commerce and will live as servants, that is, following various possessions. The leaders, with the excuses of fiscal need, will rob and despoil their subjects and take away private property. Moral values and the rule of law will lessen from day to day until the world will be completely perverted and agnosticism will gain the day among men.

There are many other references to this division of time. For instance, in the Bible, Nebuchadnezzar's dream (Daniel 2:31 – 45) was of a bright and terrible image with a head of finest gold, chest of silver, hips of brass and legs of iron. The feet and toes were of iron mixed with clay. This image was destroyed by a stone which crushed the feet to dust, and the pieces blew away in the wind. Although Daniel the prophet interpreted the various metals as the world empires that succeeded Babylon (the head of gold), the dream also has a more universal meaning. It represents the great *Yugas*. The iron legs are the Iron Age of *Kali Yuga*, which deteriorates at the end of its cycle into the present unstable civilization symbolized by the feet of iron and clay. The prophet interpreted the stone as the true kingdom of God, which would replace the other civilizations as the real and lasting Kingdom.

In the Americas, the Hopi creation story tells of four successive worlds, which are identified, as in the Hindu scriptures, with gold, silver, copper and a mineral mixed with clay. These worlds were destroyed because people had grown away from the Creator's instructions. They say we inhabit the fourth world, which is about to be 'purified' again by the Great Spirit.[1]

The Incas left records of cosmic upheavals that ended previous world ages.[2] Brasseur, in his *Histoire des Nations Civilisées du Mexique*, recounts that Mexican chronicles state, 'The ancients knew that before the present sky and earth were formed, man was already created and life had manifested itself four times.' Researching the same subject, the author in a later work says that the Maya counted their ages by the names of their consecutive suns: Water, Earthquake, Hurricane and Fire Sun. 'These suns mark the epochs to which are attributed the various catastrophes the world has suffered.'[3] The famous Maya calendar forecasts the end of the present cycle on December 21, 2012. Gomara, the sixteenth century Spanish writer, said that according to their hieroglyphic paintings, the nation of *Culhua* or Mexico believed that four previous suns had already been extinguished. The four suns were as many ages, in which the human species was wiped out by inundations, earthquakes, general conflagration and tempests.[4] In the *Visuddi-Magga,* sacred book of the Buddhists, a section on world cycles speaks of seven suns or ages, each of which terminated with fire, water, or wind. Meanwhile, aborigines of British North Borneo still hold that the sky originally was low, and that six suns have already shone in the sky prior to this one.[5] One of the earliest Greek authors, Hesiod, wrote in his *Theogony* about four ages and generations of men that were destroyed by the anger of planetary gods, the fifth and present one being the Age of Iron.

As the current cycle reaches its final phase and Earth draws closer to the light region of the galaxy, negativity in all its forms is being revealed in the 'purging' brought about by the higher vibration of the light. Earth is progressing toward a higher orbital frequency. And this process is already affecting psyches and bodies in many ways, helped along by new kinds of solar activity that are not yet fully understood.

According to extensive research published by the Foundation for the Study of Cycles, sunspot activity is intimately related to important mass historical events such as wars, epidemics and cycles of human behaviour.[6] Records from seventy-two countries were studied, back to 500 BC, which showed periods of minimum, maximum and declining excitability in human affairs during the eleven year sunspot cycle.

Soviet researchers used Kirlian photography to study the bioelectrical energy field around living things, and found that the fields flare up brightly to correspond with flares on the sun's surface. The magnetic field of the entire planet reacts to solar flares in various ways, as does the human organism via its own aura.

It is thought that the influence of the sun's maximum vivacity upon the centres of the nervous system lends energy to impulses arising from the mass unconscious and transforms potential energy into especially significant forms of kinetic energy. In other words, it excites us to *action*. However, since humanity as a whole usually takes the path of least resistance, the action to which we are excited all too often has led to bloodshed. It may be prophetically relevant that the Gulf War in the Middle East resulted from Iraq's invasion of Kuwait in 1990, just six months after a cycle of the most turbulent solar storms known in history!

The return of the light at this time in history is having intense effects upon our consciousness – a growing spiritual awakening on the one hand, and a disturbing rise in crime and general confusion on the other. In discussing the reason for this polarization of consciousness, it is useful to refer again to Eastern philosophy. Hinduism identifies three basic manifestations of life and consciousness, which are known as the three *gunas:* Sattva, Rajas and Tamas. Each person and condition in life fluctuates between each of these three expressions, and it is the play between them that gives rise to the 'phenomena' of the world and of consciousness.[7]

Sattva guna represents the spiritual aspect of life and awareness – beauty, the ideal of perfection, rhythm, harmony, a healthy nature and intelligence. Sattvic consciousness is basically intelligent, calm, clear, balanced, compassionate, loving, and is demonstrative of the higher Self.

Rajas guna represents the average state of awareness, and the average quality of life. Rajas is the landscape of existence crisscrossed by freeway vectors of the mass mind. It is the dissonance of commercials and static that interrupts the wave band of coherent thought. Rajas is the roller coaster between extremes, the veil of illusion, and the ego that blocks the view. It is the fads and fashions, glitter and crises, and all the things that grab our attention and seduce our senses – in other words, 'reality' as most people know it. Rajas consciousness is the vortex of the mass mind; the bumpy cruising space between the serene altitude of the higher self and the turbulent undertow of the lower self. This guna is associated with motor energy, activity of the mind and senses, passions, attachment, egocentricity and so on. Rajastic consciousness is unstable, uncertain, agitated, tense and willful.

Tamas guna relates to the density of matter. In humans it is characterized by expressions of the lower self – darkness of consciousness, ignorance, torpor, degeneracy, inertia and the grosser tendencies. Tamasic consciousness is ego-driven, confused, selfish, gross, addictive, violent, etc.

Because of the influence of increasing light vibration upon the collective consciousness now, it has become very important for us to understand its effect upon these three aspects of our nature. The sattvic or pure aspects of one's being and awareness will gain in health, understanding, wisdom and spirituality as the light vibration continues to increase. To the extent that rajas aspects of consciousness predominate, one may experience dissipation of vital energy and anxiety as negative qualities surface, causing stress, agitation, confusion, or disorientation. Residual, tamasic tendencies of the lower self are distilled to the surface by the higher frequency and experienced as inertia, sickness, emotional trauma, delusions, or violence.

The awakening of the light is a two-edged sword; the light that illumines can also blind. Vibrational acceleration nourishes and evolves pure conditions – and purifies that which is unlike love and harmony, and which does not serve the greater whole of life. So, it becomes important that we use this historical moment well, put our full conscious attention on the transformative value of prayer, meditation, body work, all forms of physical and emotional clearing, service, etc., in order to heal ourselves and our planet before

Actuating force	Predominance of Sattva/Purity	Predominance of Rajas/Inertia	Predominance of Tamas/Regression
Expression	Firmly confident but not egotistical. Unchanged by success or failure.	Swayed by emotions and motivated by ego.	Inert, selfish, stubborn, malicious.
Action	Unattached to the result.	Attached to results. Ego involvement.	Indifferent to loss or injury to others. Self centred.
Knowledge	Sees the unity of all beings and things.	Sees only the separateness and differences.	Insists his/her view is the only one.
Reason	Knowledge of power and right action.	Indifferent to ethics or morals.	Morally and ethically indifferent and confused.
Pleasure	Knowledge of the true self. Knows how to accept a disadvantage in order to enjoy its advantage.	Primarily enjoys only the senses. Unwilling to tolerate a negative to get to a positive.	Thrives on discord and negativity. Enjoys grossness. Takes pleasure at others' expense.
Food	Live, raw organically grown foods. Fresh fruit and vegetables, nuts, seeds, grains. Unprocessed foods.	Dead, overcooked, flesh foods. Bitter, sour, too hot/cold, pungent, processed, sprayed or chemicalised foods.	Stale, flat, putrid, leftovers, plus all the inertia producing foods of the previous column.

The Three Gunas

a healing crisis accomplishes it for us. Our conscious participation is part of the equation; it's all factored in, and what we are supposed to be doing right now. It is all perfect. Just do it.

Surely, this is incentive enough to get ourselves together: spiritually, mentally, physically, socially and in all ways. For, in our direst projections of a catastrophic future, with major breakdowns of the system and societal panic, it is not the ensuing events themselves that most people fear (the hardship, deprivation, and confusion). What we really fear most is other people and what they will do!

4

Astrological Cycles

Within the major cosmic cycles are minor ones intrinsic to the course of history. Specific expressions of celestial influence are now affecting the Earth very strongly as it progresses from one astrological sign to the next. Astrology is still a controversial subject to many conservative thinkers because they have only limited acquaintance with its more sensational aspects or have been disappointed with their daily 'horrorscopes'. However, sceptics who believe astrology to be folklore or fancy frequently shift to neutral when they gain some insight into the logic of its deeper laws. Today, astrology, along with the other branches of occult knowledge, is regaining a wide recognition and appreciation. Could this be because we're entering the two-millennium period of the Age of Aquarius, which governs metaphysics and astrology? Aquarius rules the logical structure within the universal mind (the 'divine reason' of the ancients) that is the source of the laws of nature. Metaphysics and astrology assist our understanding of these laws and our inner relationship to the universe.

It is commonly believed that the constellations do not resemble their names in anything but the most arbitrary fashion. This is because the way in which traditional astronomical star maps have linked together the stars of each constellation shows a complete lack of imagination! Hans Augusto Rey, who wrote several stargazing books for children, rediscovered the ancient way of graphically depicting the constellations in perceptually recognizable configurations.[1]

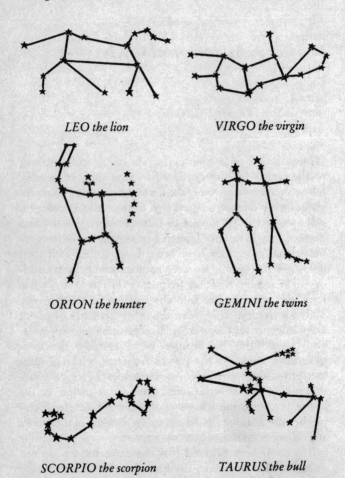

LEO the lion   *VIRGO the virgin*

ORION the hunter   *GEMINI the twins*

SCORPIO the scorpion   *TAURUS the bull*

In the writings and descriptions of almost every culture, the same creatures were used to identify the signs of the zodiac: the Native American peoples, Assyrians, Chaldeans,

Egyptians, Greeks, Israelites, Maya and Romans all shared the same circle of living creatures. They probably knew thousands of years ago something that we have only just discovered about astrological science.

If a star map is superimposed over the Earth with the pole star placed over the terrestrial North Pole, we have a celestial clock making one revolution daily. The noon point of that map (like Greenwich) is the Great Pyramid of Giza. Thousands of years ago, Egypt was known as the Land of Khem. The Khema were a group of seven major stars (in the constellation of Taurus), known today as the Pleiades. If the map is placed with the Khema over the Land of Khem (Egypt) – specifically, directly above the apex of the Great Pyramid – then Taurus falls over the Taurus Mountains of southern Turkey; Ursa Major, the Great Bear, rambles over Russia; the head of Draco the Dragon coils up over China; Orion over Iran/Iraq; Aries the Ram over Rome, and Capricorn (identified with the god Pan) falls over Panama, Panuco and Mayapan (the old name of Yucatan). Aquila the Eagle spans the United States. The analogies are obvious, and quite impressive. This is one of the clearest examples of the law of 'As Above, So Below'.

Those who designed and built the Great Pyramid understood this. As the central geodetic point and key node of the planetary grid, the Pyramid was constructed at a time when the Pleiades paused in the midheaven, directly above its apex. This enabled the descending passage of the Pyramid to be directly aligned with, and illuminated by, the pole star, indicating true North.

In order to more fully understand the influences that are now operating upon the Earth, a basic knowledge of astrological fundamentals is helpful, along with some intriguing and little-known historical background.

The word 'zodiac' is Greek for 'living creatures'. These equally spaced signs are a series of twelve star groupings circling the sky in a sixteen degree belt. Sun, moon and planets appear to be 'in' these constellations as they move against the background of these star clusters. Each sign of the zodiac makes a brief and regular appearance with the passing months of the year. Summer and winter divide the year into a combination of darkness and light. The Earth rotates on its axis twenty-three degrees to the plane of its orbit, bringing about our seasonal changes. (Without this tilt there would only be a single season, because the sun's rays would always fall directly at the equator.) The elliptical orbit of the Earth's annual rotation around the sun warms and lengthens the days approaching the summer solstice, shortens and chills them around the winter solstice. Spring and autumn equinoxes mark the midpoint between these two extremes; then, day and night are of equal duration.

This model of the celestial timetable applies on a much larger scale, too. An astrological 'age' is comprised of 2,152 years. An age is the duration of each zodiac sign, and represents a month of the cosmic year. The cosmic year, then, is comprised of the twelve zodiacal ages – a total of 25,826 years. During this great cosmic year, the Earth's axis will have pointed to each zodiac constellation in turn. This is called the precession of the equinoxes, or the equinoctial cycle. (Opinions differ as to the precise number of years in an age and an equinoctial cycle. The figures quoted here are based upon the measurements given in the geometry of the Great Pyramid.)[2]

The Age of Pisces has been with us for the past two thousand years or so. Pisces is the sign of 'self-undoing'. We've been trapped in orbit, as it were, around the materialism, competitiveness, and limitation generated by Piscean energy (and are certainly almost undone). In the Jungian sense, it could be said that because we are imperfect, we muddle along until a collective crisis occurs. This way, we unconsciously 'undo' ourselves by the end of each cycle (Pisces is the last sign of the zodiac cycle) in order to bring about enough crisis to force us through, do or die, to the next highest level. What we are now experiencing is all the surface instability, precariousness and velocity needed to break away from the confining matrix of Pisces to an expanded state of harmony and wisdom consistent with the influence of that benevolence which is Aquarius.

The mighty labour now being generated to wrest new life from the clutches of the old will not be easy. In human affairs, age tends to crystallize one's ideas; and, in the same sense, our culture is now cracking under the weight of its own senile tenacity to status quo. The task at hand is to release that which no longer serves us and retain the best from all that we have accomplished to serve as a platform upon which the 'New Order of the Ages' will be secured.

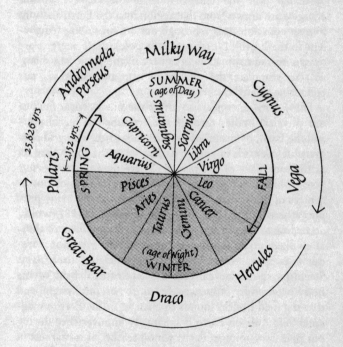

Astro Logic

Most people are familiar with the various influences brought by each of the passing zodiac signs, but little is known about the *governing* climate of influence beamed by the various pole stars throughout history. The pole star is also known as the North Star, because it is the one directly above Earth's North Pole. (Geographic North can be located at sea, or at night, by siting Polaris, our present pole star.)

As the Earth traverses the heavens during the great cycle of 25,826 years, it passes through the cosmic year's equivalent of the four seasons, each of which produces spiritual changes in the state of evolving humanity. As the tilt of Earth's axis allows its North magnetic pole to align with a particular pole star constellation of the heavens, cosmic energies are drawn from that region into the Earth and into human consciousness. Through our crown *chakra* (equivalent to the Earth's North magnetic pole), these energies are drawn into our spinal energy channel (the yogic 'shushumna') to stimulate the quality of our awareness via our endocrine-related *chakra* system.

These same energies also affect the bioelectrical field of our physical bodies through the acupuncture meridians – and the Earth by means of its 'planetary grid'. This grid is an invisible network of energy paths within the Earth that act as the meridians of the planet. Where these lines intersect geographically, they form power centres. At major power centres of the grid are located sacred sites where many people gathered for the Harmonic Convergence of 1987 (which, according to the Maya tradition, marked the climax of global civilization) to receive and amplify new vibrational frequencies now streaming from the centre of the galaxy. Scientific studies reveal that the bioelectrical field of the body profoundly influences the entire nervous system, and that the field itself responds to changes in the Earth's magnetic field. Life on Earth is spiritually impoverished during our planetary sojourn in the winter season, at its darkest in the constellation of Draco the Dragon. It is able to flourish in the light of the spirit while in the summer region, peaking closest to the Milky Way. Prophetic sources, explored later, have designated 1931 as the beginning of the Age of Light. The astrological Age of Pisces represents the dark before the dawn, and we are at the turning point of the circle, the cusp, merging into Aquarius and into the light.

The symbolic and mythical characters depicted by the constellations around the wheel of the zodiac are codes, metaphors for the evolutionary stages of progression since the beginning of our present cycle of civilization. When the Earth passes closest to the Milky Way, through the Ages of Sagittarius and Scorpio during the cosmic summer, civilization periodically attains its highest peak: the era of the recurrent Golden Age.

In his amazing biographical work, *Memories, Dreams, Reflections,* Carl Jung states, 'Only here on Earth, where the opposites clash together, can the general level of consciousness be raised. That seems to be man's metaphysical task – which he cannot accomplish without 'mythologising'. Myth is the natural and indispensable intermediate stage between unconscious and conscious cognition.'³ Like a great wind at our backs, the irrepressible evolutionary force is now preparing us to bridge that intermediate stage. How amazing it was to discover, quite by chance, the hidden meaning behind well-known characters and events of world mythology.

Tradition tells us that the Golden Age was populated by people who had realized the Self – just as it will be next time around. From the vantage point of the Astro Logic chart, you will see that when the last Golden Age faded, Earth began to align with a new pole star: Cygnus, the swan. The mythic meaning of this bird reveals the nature of human consciousness while it was the pole star.

A declining cycle of human affairs had begun. In this context, one might associate the symbol of a swan with the term 'swan song' (the sound uttered by a dying swan), as the dying Golden Age and its fading beauty. Surely, 'paradise lost' was the name of its song.

Mythically speaking, the swan was a creature of spiritual importance in the ancient world. In Hindu iconography the swan personifies 'Brahmanatman,' which is the transcendent and immanent ground of being – the Self. 'Paramahansa' (supreme swan) was a term of honour bestowed upon certain yogis (such as Paramahansa Yogananda, who brought Hinduism to the West in the 1950s) who had attained liberation from the bondage of the material world. In Black Elk's account *The Sacred Pipe: The Seven Rites of the Oglala Sioux*, he speaks of birds representing divine principles. Among the Sioux of the North American plains, the sacred white swan symbolizes the Great Spirit who 'controls all that moves and to whom prayers are offered'. In the recurrent Golden Age, people lived in peace and resonance with divine principles. It was a time when the creation existed in perfection and people lived in harmony with the natural environment and each other. The state of mind required to maintain that kind of culture we call 'Christ consciousness'. By the time the dust settles and the next Golden Age blooms, we, too, shall have acquired it.

The story of how a young man called Cygnus was transformed into a swan and became the pole star is found in Greek mythology. It is a tale of two friends, the one impetuous and headstrong, the other conservative and responsible. In this ancient version of a modern theme, Phaëthon (the headstrong one) wanted to prove to his peers that he was the son of a god, so he coerced his father, the sun god, into letting him drive the chariot of the sun across the sky for a day. The youth was overconfident and not a little reckless as he pushed the blazing steeds to their full horsepower. As he whipped the team to a frenzy, eyes wild, mouths frothing, they sped ever faster and higher in the sky. Myth has it that a scorpion (see placement of Scorpio on chart) frightened the horses in mid-gallop and that the sunchariot went berserk as they bolted in panic. Phaëthon was unable to 'pull over'. The chariot careened out of control, swerving wildly off course, and tumbled through the sky, engulfed in flames. The roar of the fire and the screams of the horses were terrible. Heaven and Earth were threatened with conflagration as the chariot began to set the sky ablaze and scorch the Earth. The Earth started to wobble dangerously in its rotation, and the poles began to ignite. According to Nonnos, the Greek writer, 'There was tumult in the sky, shaking the joints of the immovable universe, the very axle bent which runs through the middle of the revolving heavens.' At this point the Earth Mother became distraught, beseeching Zeus, father of the gods, to intervene. Desperate means were necessary to save the Earth. Phaëthon (Greek for 'the blazing one') had to be stopped, and so Zeus zapped him with a thunderbolt ... The silence was awesome as the riderless chariot gradually veered back on course, slowly disappearing as a glowing smudge over the Western horizon.

Because of his prolonged grief over the death of Phaëthon, Cygnus was transformed into a swan by Helios. After his death, the loyal Cygnus became the pole star. Ever mindful of the Earth's near-annihilation by the joyride of his friend, the 'well-balanced' Cygnus maintained cosmic order by presiding over the Age of Libra, sign of balance, symbolized by the scales.

This myth echoes a theme found within most world cultures of a time when the stability of the poles shifted and the world experienced some form of combustion or flood. The drama of Phaëthon is the recurrent story of power without maturity, human willfulness and its recurrent tragic results.

As the cosmic season of the fall drew closer, Vega became the next pole star. The dictionary says 'vega' is the Arabic word for 'fall' (and this pole star does, in fact, rule over the fall or autumn season of the great cosmic year). Other 'falls' that cycled out great civilizations were the decline of Lemuria and the sinking of Atlantis. When Vega faced the Earth about 12,400 years ago, it is believed, the last Age of Day ended with the Noachian Flood and the last known reversal of the planet's magnetic field.[4] The dictionary goes on to associate Vega specifically with 'the fall of the vulture'. This is a metaphorical reference to the fall, or decline, of the female principle in the world. Vega ruled over the Age of Virgo (the virgin). When the stars of that constellation are joined up by lines to identify its outline, a female figure is seen falling backwards. The vulture is the hieroglyph for the Egyptian deity Mut, mother of the gods. She wears a vulture headdress and is associated with maternity, as is Knekhebet, the vulture-headed goddess of childbirth. Hera, Queen of Heaven, is the Greek counterpart, as the goddess of women, light, birth and marriage. Unfortunately, her consort Zeus had many extramarital affairs, and Hera became vindictive to his children by other women, especially to those of Hercules.

Historically, it was Hercules who was destined to become the next pole star as the power of the feminine declined. He was probably the most famous of all the Greek heroes, because of his twelve labours – which came with the territory of his new role as pole star. The first Herculean labour was to kill the Nemean lion (notice that Leo, the lion, is the first age under his rule). Hera, as the Greek archetype of the feminine principle, began efforts to resist the ascendancy of the male principle represented by Hercules. Looking ahead to the Age of Cancer, the crab (and mindful that Achilles had been killed by an arrow wound in his heel), she dispatched a crab to bite Hercules's heel. Hercules, however, was not to be deterred in his rise to power. He felt his great strength was needed to perform his twelve labours and to slay dragons – symbolic of his mission to stop the world from sinking further into the domain of the dragon constellation. Draco personified the negative force and presided over the darkness of cosmic winter. So the Gemini twins, Castor and Pollux, taught Hercules how to fight before he went on to capture the sacred Cretan Bull (see Taurus, the bull). Ultimately, Hercules failed to hold out against the Dragon, although he put up a valiant fight. Stories from Greek mythology are replete with accounts of Hercules's many dealings with monsters, serpents, and dragons as he fought with his great might to hold back the winter season and the Age of Night. But darkness irrevocably enveloped the world, and the cosmic winter engulfed humanity in its deepest psychic and spiritual darkness. Like a door slammed shut against a bitter wind, the consciousness of the people drew in, became hardened and dull. Warlords plundered and laid waste the land. Life was as stale and hard as the bread; suffering great, survival difficult. The holders of the ancient wisdom were silent.

With the Age of Aries, cosmic springtime began to stir,

and the Great Bear, who hibernates through-the winter, awoke to the business of becoming the 'polar bear'. The Aztecs perceived the Great Bear constellation (Ursa Major) as the Jaguar God of Night and the stars of the night sky as his spots – a concept that had originated with the Jaguar cult of the Olmecs around 1000 BC.

Polaris, our present polar star, represents the point of polarity between cosmic winter/summer, night/day, Pisces/Aquarius. It governs the repolarization of Earth's consciousness, and also the hemispherical poles, i.e., the balance of our planet's geographic poles. The celestial event celebrated in 1987 as Harmonic Convergence (discussed in the 'Maya Prophecy' chapter) accomplished the evolutionary imperative of aligning human consciousness with the new energies emanating from the galactic core, the centre of the Milky Way, in Sagittarius. Regulus (from the Latin root 'regula', to rule, or 'regere', to lead straight), the pole star of the ecliptic, will be positioning on the Leo/Virgo cusp around the turn of the century – directly opposite Polaris. We can infer from this positioning that the intense and possibly cataclysmic polarization between opposites (the Armageddon/ purification period) is being regulated, mediated by the influence of this polar opposite star. As Aquarius pours forth the waters of life from the fullness of his vessel, the Earth will be purified by his gift. But when the waters settle and become calm, we shall see reflected in their stillness a new reality. An expanded state of harmony and wisdom awaits as the New Order of the Ages stabilizes.

With continued reference to the Astro Logic chart, we are seen moving toward the double pole star system of Perseus and Andromeda. Perseus has been called a model for the career of a perfect hero, one of the best-known, pleasant, well-adjusted, 'right-on,' all-American heroes of Greek mythology! Perseus was a champion of the feminine. He killed the snake-haired Medusa, whose looks could literally kill, and presented her head to Athena Nike, transcendent goddess of Victory, that she might mount it upon her shield to petrify her enemies. Perseus also rescued his mother from

the evil intentions of an unwelcome suitor. Most importantly, 'as he bestrode the lazy pacing clouds and rode upon the
bosom of the air' on the winged steed, Pegasus, he glanced
down to where the ocean crashed against the cliffs along the
rugged Aegean shore. There, in the distance, he saw the figure of a woman chained to the rocks at the ocean's edge. It
was Andromeda, bound as a sacrifice of appeasement to
Neptune, the sea god. She had been left there to await her
fate as a gourmet treat for the sea monster. Perseus swooped
down to release her chains – and fell in love with her. Here
we see final liberation from the chains of harsh restrictions
historically imposed upon female energy, as well as freedom
from the chains of limitation imposed by the old Piscean
matrix.

Andromeda beckons. Throughout nature, the yin force is
stirring. The Goddess is emergent. She is timely and elo-
quent in her return, rising powerful and beautiful once more
after her long sojourn through the season of darkness, when
she fell like a wounded bird half a precessional cycle ago. As
the Astro Logic chart shows, the ascendancy of the male
principle, championed by pole star Hercules, is directly
opposite Andromeda.

As the Phoenix rises, so will She soar again. This is another way of explaining the mystery teachings' prophecy of the
emergence of the 'feminine ray'. The return of the Great
Goddess is the return of the light. And, because now is a
unique historical moment for resolving world karma, we are
preparing for a really great finale – a quantum shift to a
completely new cycle. So, the light that began to return with
the Harmonic Convergence is of a frequency never before
experienced. It emanates from the centre of our galaxy and
is intended to aid our transition to the required vibrational
level of the next phase of our evolution. As the prophecies
of the following chapters unfold, this concept will become
clearer.

The new 'feminine ray' will be identified by the arrival of
a new colour into the visible light spectrum. New light, of
course, enters the spectrum at the ultraviolet end, so the new

colour will be an extension of ultraviolet – iridescent mother of pearl. Ultraviolet is the colour frequency of the sixth *chakra,* our centre of direct knowing and spiritual unfoldment, the third eye. The influx of new energy from the galactic core, which began at the Harmonic Convergence, is an evolutionary force stimulating our higher centres of awareness, particularly the brow *chakra.* This new light will accelerate into our experience the qualities of that *chakra* – intuition, spiritual power and enlightened awareness. Externally, this new energy aligns us with its source – a kind of drawing us home. Inwardly, it aligns consciousness with the crown *chakra,* our connection to the cosmos, inner dimensions and illumination.

At this time, another image arises from the mists of the collective unconsciousness to assist our progress into the Light. The 'Divine Woman' of the Bible's Book of Revelation (a mystical account of the 'end times') is the archetype we move toward as Andromeda prepares to reign overhead. This divine woman wears a crown of twelve stars; the sun shines above her, and the moon reflects beneath her feet. She is about to give birth to the Christ child, and Satan is waiting to devour the child as it is born. However, he does not succeed, because both mother and child are spirited away and protected at the throne of God.

Interpretation of this symbolism casts the crown as the circle of the zodiac and its twelve stars as the twelve astrological constellations. The sun and moon above and below the woman are found in ancient alchemical texts and act as descriptors of the archetype of the spiritually evolved woman who has balanced the polarities of the phenomenal world within herself. Her very name, Andromeda, is derived from the same route as 'androgyny,' which means having the characteristics of both sexes. It is further broken down as originating from the Latin 'andr-,' meaning 'man' (derived from 'stem'); 'o' is the combining form, and 'med' means 'middle', while the ending 'a' is the feminine suffix. 'Andromeda,' then, is the centre of the generative principle, just as 'Psyche' of Greek mythology ('female soul') is the point of light within the mind, and 'Su' in Japanese is the seed of light, or spirit, within matter.

A concept that Christian orthodoxy is having difficulty with today is this idea of the universal feminine principle as an aspect of the Trinity, the Holy Ghost. The Divine Woman is also the Shekinah, the Divine Mother, whose mission it is to channel through her creative expression and generative power the Christ consciousness on the planet. One is considered 'Christed' when awareness has stabilized at the spiritual centre in the forehead, the sixth *chakra*. (Jesus held the title of 'Christ' because he was a living example of one manifesting completely at that level of enlightened awareness.) Interestingly, anointing is performed at the site of the third eye. In Hebrew, 'Messiah' means 'the anointed one'. The Greek equivalent is 'Kristos,' or Christ. Christ consciousness, then, is a universal force to be experienced in due time by each of us as we accomplish mastery and realize the Self.

It should be understood that the global purification we are now embarked upon is the externalization of our collective shadow. It is a process both wonderful and terrible. The return of the light disturbs the darkness, penetrates the density, stirs the stagnant depths. It exposes, naked and thrashing, that which we have hidden and denied. Many states of awareness are being experienced simultaneously in the world today because of this. While apocalyptic horsemen thunder forth, instincts keen, with the stench of burning oil upon the wind, veils are also being lifted from people's eyes. Leaps of consciousness are cracking the crust off brains, and awareness is bursting forth into the light, blinking and gasping with the ecstasy of it all. We should remember that purification and healing take many forms and are experienced on many levels, both inner and outer. They always restore equilibrium, and they always carry us toward wholeness.

Perseus married Andromeda, his soulmate, and was always faithful (fidelity being almost unheard of in Greek mythology). It was a perfect match, and their union was happy and exemplary. After their death, they were both transformed into constellations. The couple represent the dynamic integration of consciousness, although it should be recognized that each of them is also individuated and can stand alone if necessary. Their power is potentiated when they 'marry'. Therefore, in the union of opposites, female energy is liberated to equal status with the male counterpart for maximum harmonizing of species/planet energies. We can also understand this union as left/right brain hemisynch, the 'rainbow bridge' (antakarana) of Hinduism where the consciousness of the head and the heart merge in perfect union to ignite the threefold flame: love, wisdom and power. Such an achievement is the accomplishment of the initiate – one who has attained the highest degree of spiritual development. It would appear that we are indeed moving toward our highest, most integrated and harmonious good, when we align with the next dual pole star combination of Perseus and Andromeda.

In the mythology, Cygnus, pole star of the post-Golden Age era, was the son of Sthenelos. Who was Sthenelos? He was the son of Perseus and Andromeda. Cygnus was, therefore, the *grandson* of Perseus and Andromeda. So you see, the prophecy cycle told by the pole stars repeats predictably throughout the endless turning of the Great Year of the precession.

By the time find we find ourselves beneath the final pole star of this cycle of human history, the New order of the Ages will also have become anchored and fully manifest upon our planet. The final pole star will be the centre of our home galaxy, the Milky Way. It will preside directly over the Age of Sagittarius (sign of the higher mind), and we will bask once again in the glow of another Golden Age, illuminated spiritually and physically by a new quality of light. In living colour, the cosmic summer will once more unfold the blossoms of human consciousness – the prophesied Maya 'Age of Flowers' in all its splendour.

But all that is yet to come. Meanwhile, back in the caboose of the twentieth century, beneath the influence of

Polaris, there is a polarization to be resolved as the light challenges the darkness. So there is work to be done, mysteries to be revealed and, above all, challenges to be met.

Because existence is cyclical, the knowledge possessed by the ancients during the last Age of Light is, literally, being brought to light. Perhaps the Great Pyramid is one remaining monument of a time when the universe was understood and recorded for posterity. Great civilizations fell after the high point of achievement during the last equinoctial cycle's Age of Light. Then the Age of Night, cosmic wintertime, again enveloped a struggling humanity, and the profound knowledge of those cultures was lost. The so-called superhuman accomplishments described in books like Von Daniken's *Chariots of the Gods* may have been souvenirs of advanced space beings. But it is much more likely that many of the feats of engineering excellence and marvels of a magnitude far surpassing modern abilities are evidence of human attainments during a past cycle more advanced than our own. In another 6,000 years, we shall have reached the zenith of this particular spiral of existence.

It is also important to understand that Earth is part of a spiritual/physical testing zone, the inhabitants of which have been set the task of freeing themselves from the tyranny of matter controlled by the 'fallen' hierarchies inhabiting key regions of the universe. According to a major wisdom source of our time,[5] these negative powers and principalities rule the Age of Night and the constellations of Ursa Minor, Ursa Major, Thuban – at the head of Draco the Dragon and our pole star, Polaris. These realms contain intelligences of the negative hierarchy, administrators of the dark force, who have used their might to establish themselves as powers over the physical plane.

The Battle of Armageddon, therefore, is the scene of the final conflict between the forces of good and evil described in the Bible's Book of Revelation. As the 'bad guys' are cast out of the higher heavens into the lower levels of creation, great imbalance will result on the Earth plane. The great clash of celestial and negative forces will then ('as above, so below') have its counterpart on Earth. It is the great purification that all of creation must experience in order that the negative forces be ousted and replaced by graduating beings of perfect light bodies whose will it is to restore harmony and balance to the highest purpose.

5

Evolution and Involution

We are not human beings having a spiritual experience
but spiritual beings having a human one.

Georges I. Gurdjieff

An accurate account of the descent of spirit into matter and
its long journey through mass, energy, space and time, must
be written at some future time by another – wiser than
Darwin, more visionary than Galileo or Einstein. We cannot
state empirically the exact nature of evolution in its totality,
but we can discuss some general premises that stand the test
of current logic and convey schematically the nature of life's
progression to completion of expression on the physical
plane.

We refer to history and the origin of species as evolution.
It is life in the process of becoming – and it moves in a spiral,
not the linear strip many people think of as the conveyor
belt of time.

Described here are the six kingdoms of creation. Energy,
which forms the first and most subtle wave of life, becomes
progressively more intricate as it transmutes into ever more
wonderful and complex forms – gases, minerals, plants, animals. The high point of creation is achieved at the sixth stage
of development, in the form of human beings who function
with erect spines and creative minds. In this sense, the human
form comes *out* of the world, and not into it. We

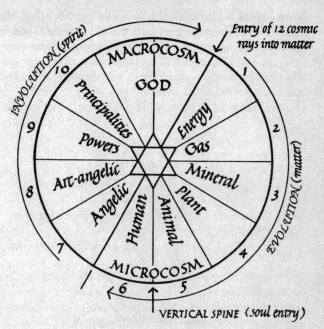

Evolution/Involution

represent a direct metamorphosis of the soil; we are not sep-arate. Energy gives birth to gases, which form minerals. These minerals, inherent in the soil, nurture plants, which then feed animals. We, in turn, are sustained by these plants and animals. From this stage onward, we can be said to 'invo-lute', since matter, upon reaching its most complete expres-sion, is at its most complex and tends to its point of origin by way of refinement. We grow up and return home, as it were. The human organism, then, begins the return to its source, taking with it the entire knowledge and wisdom accumulated and integrated into its psyche during all life's experiences. Matter once again merges gently back into spirit.

Traditional esotericism defines the outward bound jour-ney of spirit into matter as a 'masculine' process. The point where the process reverses and matter begins to indraw back toward spirit is identified as a 'feminine' process called 'the return'. This return brings at once the return of the Goddess and the awakening of the serpentine *kundalini (shakti)* energy at the base of the spine. This transformative force gradually ascends the spine, purifying its way through the *chakras* and brings enlightened consciousness when it reaches the crown of the head.

The marriage of the physical and divine forces within us combines the inner and outer realities in divine synthesis, creating new consciousness, the new Being. This is the meaning of the Biblical exhortation to be 'reborn' and explains the mystical union of the Hindu Shiva and Shakti.

Here, at the sixth evolutionary level, humans exist at varying stages of personal development. Those whose consciousness is still in the early stages of awakening represent the 'human-animal' nature inasmuch as the ego is still focused in upon itself and its own needs, largely to the exclusion of the welfare of others. It knows nothing of the higher principles nor does it care to learn, being primarily fixated upon the lower centres of consciousness characterized by security, sex and power. As life's experiences and hardships give us some social smarts and teach us to 'do as we would be done by', sensitivity grows, awareness expands, and the ego diffuses itself vicariously as a conscious part of the all. Once the intelligence of the heart has become awakened, creativity expands and knowledge of the higher wisdom is sought. As this process unfolds the human being can be described as 'human-divine'.

The sixth stage of evolution is the turning or repolarization point between darkness and light, matter and spirit. Numerologically, knowledge and power (probably the most dominant expressions of our civilization) are characteristics of the number six, which is related to the Law of Vibration and is designated as 'the number of return'. To explain this, we can refer to the I *Ching*, which has served as a rich source of Confucian and Taoist wisdom for more than two thousand years. Here is what it has to say about the sixth stage of evolution and how it acts as a turning point.

24. Fu / Return (The Turning Point)

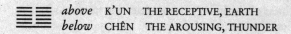 *above* K'UN THE RECEPTIVE, EARTH
below CHÊN THE AROUSING, THUNDER

> *The idea of a turning point arises from the fact that after the dark (broken) lines have pushed all of the light lines upward and out of the hexagram, another (unbroken) light line enters from below. The time of darkness is past, the winter solstice brings the victory of light.*[1]

The unbroken line at the base of the hexagram introduces the principle of light and its ascendancy in the scheme of things, like the return of the light after the winter solstice. The upper trigram describes the 'Receptive Earth' and the lower trigram the 'Arousing Thunder'. In winter, the life energy, symbolized here by thunder (that which arouses) is still quiescent within the Earth. Looking at this hexagram as the key to the image of 'return' and the transformative energies now influencing our planet, it can be deduced that light is being released from within the depths of matter. It will move upward through the 'Receptive Earth' and through every created atom of matter, transforming inertia and darkness into new life. This powerful ascendancy of the light leads, ultimately, to the return of the Christ spirit, as the powers of nature and the forces that move through us open the way for the approaching new evolutionary phase, or Golden Age.

Visionary philosopher Vincent Selleck explains in his *Global Link* networking journal (see Part V, Resources), 'For this great purpose we must resonate with the web of nature, feeling our essence in the depths of the sacred ground … Therefore, the six hexagram lines can be seen to interface with the seven chakras. The heart chakra is the magnetism which holds the three upper and three lower chakras *and* the two trigrams in relationship. Return represents the activation of the base chakra, the centre controlling the kundalini …' The base *chakra is,* among other things, the repository of our racial memory. This memory seed is awakened in the 'return' process – which is why the new recognition of mythology is now releasing to our conscious awareness the 'return' of the primal archetypal personifications called gods and goddesses and, therefore, a deeper understanding of human nature. Continuing from hexagram 24 of the *I Ching,* Fu/Return (the turning point) we read:

After a time of decay comes the turning point. The powerful light that has been banished returns. There is movement but it is not brought about by force. The upper trigram … is characterized by devotion; thus the movement is natural, arising spontaneously. For this reason the transformation of the old becomes easy. The old is discarded and the new is introduced. Both measures accord with the time; therefore, no harm results. Societies of people sharing the same views are formed. But since these groups come together in full public knowledge and are in harmony with the time, all selfish separatist tendencies are excluded, and no mistake is made.[2]

Today we are seeing these words come to life. The time of decay is *now*, in the sense of our ravished environment and the failure or decline of many traditional institutions and value systems. And it is *now* that a great spiritual rebirth is occurring on the planet, which is gradually transforming our consciousness. These ancient words describe, in practical terms, the movement that occurs within individuals and society as the light returns.

Along with our collective, confessed recognition of planetary crisis arose a psychological readiness within great numbers of people to replace the fears and separations that divide us with the love and empathy that unite us. In response to the growing light, a certain ordering principle has emerged from the chaos of our previous endarkened state. As the final decade of the century dawned, a new psychological climate became the matrix within which epochal events suddenly and profoundly changed the geopolitical face of Eastern Europe. A planetwide sociocultural cohesion has commenced. And intense changes are occurring in our world and in our lives, whether we like it or not. Elucidating this turning point, the *I Ching* continues:

> Return always calls for a decision and is an act of self-mastery. It is made easier if a man is in good company. If he can bring himself to put aside pride and follow the example of good men, good fortune results.[3]

Those who remain attached to the apparent benefits of personal gain at the expense of the greater good can ponder the oracle's words, because disaster can overtake those who are ignorant or indifferent to the needs of the times.

When the time for return has come, a man should not take shelter in trivial excuses, but should look within and examine himself ... If a man misses the right time for return, he meets with misfortune. The misfortune has its inner cause in a wrong attitude toward the world. The misfortune coming upon him from without results from his wrong attitude. What is pictured here is blind obstinacy and the judgment visited upon it.[4]

You may recall that in the Bible, the plagues of The Revelation are special packages of returning karma, rude awakenings, visited upon the obstinate to shock them into awareness. Humans are the most versatile of all the animals, and yet they always resist change. As the late philosopher, poet, and scientist Dr Jacob Bronowski described it in *The Ascent of Man*, 'We live our past in the present from the ragbag of fixed and obsolete ideas.' Animals that don't adapt become extinct. Remember? Is that why dinosaurs are so popular today? Is our collective subconscious trying to bring something to our attention? Survival today means understanding and responding to change within the context of an 'internal revolution' and preparing ourselves accordingly. Above all, it definitely means an inner commitment to the Light, to reconnecting with the Earth and each other, to spiritual growth and a new phase of human evolution. To deny or avoid the transformative spirit at work in the world today is to vote 'No' on 'Yes'; it is to resist the force of evolution. And it leads to catastrophic outcome.

Involution, the return of matter back to spirit, stirs when a significant number of the sixth kingdom of creation begins to realize its species' potential. The involutionary force takes us on to the seventh level, where the soul learns spirituality, finally passing from the material plane to the subtle realm whence it came. The seventh stage will burgeon when a necessary period of purification has healed and readied the world for its 'leap' to that next level.

Seven is not often found within the physical world of nature; it is much more related to spiritual forces that regulate the cycles of time and human development. Seven is the number of perfection and completion, as expressed in the seven symbolic days of creation, seven days of the week, seven rays, seven *chakras*, seven biological systems of the human body, seven seals of Revelation which complete the action, and the seven of the Kabalistic Tree of Life, representing the 'Triumph of Endurance' or 'Victory'. Thus, six, the image of Return, merges into seven, the victory of the Light.

This model for physical and spiritual evolution also applies macrocosmically to the twenty-six thousand year cycle of the equinox precession. As described in the preceding chapter, this 'great cosmic year' with its twelve astrological 'ages' also comprises the four seasons. So, about thirteen thousand years ago at a time consistent with the cosmic fall equinox, after the great flood and the sinking of Atlantis, a new cycle of civilization began in the Age of Leo. It took six astrological ages to arrive at Pisces, and we are now leaving that sign, traversing the threshold to Aquarius, the seventh age. What is noteworthy about this seventh age is that it will provide the tools of our transition from our present physical experience in a world of dense matter to a subtler, more spiritual vibration. This means that civilization now rides the great wheel of time at a position equivalent to the spring equinox of the cosmic year – a time when the light ascends and the darkness must yield. At such times, the ancient, mythic theme of the conflict between the forces of good and evil again plays itself out in the world. We call it Armageddon.

A primal drama has begun. Through us, as spectators or players, the will of the world unfolds. 'All the world's a stage,' said Shakespeare, and the idea of the physical world really being a play of illusion is fundamental to many religions. So here we are at the play, and in the play. The orchestra has already struck up – deep, resonant chords that capture our attention and vibrate our very sinews. The archetype is beginning to emerge – so darkly fierce, most shade their eyes with their programme and dare not look. Some know the score and sing along. The chaos plays its role, and, against a backdrop of diffused light, casts before itself apocalyptic shadows. From that deep place where light and shadow blend, the ancient knowledge of our ancestors cries out: 'Stop! Stop and look back! Look to the harmony and harmonize!'

So, we are stopping. We are looking back. We do seek the harmony. And we will harmonize. The following chapters are presented as a script so that you, the reader, may preview this cosmic drama in which you have chosen to play a part.

When the play ends, physical creation is fully perfected and completed upon the Earth, drawing the present era to a close. The class of the *Kali Yuga* graduates to planes of existence more suited to its new unfoldment, and God says He will 'wipe away all tears from their eyes; and there shall be no more death, neither sorrow, nor crying, neither shall there be any more pain: for the former things are passed away' (Revelation 21:4).

Then, a new play will begin. It's called 'The Golden Age.'

6

Pole Shift

Our home the Earth, that blue and green globe in space, is a living organism of great energy and beauty. Being a negatively charged planetary body, it was declared female, and because she generated and sustained all living things, she was called Mother Earth: Gaia. Through her oceans and flowing rivers, she circulates her life force over seven-tenths of her surface and the capillaries of the land. Her mighty digestive system enriches the soil, eventually returning all life forms and matter back to the receptive Earth. Sometimes she rumbles deep inside, and sometimes she excretes hot gasses and molten lava from the pinched-up wrinkles of her rocky skin. With the passing of the ages, her breathing has shifted whole continents and ocean beds, nudging them to new geography. The ancients knew and understood her nervous system and built temples of healing and worship in quiet places of the spirit; energy sources of such discreet and refined vibration that they became holy places, linked by paths of pilgrimage and trade. We recognize this network as the 'planetary grid'. The human body contains the same network in the form of meridians along which foci of energy can be specially photographed as points of light and stimulated by needles or pressure to heal and regenerate. Through us, the Earth becomes self-conscious.

The weather is an outlet for Gaia's emotional nature but we, as her children, have ignorantly disrupted and destroyed the integrity of her nurturing whole systems. So, if She cries and rages, floods and erupts, trembles or begins to flip out (or over), we should take notice and learn why. The Earth does have a tolerance flashpoint and is responsive to stress. Apparently, there is a limit to how much land can be stripped of resources, coal, trees, vegetation, topsoil and species, and how much land, air and water can be polluted to support the equation of 'progress, progress, progress = survival'. Evidently we do not know what that limit is, but the Earth does, and She's trying to tell us. 'Now.'

There have been many other civilizations that reached great cultural peaks and dissolved into faded records on ancient papyri: thousands of years reduced to a reference, great upheavals retold as myth, folklore based on fact or fantasy. We've never really been sure about any of this, but research by the major Earth sciences in recent decades has placed at our disposal many missing pieces of the puzzle.

Legend, historical records and geological evidence reveal that during the approximate three and a half billion years of Earth's existence there have, in fact, been many reversals of the Earth's geographical poles. They caused cataclysmic upheavals, which deluged entire continents, made mountains out of molehills and seabeds, and razed civilizations to rubble and humanity to recurrent grubbing around with stones.

Even within recent memory, the theory of continental drift (the slow shifting of continents owing to weakness in the suboceanic crust) was controversial. Today, there is agreement on its validity. The theory of terrestrial pole reversal is a similar situation (but more serious in that the available evidence may well continue to be dismissed as anecdotal, right up until the occurrence of the next shift!).

Wandering of the magnetic poles, however, is a well-established geophysical fact. Opinion is divided amongst adherents of terrestrial pole reversal theory as to how it happened in the past, and whether it occurred simultaneously with magnetic reversals, or independently. There seems to be evidence to support both conclusions. This theme is a crucial factor in terms of evolutionary progression. External occurrences in the material world, of course, have their mythic and psychological counterpart within the human psyche. Important prophecies on the subject may prove more meaningful, then, if we first discuss the physical basis of their probability.

It should be noted that the traditional scientific view of major geologic Earth changes occurring only slowly over long periods of geologic time has been effectively challenged since the 1980s. Although not without its critics, the theory of 'catastrophism' nevertheless has been established as an evolutionary force to be reckoned with. Agents of catastrophe range from Apollo class asteroid impacts of the Earth to lethal radiation from supernova explosions.

It might be helpful to start off with some third-party credibility, inasmuch as the late Dr Albert Einstein endorsed the theory of geographic polar reversal and wrote the Foreword to the first edition of *The Path of the Pole* by Charles H. Hapgood. This impressive work defines a phenomenon, polar shifting, which occurs when the rigid outer crust of the Earth periodically undergoes extensive displacement over the viscous and possibly fluid inner layers. In appraisal of Hapgood's treatise, Einstein wrote, 'Such displacements may take place as the consequence of comparatively slight forces exerted on the crust, derived from the earth's momentum of rotation, which in turn will tend to alter the axis of rotation of the earth's crust.'

In discussing the dynamics of the Earth as a living organism, we will explore reversal of the magnetic poles and how the magnetic field is generated, and the fact that over the years it appears to have weakened greatly. We will present several theories to account for this, but isolate no singular stimulus, because all geophysical events are interrelated and of cumulative influence. We will also cite geographical and historical evidence to confirm our assertion that the terrestrial poles have also about-faced, and may well give an encore – within our own lifetime. The physical process involved in such a happening is outlined, together with future influences that could contribute to history repeating itself. We shall also touch upon a new theory of rotation.

The magnetic poles are not in quite the same place as the geographic poles. They wander around somewhat randomly, and during the one hundred years between 1850 and 1950, their customary meandering averaged but two miles each year.[1] However, since 1950 (the time when Earth's cooling and increased volcanic activity began), the North magnetic pole has moved more than 200 miles – a four hundred-percent increase of declination. The Hydrographic Office of the U.S. Navy now updates its isogonic maps every five years because the wandering has been so extreme since 1955.

Physicist Arnold Zachow, electromagnetics consultant at Villanova and Drexel Universities, states that it is the locking of the Earth's core to the mantle that is the source of the geomagnetic field. As the Earth revolves, it generates a magnetic field along the axis of rotation that both radiates and attracts energy, and serves to deflect cosmic rays away from the planet. The strength and direction of the magnetic field are influenced by the speed of the Earth's rotation, and also by solar cycles. The greatest perturbations of Earth's magnetism always accompany the appearance of large sunspots as they pass through the central meridian of the sun. This is one of several reasons for recent rotational slowing of the Earth, a phenomenon also related to the extreme wandering of the magnetic poles over the past three decades. Beginning in 1957, the number of sunspots in solar cycles has been increasing, 1990 being the highest count on record.

By examining excavated pottery shards and core samples from rock and submarine mountain ranges, 171 reversals of the Earth's magnetic poles have been documented. Iron oxides in lava or igneous rock are nonmagnetic when liquified by extreme heat, but they acquire a magnetic orientation and, upon cooling, fossilize into an alignment that matches the Earth's own polarity at any given time. Based on the evidence from geological core samples, the end of the last known reversal period has been calculated to have occurred 12,400 years ago.[2] And a brief anomaly has been dated around 860 B.C.[3] – the time of the great cosmic upheavals described in detail in Velikovsky's *Worlds in Collision.*[4]

It is confusing to scientists that the great majority of rocks with inverted magnetic polarity are charged up to one hundred times more strongly than could have been produced by terrestrial magnetism.[5] Certainly, there is speculation as to the nature of the forces that could involve such massive magnetic exaggeration. Is this evidence that the Earth at one time revolved faster, and thereby generated a stronger protective magnetic field? During the past 1,800 years, this field is estimated to have fallen to less than two-thirds of its original strength.[6] We know that magnetic field reversals were accompanied by declines in intensity, which may have persisted, and that in the last one hundred years alone, the field strength has decreased by more than ten percent.[7]

The significance of this data is that it indicates an increase in the amount of radiation now reaching the Earth's surface from space, because the strength of the protective magnetic shield is proportionate to the speed of Earth's rotation. This is probably all right if we are to mutate and evolve at a satisfactory predetermined pace, but how dangerous is this trend combined with depletion of the delicate ozonosphere that protects Earth life from lethal ultraviolet radiation? The extinction of entire species (especially marine) has been linked to magnetic reversals. Reduction or cessation of the geomagnetic field is thought to have accompanied the reversals, allowing lethal amounts of solar radiation to penetrate the Earth, destroying many life forms.

A theory now gaining support suggests that the great glacial ages of the past were caused by irregularities in the tilt of the Earth's rotational axis, which produced great earthquakes and inhospitable weather. There is evidence that the radical weather changes and the increase of earthquakes since 1976 are related to these factors.

The Paris Observatory, which uses atomic clocks to keep official time for the whole world, began delaying the New

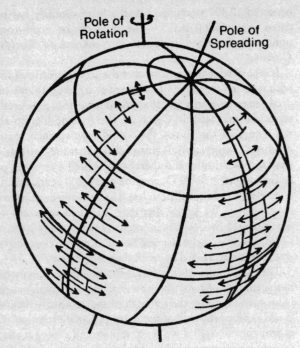

*The greatest and fastest areas of ridge spreading occur in most
ocean beds closest to the equator, rather as if the globe were
splitting like a huge squashed orange, the rate decreasing
regularly with distance from it. This can be attributed to the fact
that the Earth is very slightly pear-shaped, being about 30 miles
fatter in diameter just below the equator, and flatter at the poles,
due to the greater centrifugal force of rotation there. As the
earth expands this way it slows down.[8]*

Year in 1971. At the end of 1979 the United States Commerce Department issued a statement about an annual loss
of time. A spokesperson said a discrepancy existed between
solar and atomic time and that 'the earth doesn't spin on its
axis at a constant rate. It slows down and speeds up at
unpredictable times and for the past few decades it has been

slowing down.'" The following year, 1980, the Magsat satellite was launched as part of a project to investigate the erratic migrations of the magnetic poles and measure length of day. It fell back to Earth after eight months. We don't know how the satellite's data was interpreted, but an additional second of 'leap' time at year-end is now necessary. On the eve of 1990, network TV news reported from the U.S. National Bureau of Standards that 'the Earth is slowing down enough that extra time is needed to keep atomic clocks synchronized to the spin of the Earth'. To scientists, the rotational loss of even a second is considered immensely significant.

The next question is, what exactly causes reversals of the magnetic poles? Scientists still do not know how or why the magnetic poles reversed, only that they did. Polarity within an electromagnetic device can be achieved by reversing the current instead of turning the core over, and a thunderbolt striking a magnet theoretically can effect the same result. The planet has the properties of a huge magnet, so a short circuit between it and a transiting celestial body could result in magnetic pole reversal. For instance, we know that tremendously powerful arcs of electrical charges are continually sparking between Jupiter and one of its moons, Io. In the case of the Earth, if the passing sphere were a comet, dense clouds of magnetic debris from its tail could have been electrically charged, the strength of its magnetic field depending upon its charge.[10] This would account theoretically for magnetic pole reversals of the past, as well as the mystery of rocks with reversed magnetic polarity up to one hundred times stronger than normal.

Astronomer Michael Papagiannis of Boston University postulates that the constant stream of energized solar particles that produces the solar wind thrusts on earthward, causing a torque that can influence the magnetic poles and their meanderings.[11] Dr Immanuel Velikovsky, in his monumental works, *Worlds in Collision* and *Earth in Upheaval*, provides fascinating historical documentation and theory to explain a number of these events, which may have accompanied actual transposition of the terrestrial poles as well. Venus, originally a comet from Jupiter, struck the Earth and the planet Mars several times, causing the aerial phenomena and global terror alluded to in the lore of most ancient peoples. These convergent phenomena resulted in Venus's orbital stability as a planet. Mars also encroached upon Earth's gravitational field several times, triggering exactly – the kind of apocalyptic havoc outlined in the Bible's Book of Revelation. In this regard, we are reminded of one of Nostradamus's prophecies:

The year 1999, seventh month,
A great king of terror will descend from the skies
To resuscitate the great king of Angolmois,
Around this time Mars will reign for the good cause.

Could this quatrain refer to the possible liberation of Mars's satellite, Phobos (meaning 'terror') from its orbit? Phobos revolves centrifugally, which means it is straining to get out of orbit. It is a relatively dense body, and, were it to escape (let's hope we are all sitting down at the time), it would gravitate toward the centre of the solar system, passing close to or even colliding with Earth.

Riley Hansard Crabb, director of Borderland Sciences Research Foundation, has information on this subject from sources other than Nostradamus. His source suggests this satellite of Mars may stray within Earth's atmosphere and surprise our planet into a reluctant orbit out between Mars and Jupiter, and that Pluto may be lost from the solar system. It is known, moreover, that up to a thousand times more meteors impact the Earth from Mars than from the closer proximity of the moon.[12]

Scientists confirm that the Earth's geomagnetic reversals were often accompanied by rains of meteorites and tektites. This fact is immensely important to the overall theory of geographic pole reversal, since historical accounts of cataclysm, as well as prophecies about the future, include mention of hail from heaven or stars falling upon the Earth like a plague. At least four such occasions have been extensively documented. Samplings from the ocean floors indicate that at least a quarter of a billion tons of these fragments covered almost a tenth of the Earth's surface at the time of the last magnetic polarity reversal.[13] Scientists also acknowledge that cosmic debris in the form of falling meteors and tektites not only slows the Earth's rotation, but can influence its actual orbit. Don't miss that! This indicates that magnetic and geographical poles may have shifted at the same time.

Marine geologists have now studied the occurrence extensively, attributing meteoric tektite rains to the impact of a cosmic body entering Earth's atmosphere periodically, specifically, at the time of the last reversal of the Earth's bipolar magnetic field. Over the decades, magnetic reversals have increased, with the interval between sometimes no more than ten thousand years. Many scientists agree that the next reversal would seem to be due, even overdue.[14] The implication is that this 'overdueness' may well be related to the recent extremes in pole wandering.

Accounts of great cataclysms on the Earth almost always appear to have been accompanied by meteor showers and heavy hailstones. It has become generally accepted that major extinctions, like the disappearance of the dinosaurs, correspond to impacts of large extraterrestrial bodies on the Earth.[15] Deposits of stishovite (a dense form of silica formed by extreme pressures, only found at impact sites), iron-rich H-chondrites (stones of meteoric origin), and iridium (mostly found in objects from space) correspond with extinctions and the boundaries of the last two of the major geologic ages. Evidence now suggests that an asteroid crashed into the Earth and actually *caused* the worldwide changes that terminated the Cretaceous period and began the Tertiary geologic age. Additionally, red clay excavated from the Cretaceous-Tertiary boundary period has also been correlated with a seventy percent extinction of all plant and animal life. Perhaps this red clay is also a clue to the prophecies of Nostradamus and the Bible about rivers turning to blood at the time of a great future cataclysm.

And so, the seemingly surreal or weird events from the Bible become more understandable when viewed with the correct perspective. In the Old Testament, Israel's enemies, the Amorites, were killed when 'the Lord cast down great hailstones from heaven upon them', while at Joshua's command, the sun and moon stood still for an extra day (Joshua 10:11–13). Referring to the 'last days', Jesus prophesies: 'Immediately after the tribulation of those days ... the sun and moon will be darkened ... the stars shall fall from heaven, and the powers of the heavens shall be shaken' (Matthew 24:29). At the end of the Bible, tektite falls and polar reversals appear again: 'The stars of heaven fell unto the earth, even as a fig tree casteth her untimely figs, when she is shaken of a mighty wind./And the heaven departed as a scroll when it is rolled together; and every mountain and island were moved out of their places' (Revelation 6:13–14). Or, in 16:21: 'And there fell upon men a great hail out of heaven, *every stone* about the weight of a talent ... for the plague thereof was exceeding great.' With a talent weighing seventy-five pounds, we bet it *was*.[16] Nostradamus prophesied (X:67) that at some point in the future, during the month of May, 'a very mighty trembling' would occur, accompanied by 'hail, larger than an egg'.

Even minor changes in the Earth's axis of rotation or 'wobble' can affect 'to a surprising extent both the climate at the surface of the Earth and the forces and stresses within it', says physicist Heirtzler.[17] There seems to be no set linear progression to the Earth's changing dynamics, but rather an interaction and synergistic fusion of geophysical events such as earthquakes, volcanic eruptions, weather changes, solar activity and rotational changes. Evidence suggests that earthquakes of 7.5 Richter magnitude are either the cause or the effect of an irregular wobble described by the North pole of rotation. Since 1900, this rotational irregularity has been measured by astronomers, who say that it reaches a maximum every seven years – a periodicity correlated with peaks of earthquake activity.[18]

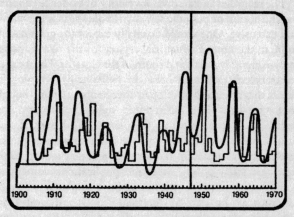

Earthquake energy and mean daily shift of the polar wobble:
'A definite correlation.'

We do not know for sure whether radical changes of Earth's geographic axis of rotation and the magnetic dipole reversals were simultaneous, but, from the evidence available, it appears theoretically possible, and even likely. One should bear in mind that the existence of flying saucers is not officially acknowledged in spite of the now overwhelming evidence that they exist; the theory of continental drift was not acknowledged, either; nor was acupuncture; or ESP. Venus was doggedly declared to have a surface of swirling gas until Russian satellite pictures established a solid rocky one. Examples are numerous, and encourage us to keep an open mind.

If it is true that the planet's poles have periodically, radically, rolled around, producing immediate displacement of geological features and climates, the upheaval must have been of gargantuan proportions. We can assume abrupt extinction of countless species and life forms as they were swept up in the folding of ocean beds, ice sheets and forest cover, bombarded by molten detritus or swallowed by rupturing land masses. Evidence comes from various sources.

The recorded and archival inventory of evidence supporting the notion of periodic terrestrial pole shifts is persuasive
and extensive. One would normally expect the great deserts
to be in the hottest equatorial regions of the world instead
of considerably north and south of the equator. The ice ages,
contrary to traditional belief in millennially creeping ice
sheets that gradually enveloped continents, are now thought
to have taken place much more suddenly, perhaps even
'ready-made' (inasmuch as the planet rolled over, its ice-
capped poles settled at the equator, and evaporation quickly
caused icy precipitation and formation of new ice caps at the
new terrestrial poles). Scientific publications contain no
scarcity of relevant information about enigmatic discoveries, such as the 1957-58 International Geophysical Year's
data that oceans all over the world suddenly rose two hundred feet about thirteen thousand years ago – a period
thought contiguous with the biblical Flood. And, as mentioned previously, the last known full reversal of Earth's
magnetic field is calculated to have occurred around 12,400
years ago (although a brief reversal anomaly is also thought
to have occurred in approximately 860 BC). Then, there are
the intactly preserved bodies of mammoth herds found in
profusion with leaves and fir cones in the frozen tundras of
northeast Siberia;[19] shells and marine fossils discovered atop
the Himalayas and other mountain groupings; fossil trees
and coral reefs within the Arctic Circle, only 8°15' from the
North Pole;[20] quadruped species from both arctic and tropical regions found buried together in caves and excavations
in the United Kingdom and Europe,[21] and literally millions
of animals – mastodon, bison, horse, etc. – mangled and
mingled with uprooted trees, which were mined out of
miles of excavations along stream valleys near Fairbanks,
Alaska.[22] Whales, too, have been found beached several hundred feet above sea level hundreds of miles inland in various
parts of North America.[23]

Historical records also lend an interesting and supportive
perspective to this subject, and most ancient cultures have
something to contribute from their annals. The Egyptian

priests, for instance, told Herodotus that the sun had 'four times risen out of his usual quarter,' and that he had 'twice risen where he now sets and twice set where he now rises'.[24] Records of the Earth's great cycles, the profound knowledge of astronomy and astrology, as well as those principles of concealed knowledge in which humanity and the cosmos are related, are believed to have been preserved within the religious 'mysteries' of the ancient world by a hierarchy of initiates (see Chapter 8: 'The Great Pyramid').

In the tomb of Senmut, architect to the Egyptian Queen Hatshepsut, the night sky with constellations and zodiac is shown in complete reverse along the Eastern ceiling.[25] Other Egyptian documents echo this theme. Papyrus Anastasi IV, Magical Papyrus Harris, and Papyrus Ipuwer refer to the Earth being turned upside down, the seasons reversed, time disordered and the sun failing to rise.[26] And in Breasted's *Ancient Records of Egypt* III, Sec. 18, the reference 'Horakhte, he riseth in the West', appears. Horakhte was the name given to Horus, the sun god, when he rose in the morning, eastern sky.

Sura LV of the Koran speaks of the 'Lord of two Easts and of two Wests.' The Talmud says, 'Seven days before the deluge the Holy One changed the primeval order and the sun rose in the West and set in the East (Tractate Sanhedrin), and another rabbinical source declares that in the time of Moses, 'the course of the heavenly bodies became confounded'.[27] In the ancient Finnish epic poem *Kalevala*, we read that 'dreaded shades' enveloped the Earth, and 'the sun occasionally steps from his accustomed path'. The poem also describes a time when iron hailstones fell (ancient descriptions of the meteorites and tektites scientists have associated with geomagnetic reversals, and similar to biblical descriptions of hail and falling stars during events that allude to the planet rolling over) and the sun and moon were stolen from the sky, but that after a period of darkness, they were replaced by two new luminaries. The beautiful and intricate creation myth of the Hopi tells of twin beings stationed by the creator at the North and South Poles, jointly to keep the world rotating and ensure stability of land and gentleness of air movement. At the end of the first three worlds, they were instructed to leave their positions. The world, left to function without polar supervision, was plunged into chaos 'and rolled over twice', after which a new world was born.

These references are not entirely restricted to historical data, either. Persons of vision have always been attuned to reality beyond the range of the ordinary senses. Shortly before his death in a San Francisco hospital in 1971, Murshid Samuel L. Lewis, spiritual leader of the Chisti Order of Sufis, said that the 'sheep had been separated from the goats', and that the world would very soon know about it. This was a biblical reference to the sorting out of people at the Last Judgment. His grave marker, located in the rolling foothills of the Sangre de Cristo Mountains in northern New Mexico, bears this simple inscription: 'And on that day, the sun will rise in the West, and all men, seeing, will believe.'

Edgar Cayce, the 'sleeping prophet,' said in one of his 1932 readings that 'the extreme Northern portions of the Earth were then the Southern portions – or the polar regions were then turned to where they occupied more of the tropical and semi-tropical regions'.

Perhaps accounts from the Bible such as that of Joshua commanding the sun and moon to stand still (Joshua 10:11–13), are not so farfetched when viewed in the light of these findings. If the Earth's axis tilted in the presence of a strong magnetic influence, and its rotation continued undisturbed, the sun could appear to lose its diurnal movement for an equivalent number of hours.

Just how relevant all this information is to the planet today remains to be seen. We know that when any resilient object (such as a planet) spins, it tends to flatten at the poles and acquire an equatorial bulge, becoming increasingly dislike. In this connection C. O. Dunbar of Yale University stated that when orbital momentum causes enough torque to transcend the reduced stability forces, polar shifts

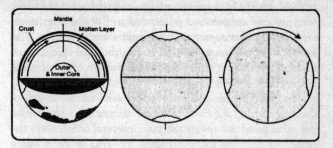

occur.[28] Combine those ingredients with some unusual planetary alignments and rapid changes in polar ice cover, and you have the makings of a very precarious axis!

The process of acquired shape and spin, combined with weight of polar ice coverage and external astronomical influences, is thought to cause sporadic shifts in the Earth's axis of rotation. The late Hugh Auchincloss Brown, engineer and author of *Cataclysms of the Earth*, and UCLA researcher and instructor Chan Thomas, both independently studied this subject for decades; they maintain that every few millennia the polar ice caps reach a weight which, aggravated by the Earth's wobble, spins the poles around, causing the shell to slide over its molten layers. Outer equatorial layers of the rotating globe move at a higher linear velocity than points on the inner layers, but at the same angular speed. If the Earth were to decelerate suddenly because of external celestial influences, the inner layers would slow down or come to rest, while the outer layers would tend to continue rotating, causing friction between the various liquid and semi-liquid layers, and produce heat. Brown and Thomas assert that the outermost solid layers would be torn apart, causing mountains, even continents, to rise and fall.

There follows some dramatic graphic evidence of existing polar motion disturbances.

It can be observed that during 1912–1918, the North geographic pole was contained within the centre of Earth's axial spin, designated by the intersection of x and y coordinates.

In 1962–69, the spin appears erratic, rolling back upon itself, creating earthquakes and a decrease in the stability necessary to maintain consistent momentum about its axis. The North Pole, no longer centred within the axial spin, is now at the extreme right of the chart, and the path of the pole has become less circular. This decrease in rotation rate accompanied an increase in spin wobble that affected the length of the day, causing the magnetosphere to weaken and increase the likelihood of magnetic pole reversal. However, the centre of this tracing represents the year 1969, when a massive, anomalous jerking of the Earth's magnetic field occurred – originating within the core of the Earth itself. This phenomenon was not even *talked* about until 1978. But scientists now believe that, over a period of ten to fifteen years, the jolt served to correct the Earth's rotational instability![29] The 1971–1975 and 1976–1980 tracings show that the unstable trend did continue. But, since 1980, there *has* been a marked restabilization of the wobble – but a continued drift of orbital position. The Geodetic Research and Development Laboratory of the U.S. Geodetic Survey advise that this long-term axial drift (about eleven metres) has caused the spin axis to shift and that the data should be interpreted 'with caution'. I was told that controversy exists as to whether the x/y coordinates reflect the real motion of the pole, or the shifting of the continental plates on which the polar motion siting equipment is located.

There can be no doubt that the polar motion drift is both significant and important. This drift is illustrated by the fact that in 1989 the ancient Anasazi 'Sun Dagger' calendar failed to register the summer solstice for the first time since it was created sometime between 800–1150 BC. For about one thousand years, and only on the first day of summer, a bright, vertical shaft of sunlight (the 'sun dagger') has crept to the centre of a nine-ring spiral carved on a ten-foot rock face in Fajada Butte, Chaco Canyon, New Mexico. Because the rotation of the planet has shifted, the shadow cast by the sun at the summer solstice now falls at a different angle, no longer indicating the solstice.

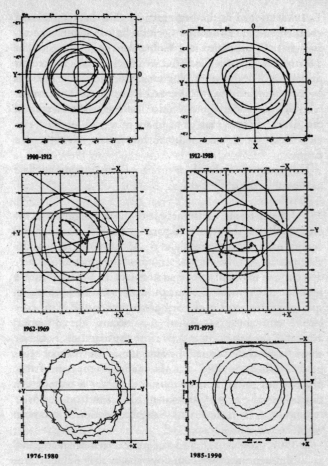

Graphs indicating changes in the stabilizing forces affecting Earth's axial spin and displacement of geographical North (intersection x and y) to right of centre. Measurements prior to 1975 contain up to 1.5 metres of error and were co-ordinated by the International Polar Motion Service from various siting stations. Measurements after 1975 contain an error range of 4–8 centimetres and were obtained by satellite laser ranging (bouncing a laser beam from Earth off a satellite).

As mentioned at the beginning of this chapter, external events have their counterpart within human consciousness. So, what *else* happened in 1969 besides the aberrant jerk in our planet's magnetic field? In 1969, men actually walked on the moon. The Earth, a blue and white jewel against the backdrop of infinity, was viewed from space. This image, relayed back to Earth and electronically reproduced around the planet, allowed each of us to see how we looked, not as individuals or separate nations, but as *one people – one world*.

This image of the Earth from space is the supreme symbol of the archetype of the Self!

Wholeness –

In Jungian terms, the archetype of the Self organizes back into wholeness the separated parts of the Self. Through the evolutionary process, spirit and consciousness flow out into the material world along the strands of the great web of life, diversifying into multiple separatenesses. At the appropriate time for the 'return' of consciousness from matter back to spirit, the archetype of the Self arises powerfully in the collective consciousness. When this occurs, the disparate aspects of the Self begin to move into the harmonic relationship of a coherent whole. The Harmonic Convergence celebrated globally in 1987 was the matured eruption of this process into external consciousness! It was a part of the function of the Maya Calendar to reach out from the past, reminding us 'It is time' with a sombre nod and a knowing wink, keeping us on track.

In 1969, people journeyed as deeply into inner space, and as far through their own consciousness, as they did into outer space. Being such a materialistic culture, it is little wonder that a materialistic approach to spirituality – LSD et *al.* – held such broad appeal for getting in touch with the inner Self and in the 'awakening' from cultural trance. In 1969 a massive social phenomenon celebrated that. It was called Woodstock. And, in 1969, in a distant subgalaxy of the Milky Way, a benign blue star was discovered, named, and unceremoniously catalogued. Little did anyone guess the

significance that obscure star would assume just two
decades later (discussed in the 'Hopi' and 'Our Prophecy'
chapters)!

Tracking the ebb and flow of events as prophecy unfolds
is sometimes scary, often inspiring, but always humbling. It
lets one know that reprieves and detours are possible, and
that when the arrow of fate does hit its mark there is *always*
a challenge and positive payoff involved, no matter what the
outer circumstances.

We now know that the relationship between changes in
the Earth's tilt, wobble, the path of its orbit around the sun,
and previous ice ages are all related to the geometry of
Earth's orbit. In 1930, Serbian geophysicist M. Milanko-
vitch said as much, but it was not until recently that there
was any validating evidence for his theory.

The 400 percent increase in magnetic polar wandering
since 1950 has helped support the theory that the Earth
spins, not, as held by traditional science, upon its stationary,
geographic, South polar axis, but upon its continuously
moving South polar *magnetic* axis. National boundaries and
the lines of latitude and longitude, obviously, are designa-
tions found on globe models only. As the late Captain Scott
would attest, it is not possible to pinpoint exact terrestrial
North; we go by our computation of it only. The magnetic
dipole, however, is a physical fact with no basis in theory – it
actually exists. The gyroscopic effect of Earth's equatorial
bulge appears to confirm that our planet does spin upon its
geographic South polar axis, but it is suggested that this very
bulge accounts for the wobbling of the geographic North
Pole when the axis of the magnetic dipole wanders. The U.S.
Geodetic Survey confirms that the longterm drift of the
North pole has caused the South polar axis to shift.
Advanced translations of geometry from the Great Pyramid
also appear to substantiate this hypothesis.[30]

The subject of pole shift lends itself to factual definition,
philosophical consideration, and that area of abstraction
which lies beyond the vanishing point: the place where
logic and intuition briefly merge before translation into the

subtler energies of a different reality. In the final analysis, things seldom happen to us; they usually happen from us. We help or hinder natural processes by the way we think and act – especially within the environment.

One may believe the cataclysmic events described in this chapter to be part of a coincident epic, unrelated to any of the discernable patterns that historical perspective finds most comfortable. But humanity, responding freely within the law of cycles, bore responsibility for events of the past, and will do so again. The first part of this book dealt with the thought-word-action chain, and how, when natural laws are ignored, chaos always results. The story continues: all energy contrary to the evolutionary life force is negatively polarized. It eventually transmigrates to lower and more destructive life and energy forms. The collective negative energy (of thoughts, words and actions), in its varying forms and degrees, descends to the appropriate vibratory frequency of less evolved forms. It can animate and energize viruses or bacteria, for instance, causing epidemics; weather, in the form of storms, floods and hurricanes; geographical upheavals within the Earth itself; and disturbances from the outer environment of space – all vehicles of negative karmic feedback. This is what Edgar Cayce meant when he said that many a land could be kept intact by the consciousness of its inhabitants. This is also why tampering with nature to modify and eradicate undesirable weather is so useless and dangerous – like dispensing drugs to treat symptoms which may or may not disappear, and creating serious side effects in the process. The negative energy will simply manifest more powerfully in another place at another time.

The daily disasters and crises of the world are not the 'acts of God' conveniently ignored by insurance companies. Ignorance and fear are the culprits, along with their companions – greed, dishonesty and just plain stupidity – a conspiracy of unconsciousness in which we have all held membership. The negative attributes of individuals seemed to become an asset once power and profits got involved. Free enterprise all too often became synonymous with getting ahead at the cost of the greater good, and objections all too often were interpreted as a threat to free enterprise because pollution and exploitation have always been someone's profit. We have begun to recognize today's technology as a usurer delivering convenience, efficiency and profits in exchange for the exorbitant dues of ecocide, human and species suffering, and estrangement from all that is natural. On a diet of natural resources, the industrial revolution's technological offspring gave birth to corporations, conglomerates, and fiscal networks so powerful that they soon transformed the face of the Earth. And its computerized nervous system crackles with superhuman intelligence as it demands aggressive gambling for oil, inspires nuclear addictions, and more and more of the failing resources that spawned its genesis.

Perhaps the most threatening of all ideas now is the belief that global problems can be solved by the right politics or technology. They not only have failed at the task so far, but have compounded the problems. As the appropriate model for culture, the failsafe ways of the natural world have been ignored, regarded as irrelevant. Physical effects always have their roots in spiritual causes. How can a bunch of 'effects' be successfully juggled to correct a 'cause'? When the fire alarm clangs so urgently, why do we repeatedly disconnect it instead of locating the fire?

If the cataclysms of the Earth and solar system are, as we assert, cyclical and according to cosmic and divine rhythms, it is human consciousness and actions which aggravate or aid the process. From the way we think to the way we treat the planet we contribute to the *degree* of potential catastrophe should Earth's poles become transposed.

To the extent that people can begin living their best basic values (irrespective of what others may be doing), break out of the old non-serving habit patterns and realign themselves with natural law and human values to the best of their ability, the future can be improved. We are creating it now, minute by minute.

And by that destiny, to perform an act,
Whereof what's past is prologue;
What to come, in yours and my discharge.
The Tempest, William Shakespeare

Our sun is the point of emergence through which light and life, mundane and divine, is channeled through the Central Sun from the other interdimensional suns beyond. *Yugas,* the great cycles of cosmic time, are related to the revolution of our sun around the Central Sun. With each complete revolution, our sun increases its vibratory frequency, passing the increased energy on to its planets. We are on the verge of an ascending spiral, and this transmission of energy already has begun. We have also noted that magnetic pole reversals are becoming more frequent as time goes by, and that the decreased intensity of the Earth's magnetic field contributed at these times to the increase of cosmic and ultraviolet radiation reaching life on Earth from the sun. This is how evolution is fostered and prospers, through the resultant mutation and survival of the fittest, both physically and spiritually.

According to the esoteric teachings of the wisdom tradition, in the process of evolutionary unfolding, major moons become major planets, generating moons of their own. It is stated that there will ultimately be a general displacement of all the bodies belonging to our solar system, including the establishment of our present moon as a planet and the creation of a new moon. This sequence of macrocosmic events is analogous to the microcosmic quantum leap where electrons appear to jump into closer orbits around an atom's nucleus – a phenomenon as little understood as the evolution of a solar system or the shifting of the poles. It is all to do with transmutation. Transmutation is the science of naturally occurring changes within the atom's nucleus, one that provides the missing link between matter and spirit.[31] According to the rhythmic pulsations of evolution, each element is not fixed and immutable, but transmutes in its appointed time and way into the next and more complex one. From hydrogen, the simplest element, on up the spiral to the human organism, the most materially complete and complex, the process unfolds. According to the same Law, the planet itself is like an atom in the body of the universe and is transformed physically by the evolution of its elements and spiritually by the consciousness level of the beings who inhabit it.

Major planets eventually become suns, which in time become supersuns. When the Central Sun was a physical plane sun, our sun was one of its planets. In discussing the fact that Earth may be subject to forces which can bring about its displacement into a new orbit, promote our moon to planetary status, bring about a new moon, and leave Pluto to fret somewhere in distant space, the following may provide a basis for understanding these deeper mysteries.

In talking of the birth of a new moon, we should point out that areas of seismic activity are located primarily along the edges of the Earth's tectonic plates, which slowly heave against each other until pressure and slippage cause relief through volcanic eruptions or earthquakes.

The Ring of Fire is a circle of volcanic and seismic activity around the Pacific rim that contains about 80 percent of the world's volcanoes. It coincides with the outline of the central Pacific plate, which is slowly edging northwest against the stubborn thrust of the Eurasian plate. Emerging from the centre of this ring (like the knob of a saucepan lid) are the Hawaiian Islands, which, measured from the ocean floor, represent the highest points on the Earth's crust – five hundred feet taller than Everest.

If it is true that Earth is destined to receive a new moon when the time is cosmically ripe and/or sufficiently cataclysmic, it will undoubtedly be sucked, hurtling molten, into space from that area now defined as the Ring of Fire. There may even be evidence of just such a process in our solar system.

The myth of Minerva, who was born, fully mature, from the head of Jupiter, father of the Gods, may be a disguised metaphor for the factual birth of Venus as an errant comet

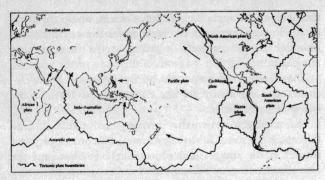

The 'Ring of Fire'. Worldwide distribution of shallow earthquakes and tectonic plates.

from the celestial body of Jupiter, largest planet of our solar system. By somewhat circuitous research, it is demonstrated that the planet Venus was identified by the Babylonians with Astarte, who was known to the Romans as Minerva and to the Greeks as Athena.[32] Athena was recognized by the Iranians as Anaites, whom they identified with – you guessed it – the planet Venus.[33] The enigmatic 'red spot' on Jupiter may be the turbulent scar of Venus's cataclysmic separation. It is believed that Venus subsequently caused terror on Earth and havoc in the solar system until stabilized into orbit as a planet.[34] Scientists have concluded that Venus was formed in an entirely different manner, or from different material, than the rest of the solar system, because concentrations of an inert gas called argon 36, a hundred times greater than on Earth or Mars, were discovered by the 1979 Venus mission.

Jim Hurtak of the Academy of Future Science describes the characteristics of the major nodes of the planetary grid. He states that Earth's magnetic fields are aligned through aerials of magnetic energy marking the points where energies from deep space pour into the Earth's surface. These aerials are balanced on the Earth by the magnetic North and South poles, and at a particular time in the future when unusually turbulent solar flare radiations bombard the magnetic points of the Earth, its magnetic fields may be thrown into imbalance, causing a spinning of the shell to new meridians.[35]

The magnetic fields are already in a severe state of imbalance. Australian researcher Bruce Cathie, in his works *Harmonic 66* and *Harmonic 695*,[36] lends scientific amplification to the subject, asserting that atomic bomb detonations at key nodes of the planetary grid have disrupted the grid's natural Earth energy frequencies and created a massive effect akin to the static in the circuits. Many of the aerials mentioned above (the function of which is to keep in alignment the terrestrial and celestial magnetic fields associated with Earth and to channel specific cosmic frequencies into the grid network) have been obliterated.

There is a strong correlation here between the celestial grid associated with Earth and the etheric body that interpenetrates and energizes the human physical body. Psychics see this etheric sheath as a web of fine light fibres. Serious mental and emotional problems are sometimes the result of these two bodies becoming misaligned with each other. When this *is* the case, and on occasions when electroshock therapy *is* successful, it is thought by some to be due to the shocking of the etheric and physical bodies back into correct juxtaposition. The planet appears to have a similar problem, with its physical and etheric fields out of synchronization. UFOs apparently utilize the celestial grid to negotiate interstellar space, and it is author Cathie's view that one of their main missions regarding our planet is to assist in realignment of the planetary and celestial grids – for their own ends as well as ours.

The strange and sudden reactions of nature, geophysical and climatic problems may be symptomatic of this little-understood imbalance. Perhaps an eventual pole shift will be the 'electroshock' necessary to restore cosmological and biospherical harmony.

We cannot state categorically when the foregoing events will occur, but only that they are cosmically scheduled within the great plan of evolutionary unfolding and that they can be logically accounted for right now within our own lifetime.

Magnetic anomalies are found at twelve key nodes of the grid. These geomantic coordinates include areas such as the Bermuda Triangle and part of the Great Lakes where air and sea craft inexplicably have disappeared. The other nodes are the North and South poles, and various sacred sites, such as Stonehenge, Machu Picchu and the Great Pyramid. This is valuable backup data for the esoteric information that shifting of the Earth's geographic poles will act to realign these twelve major magnetic vortex nodes with a higher vibrational frequency of existence. In this sense they act like valves to a new time-space continuum, like timewarp locks to the next evolutionary level. The Bible's Revelation (21:12) describes the New Jerusalem descending from the heavens after the battle of Armageddon, prepared for residence by the righteous. It has twelve gates, complemental to the twelve nodes of the grid that will realign the Earth at its polar shifting with the twelve points of the new dimension, as we ascend into the new reality that descends upon us.

Only when all planets of the solar system have their axes aligned with that of the sun, and the sun has its own axis pointing toward the Central Sun (of which it is a satellite), can the sun increase its own vibratory rate and progress towards Central Sun status. This cannot be accomplished, however, until all life on each and any of the planets has cultivated the capacity to sustain that higher frequency, or life unsuited to it has been removed. This is the nature of today's accelerated changes, the consciousness revolution, and the distress which will result from not understanding the process that is at work. The purpose of the Earth's repositioning is to align its axis more closely with that of the sun, and its life with that of the appropriate vibrational frequency for its expanding consciousness. The New Jerusalem, the new Heaven and new Earth, are invisibly present. They await us as the new reality, a world in which we are about to be reborn when we have purified our physical bodies and developed our Light bodies well enough to function in them.

> God will call out of the nations of the world a chosen people who will generate a new race to inherit a new Earth that will grow out of the old. It will be a planet of Light, like the Sun, brilliant and fiery, under the direct rulership of God. Man will save himself by generating a new body of Light.[37]

For them which shall remain ... shall be made whole, and they shall be as new. The Earth shall be purified and it shall give forth a new Light from the place which is appointed Her within the firmament. There shall be a new Moon – and She shall have a new Sun, and in turn She shall be a Sun unto lesser worlds – for that is She being prepared.[38]

Do not, then, think of the future as 'the end of the world' in the negative sense, but remember that its destructive aspect is but a healing crisis within the natural order of cosmic progression. It is an occasion for the advancement of humanity as spiritual beings, renewal for the planet and evolution for the solar system. A new beginning is stirring even now, and all you have to do to be a part of it is to get it together in the best way you know how!

PART THREE
Timetable and Guidebook

7

Prophecy and Pragmatism

Prediction and prophecy have fallen into disrepute in this century largely because science, with its own built-in aspect of predictability, has replaced the need within the human psyche. Then, too, prophecies in general have had a notorious reputation for not coming true, or for simply fulfilling themselves at the wrong time, in the wrong place and under different circumstances. Sometimes they appear to be plain irrelevant. This did not seem to bother primitive people, with their unreasoning belief in omens; the Gods simply had changed their minds. Even amongst cultures and societies only slightly less sophisticated than our own, prophecy still has its place of respect as an extension of the religious impulse. But, for those brave souls caught up in the paradigm of logic and reason, there seems to be no place or need for the message of such a medium.

The rapid changes of fast-paced urban living and '9 to 5-ing' snatch most of us into the freneticism of a Keystone Cops scenario at least several times a week. As the Red Queen said to Alice, 'It takes all the running you can do to keep in the same place. If you want to get somewhere else, you must run at least twice as fast as that!' Is it any wonder that predicting the future has been making a slight comeback amongst those practitioners of 'escapism' who still have enough of that ancient instinctual reliance upon providence? Escapism, to some, means faster linear progress, as they rush to meet the future with its technological magnificence. To others, it can mean a change of perspective, another kind of reconnaissance through the looking glass.

The trouble with prophecy has always been that the laws of prediction have not generally been understood – even by the prophets themselves. If a stone age tribe (better described as an isolated group of people simply doing their own thing in their own way) came upon a discarded transistor radio and their shaman said it was a talking box and that a certain man would speak through it at the next full moon, he could be right. However, if the batteries were run down or the programme had been pre-empted, the tribe would believe him to have been mistaken. Then, if a neighbouring tribe were to report that a foraging party had discovered an abandoned automobile and their medicine person had declared it to be a horseless chariot, capable of carrying persons at great speeds, they would think it mighty suspicious if it did not move in spite of his best efforts and incantations. As the tribe moved into closer peripheral contact with civilization and found more artifacts, their soothsayer could soon be in big trouble, even if the divination of the objects were correct.

This analogy holds good for modern prophecy, too. Many times, the prophetic vision, when received, has simply been too advanced to fit into the cultural matrix of the times. As a result, the description of the vision was couched in such limited vocabulary as to be unintelligible, even to people living in the period when the prophecy was supposed to occur. The story of Ezekiel's wheel in the Bible may have been an account of some subjective weirdness that Ezekiel underwent after a breakfast of wild mushrooms, or it may have represented an encounter with beings from space who were transported from the heavens in a circular craft. He did not understand what he saw, so, reading his description, we don't either!

Knowing the principle or law governing a phenomenon allows a greater margin of certainty when faced with a seeming paradox or lack of substantive detail. For instance, when a prediction fails to materialize, there is a natural tendency to refute its validity. It could well be a dumb divination, but one should also consider that the seer was seeing the future correctly, but not understanding it, or misinterpreting it. How can a no-show prophecy be true and correct? In logical thinking, this is indeed a contradiction, but understanding certain principles can reveal how, from a different vantage point, the apparent dilemma is resolved.

A prophecy can be averted because of the interaction of the karma and/or free will of those involved in the chain of events leading to its fulfillment. This is seldom done consciously (unfortunately), but when there's a nonevent, this is sometimes the reason. Let's say, an event was presaged in the year 1911, due to materialize in 1925. That is to say, if circumstances were to unfold as a logical chain of events, 1925 would see the fruition of the prediction. However, the future contains not only that which *will* be, but also everything else that may be. For instance, it would be logical for the humblest or dimmest of oracles to forecast that a blind man walking in a straight line toward the edge of a cliff will, very shortly, disappear over the edge to his death. That is the prediction. However, the blind man could suddenly change his mind and alter direction, based on nothing more than his personal whim. The prediction would then prove 'false', due exclusively to free will. Taking this same circumstance again, the blind person could avert the prophecy if it wasn't his karmic destiny to 'go' at that time. He might unexpectedly remember that he had left his dinner on the stove, and turn back just as he reached the edge. If it were his fate to fall off the cliff, an example of the saving grace of good karma might be that he stepped over the edge as predicted, but landed on a ledge, where he was discovered by a passing sheepherder who led him to safety!

Humanity has the facility of free will, but is still subject to those whims of fortune known as destiny or fate. The Greek translation for destiny is 'Moira', which also means 'the sum total of one's experience'. Two thousand years ago, Heraclitus said it: 'A man's character is his destiny.' From a psychological viewpoint, character could be defined as a combination of heredity and environment, tempered by desires, fears, attitudes and all the learning and acquired marks of personality that make each of us so interesting and unique. These factors subtly motivate actions and steer our course through life, guiding our destiny within certain flexible bounds. But it is the faculty of free will, governed by the elements intrinsic to our nature, that enables us to soar beyond these limits and to triumph, in spite of adversity, over our circumstances.

Fate, returning bad karma, the events of destiny, can only be cancelled by the divine dispensation known as Grace ... A merchant was told by the oracle that he would meet with death in Baghdad. Not wishing to meet with his fate so soon, and planning to avert the encounter, he travelled instead to a far-distant city. And he entered in by the north gate and mingled a while in the marketplace. Quite suddenly, there in the crowd, he saw Death staring at him with pale eyes, and he was afraid. And Death said unto him, 'Boy! Am I ever surprised to see you here. I was just on my way to Baghdad to meet you!' Apparently Grace was not forthcoming for our merchant. If it had all would have been well.

If prophecies have any useful function at all, it is to reveal a glimpse of the future for examination, now. In life, if we don't like the preview, we don't have to see the film. If we do not understand it, we can still attend or wait for it to go away. With a prophecy it's not that simple, but in the case of a particularly fearful augury we can ignore it or try to understand its practical implications. These would be a) to warn, b) to prepare, and c) to provide an opportunity in the present for changing the future. The destiny of a nation can be modified by the collective free will of its people, and the fate of a planet can be changed by the collective free will of its nations. And that is what the following prophecies all have in common.

We can sail the boat of free will anywhere within the shores of destiny. It is when we fail to change course that we end up where we are headed! Prophecy previews an outcome we may or may not welcome. It's really a gift that makes us conscious of what is in motion and invites our response. The purpose of prophecy is to empower, not paralyze. Therefore, if we are already moving toward an undesirable future, whatever we can do to change course will affect the final outcome. In that sense, the fulfilled negative prophecy is actually a prophecy that failed.

'Predictions' tend to be made by individuals (i.e., persons without a large ideological support group) using a divination method. Predictions are more often of short-term and limited profundity range, and affect individuals or relatively small groups of people. 'Prophecy,' by contrast, deals more with the distant future, and has epochal implications affecting great numbers of people. Characteristically, prophecies issue from a religious or spiritual impulse and a connectedness with tradition. A prophecy resonates a deep chord in the collective psyche.

Each of the following prophecies originated in different times from a variety of diverse, respected, cultural traditions. Together, they constitute a coherent, solid body of world prophecy relevant to our times. Different descriptions of the same picture are presented, but what emerges is a single prophecy, a single theme. Its message is clear and the conclusion unmistakable.

Let us then be warned. Let us also be prepared; and, above all, let us realize this opportunity now to work together and influence destiny.

8

The Great Pyramid

From the most ancient times, one structure above all others has inspired and intrigued scientists, archaeologists, researchers and seekers of truth alike: the Great Pyramid of Giza. This Pyramid was named after the pharaoh Khufu (Cheops), who lived around 2575 BC. It stands on thirteen square acres on the Giza Plateau, three miles southwest of Cairo, on the bank of the Nile. As a gift to future generations from the masterminds who conceived and built it, the achievement that is the Great Pyramid stands alone as *the* Wonder of the World.

Controversy surrounds the age and purpose of the Great Pyramid. Academia holds that the structure is nothing more than Khufu's tomb. Others reject this idea and maintain that millennia before Khufu's reign, the Pyramid served as a centre of initiation in the ancient world. There is also a theory that Egyptian culture was inherited from an Atlantean exodus. Throughout the mystery tradition there is a persistent echo that Thoth, known as the Master Initiator, and originally an Atlantean mentor of Egyptian culture, was the designer and architect of the Great Pyramid.[1]

The monument's overall design, architecture, engineering and construction represented pyramid building at its very zenith. There has never been anything even remotely like it – as a repository of geodetic data, as an astronomical calendar and observatory, as a prophetic blueprint, and as a place of initiation in the ancient world.

In squaring the circle, the sum of the Pyramid's base diagonals measures 25,826.53 pyramid inches – mirroring the 25,826.53 year precession of the equinoxes, the Great Year. It seems clear that the architects of this structure understood their place in the cosmic scheme of things and that the Pyramid represented a good deal more than we can presently comprehend.

Ancient Arabic legends and Greek chroniclers tell various versions of the Great Pyramid's origin. However, one of these stories is worth repeating here, since surprisingly, it seems to corroborate a now familiar theme.

In 1646, John Greaves, a professor of astronomy at Oxford University, translated the most prominent of the Arabic writings, which the greatest number of the chronologers agreed upon, concerning the origins of the Great Pyramid.[2] This legend, recorded by one Ibn Abd Alhokm, recounted how the Pyramids were built by a king of Egypt three hundred years before the flood (approx. 11,000 BC). Greaves wrote carefully in his sixteenth-century archaic English script that the king was greatly disturbed by a night vision, a premonition in which 'the whole earth was turned over, and the stars falling downe and striking one another, with a terrible noise ... [and] the fixt stars falling to the earth ... and the shining stars made darke'. As we have already discussed, this business about the Earth turning over and the stars falling from the sky is a repeated theme in the legends and prophecies of major cultures throughout the world.

The King consulted with the chief priests of all the Egyptian provinces, and it was agreed that an underground system of cisterns and waterways should be built to disperse the flooding of the Nile (the assumed source of the coming flood) into a region to the West. (Is this, perhaps, why the Egyptian priests told Herodotus that Khufu was buried *beneath* the Pyramid [not *in* it] in an underground chamber on a subterranean island surrounded by the waters of the Nile?)

Then, to protect the cultural heritage of his times, the King and his advisor priests planned the construction of three massive pyramids as safe repositories for 'all the things that were told him by the wise men, as also all profound sciences, the ... science of Astrology, and of Arithmeticke, and of Geometry, and of Physicke. All this may be interpreted by him that knowes their characters, and language.' The foundations of the pyramids were described as fastened together with lead and iron; the gates were built forty cubits (about seventy feet) underground, and 'the beginning of this building was in a fortunate horoscope'. After describing a huge festival, to which all Egypt was invited, when the pyramids were complete, Greaves writes that Alhokm enumerated the contents of each structure.

'In the Westerne Pyramid 30 treasures, filled with store of riches, and utensils, and with signatures made of precious stones, and with instruments of iron, and vessels of earth, and with a metal which rusts not, and with glasse which might be bended, and yet not broken, and with strange spells, and with several kinds of [elixirs?] and deadly poisons. (Does this mean they had aluminum, plastic, and drugs back then, too?!) He made also in the East Pyramid, divers celestial spheres, and stars, and what they severally operate, in their aspects; and ... the books which treat of these matters. He put also in the coloured Pyramid (the exterior of Kephren's pyramid is known to have been red at one time) the commentaries of the Priests, in chests of black marble, and with every Priest a booke, in which were the wonders of his profession, and of his actions, and of his nature, and what was done in his time, and what is, and what shall be, from the beginning of time, to the end of it.'

Could this be the oldest historical account of the concealed 'Hall of Records' referred to by Edgar Cayce, and predicted to be discovered within the Great Pyramid or beneath the Giza Plateau around the turn of the century?

Edgar Cayce spoke of the Great Pyramid and described its function as a centre of initiation in a 1932 reading: '... the building of that now called Gizek ... the Hall of the Initiates ... receives all the records from the beginnings of that given by the priest ... to that period when there is to be the change in the Earth's position and the return of the Great Initiate to that and other lands for the folding up of those prophecies that are depicted there. All changes that came in religious thought in the world are shown there, in the variations in which the passage through same is reached, from the base to ... the open tomb and the top. This then is the purpose, for the record and the meaning to be interpreted by those that have come and do come as the teachers of the various periods, in the experience of this present position, of the activity of the spheres of the earth ...'

Further light is shed upon the Pyramid's initiatory aspect by the ambiguous nature of the Egyptian *Book of the Dead*, which is ultimately associated with the Osirian mysteries and the central theme of resurrection. Many scholars regard the text as an initiatory manual for the living. The work is basically a random compilation of funerary texts, spells, prayers, hymns, magical formulas and other ancient papyri. Many of its sections are directly attributed to Thoth. These collected texts are more correctly titled, 'The Coming Forth by Day,' which is what Ra, the Egyptian solar deity, did each morning as he illumined the dawn horizon after his difficult nocturnal journey through the underworld. So, too, the Egyptians believed, did the soul traverse the dark and dangerous regions of the underworld before being reborn into the light of a new day in the world of the living.

However and whenever the Great Pyramid was constructed is still a matter of conjecture, but we are sure of one thing, the knowledge of the Pyramid's builders was, without a doubt, more advanced than our own. Many of the Earth's exact dimensions, as disclosed by the Pyramid, were not verified by modern science until after the first satellite was launched during the International Geophysical Year in 1957–58. By now, the Great Pyramid is probably the most measured structure in history. Nevertheless, critics have tended to isolate apparent inconsistencies or lack of precision in measurements as proof that its statistics are contrived generalities and not specifics. One glaring instance is the general belief that the Pyramid stands in 'the exact centre' of the Earth's dry land mass. If this were true, the Pyramid would be located at 30° x 30° instead of where it is – at latitude 29°58'51" N (or 01'9" less than the thirtieth parallel) and longitude 31°09'00" E. It is particularly interesting that the sine of the Pyramid's North geographic latitude is .4997139. The sine of the 'perfect' centred location of 30 degrees is .500000. Subtracting the former sine figure from the latter gives .0002861.[3] (In esoteric numerology it is acceptable to shift decimals and drop zeros.) The result is 286.1 – the factor of displacement.

The factor of displacement is also known as the golden section or golden proportion and is represented by the ratio between the two divisions of a line such that the smaller is to the larger as the larger is to the sum of the two; roughly a three to five ratio. The golden proportion represents the spiralic form found throughout nature – the helical strands of the DNA, the measured chambers of the nautilus shell, the mathematical precision of pine cone formation, and the delicate spacing of plant leaves as they curl around the stem toward the light. It is the factor of displacement that prevents a spiral from becoming a closed circle. Without it there is only a closed system, and evolution cannot occur. Thus, the Pyramid itself was built at that precise location 'just short of perfection'. The golden proportion, 286.1, appears repeatedly throughout the Pyramid's geometry because it represents the evolutionary process. And, as we shall see, evolutionary process is what the Great Pyramid is all about.

Early evidence of that statement came in 1925, when the research of Dave Davidson – a structural engineer who had studied the Great Pyramid for twenty-four years[4] – confirmed a six thousand year system of prophetic dates, beginning in 3999 BC and ending in 2001 AD, contained within the structure of the Pyramid. The dates, which comprised a

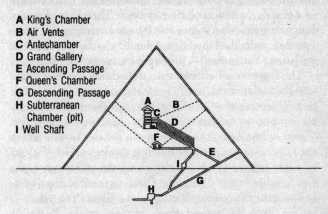

A King's Chamber
B Air Vents
C Antechamber
D Grand Gallery
E Ascending Passage
F Queen's Chamber
G Descending Passage
H Subterranean
   Chamber (pit)
I Well Shaft

Cross-Section of Great Pyramid

chronological time scale, were derived from mathematics of the Pyramid's astronomical alignment, and its geometry. Additional dates, obtained from the geometrical features of the Pyramid, served to emphasize the importance of, or complement, the time scale dates. Factors such as the types of stone used, their colour, layering, and the direction in which the passages turn, were also found to be symbolically meaningful. The ratio of one pyramidal inch to one year is the basis of the mathematically deducible dates of the time scale. Numbers are not carved into the masonry; the time scale does not provide details of historic events – it is the historical events themselves that provide the details, of course, and history has established their significance and importance.

When the intramural design of the Great Pyramid is understood as template, its deepest, most secret gift stands clearly revealed in the light of its own truth. Symbol and meaning correlate the exoteric funerary rites and esoteric initiatory rites from the *Book of the Dead* with the prophetic time scale. In other words, the afterworld experience of the deceased and the spiritual purifications of the initiate parallel the labour of humanity through the darkness of the ages toward the bright horizon, the 'turning point' into the light of a new day, a new evolutionary cycle. These three levels of function synthesize within the Pyramid's design, yet maintain their individual integrity. A tomb? Certainly! A place of initiation? Yes, indeed! A prophetic blueprint? You bet!

The Egyptians believed that after death one descended into the underworld, was judged, and, if found worthy, ultimately became 'the Osiris', i.e., the regenerated or resurrected one who would rise through the stars to the solar realm. The pole star, being the still point in the sky around which the heavens rotate, was the opening through which the soul rose into heaven. It was not surprising, therefore, that Alpha Draconis (pole star during the Old Kingdom) shone directly down the Descending Passage of the Great Pyramid.

Two vertically scored lines, just inside the Pyramid's entrance, proved to be the key to establishing the time scale. Only once during each equinoctial cycle (25,826 years), Alcyone of the Pleiades is in the midheaven, directly above the apex of the Great Pyramid and aligned with the two scored lines. (The Pleiades were known as the Khema in ancient Egypt, and Egypt itself was called the land of Khem [see 'Astrological Cycles' chapter].) At the same time, Kesil, the Egyptian name of Orion, was aligned with the air vent in the south wall of the King's chamber, and the pole star of that era, Alpha Draconis, locks into alignment with the Pyramid by beaming down the Descending Passage to the Pit entrance, deep into the Earth beneath the Pyramid. Thus the Great Pyramid fulfilled the function of the bond between heaven and Earth, locking Pyramid and cosmos into a synchronous relationship. The last time this configuration occurred was noon on the vernal equinox, March 21, 2141 BC.[5] Measuring backwards from the scored lines to the Pyramid's entrance establishes the date 2623 BC – believed to be the year of Khufu's death. Since, according to the approximate date of the Manetho King lists, his accession was around 2575 BC.

THE DESCENDING PASSAGE is indicative of the descent of spirit into matter, light into darkness. The *Book of the Dead* refers to 'The Descent' by which a person arrives in the underworld, or astral realms. Individually, we descend into physical form, become established on life's path and then, at maturity, face key decisions that affect our life and the world around us. So, too, one enters the Pyramid down the Descending Passage until arriving at its junction with the Ascending Passage where one must decide whether to continue on down or ascend. Both passages diverge from each other at an identical angle of slope. This junction is important, for it shows us a critical choice between two paths, a choice that resurfaces again and again throughout the prophecies examined in this book. The Descending Passage, then, symbolizes the material life, ignorant or indifferent to the higher principles. It bypasses the Ascending Passage and steadily slopes downward into the Pit.

THE PIT is a subterranean chamber with rocky floor and low ceiling. The Egyptian texts call it variously The Chamber of Ordeal, the Chamber of the Shadow, and the Chamber of Central Fire.

The initiatory journey begun at the Pit level symbolizes the ordeal one faces after death in the underworld (hence its name as the Chamber of Ordeal). Common to many religions is the idea of the afterworld as a place of purgatory, a place of self-examination, which yields a profound realization about one's life and the consequences of one's actions.

The Pit's identification as the Chamber of the Shadow reminds us that the Jungian concept of the 'shadow' is that part of ourselves we are unwilling to acknowledge and that we project instead onto others. The Pit was a place for processing denial and resistance. In order to become whole we must accept, reown, become accountable for our shadow. This is a prerequisite to personal and planetary healing – and to initiation.

In its capacity as the Chamber of Central Fire, the Pit fulfilled a function of purification. The 'purifying fire' consumes the corporeal dross. This fire is also recognized in yoga and Hinduism as *kundalini* or *shakti* – a force that awakens in the evolutionary purification process at the base of the spine. This *chakra* centre is the repository of 'primal fire'. It relates to such issues as survival, security and racial memory. Early experiments in 'pyramid power' showed that there are two main areas where energy concentrates within a pyramid: beneath the structure, i.e., in the area of the Pit, and off-centre, at the level of the King's Chamber. The Pit, therefore, is aptly named the Chamber of Central Fire.

It is believed that initiates entered the Pit by a secret tunnel from the Sphinx. At the far side of this chamber is a low horizontal passage. It is only large enough to crawl along, and leads to a dead end after fifty feet – a point of no return. The time scale reveals the date 1939 AD at the beginning of that passage and 1953 at its end (the same date is indicated at the far side of the King's Chamber). Consistent with the 'purifying' purpose of this chamber, 1939 in the Hindu tradition marked the beginning of the 'twilight' (the closing phase) of the *Kali Yuga*.[6] Certainly, the discovery of radar and atomic fission in 1939 set the tone of the ensuing years until 1953. This was an historical period when the security of the world was shaken by World War II, the discovery of plutonium, the atomic and hydrogen bombs, and subsequent arms race. An important cycle of the Maya calendar (Katun 16:10 Caban) ended in 1953. Arguelles's *The Mayan Factor* states, 'There is no question that events during this katun mark the most irreversible moments of the entire baktun, sealing the destiny of the remainder of the cycle.' Planetary karma evidently had been set by 1953. ('Katun' and 'baktun' are measures of Maya time, discussed in Chapter 15.)

THE ASCENDING PASSAGE is called by the Egyptian texts the Hall of Truth in Darkness. It leads past the Queen's Chamber through the Grand Gallery to the King's Chamber level. However, one must stoop to progress up this passage, because the ceiling is low and the floor steep. This difficulty implies that the pursuit of truth in darkness – going through the motions and observing only the form, by blind faith or ritual alone – is not an easy path. It makes this phase of the journey an effort of will. The texts also refer to the combined Ascending Passage and Grand Gallery as 'the Double Hall of Right and Truth'. This description distinguishes the difference between doing and being. It tells us that following the prescribed rules and 'doing the right thing' is qualitatively different from 'living in truth' (which is what the monotheistic Akhenaton said he was doing), whereby one's consciousness is illumined and one's life becomes an outward expression of one's inner connection to truth.

This Ascending Passage, or Hall of Truth in Darkness, commences with the date 1486 BC. This year has been attributed to either the Exodus or the time when Moses brought the law. Scholars have associated the pre-Exodus Egyptian plagues and the parting of the Red Sea with the volcanic eruption that birthed the island Santorin out of the Mediterranean around 1500 BC. Moses' historic presentation of the Ten Commandments was the inaugural opportunity for a new nation, about to begin a new cycle, to choose the Ascending above the Descending path. Both these key events set humanity on the 'right' path, so to speak, in preparation for the fuller and personal realizations brought by Christ.

Therefore, one might reasonably expect the place where the Hall of Truth in Darkness becomes the Hall of Truth in Light to show up on the time scale as 'year zero', denoting the birth of Christ. However, the date where the former passage opens up into the lofty vault of the latter is 4 BC. Research, however, has uncovered the fact that Jesus was born in 4 BC. This discrepancy in dates is explained by the fact that in 533 AD, Dionysius Exigus proposed that the calendar years be counted from the birth of Christ instead of from the founding of Rome. His reckoning indicated that Christ had been born during the twenty-eighth year of the reign of Augustus Caesar. He failed, however, to take into account the fact that Augustus reigned for four years under his own name of Octavian before being proclaimed Augustus by the Roman Senate.[7]

The difference between being on the path of truth in darkness or in light is the experience of being 'reborn'. Initiates are traditionally referred to as 'the twice born'. The Great Pyramid incorporates architecture to facilitate the initiatory experience of symbolic rebirth.

THE QUEEN'S CHAMBER is also called the Chamber of Rebirth/Regeneration. A step down from the horizontal entry passage to the slightly lower floor level of this chamber is, according to the *Book of the Dead*, symbolic of the last day of one's life – the 'day of stepping off' from the life of yesterday to be reborn in the afterlife of tomorrow.

The main event in the after-death experience was 'the Judgment', which also had great significance in the initiatory process of the Osirian mysteries. The central axis of the Great Pyramid bisects the centre of this chamber, which is symbolically relevant, because here the heart of the deceased, or the initiate, is weighed on the scales of justice against the feather of truth. Illustrated funerary texts typically depict variations on this theme. (Bearing in mind that the Egyptian hieroglyph for 'eternity' is a cord loop twisted three times, we find in the Greenfield Papyrus a possible example of the depth of ancient Egyptian esotericism

Anubis adjusting the scales of judgement
From the Greenfield papyrus (British Museum)

wherein the scales of Anubis show the plummet of the balance hanging from what appears to be a linked chain. But a closer look clearly shows, not links, but a double helix of seven caduceus-like coils. Could this be symbolic of the Egyptian 'Shenka' (wheels of light) – the seven *chakras* of the candidate? The ancient Egyptians loved puns, and if we read this one correctly, it tells us that if your *chakras* are in perfect balance, you live for eternity).

The Papyrus of Ani is a beautiful example of the judgment scene from the *Book of the Dead.* Anubis (guide of initiates and conductor of honest souls to the throne of Osiris) weighs the heart as two goddesses of birth look on. Meskhenet, a nurturing birth deity, also appeared at the time of death to testify on the character of the deceased before Osiris, judge of the dead. The other goddess, Renutet, encouraged the birth process and fostered the will to live; but she also controlled destiny and apportioned the lifespan. Here, the deceased recited his/her confession. And here, the initiate had to justify his or her courage and integrity before being admitted to the Grand Gallery, Hall of Truth in Light. One's words and actions in life had to express the heart's truth. Thoth stood by to record the verdict while a curious beast, 'the Devourer', crouched behind him, waiting to devour the heart of anyone judged unworthy of proceeding into the realm of Osiris. Such a person would then be condemned to the netherworld, with its lake of fire and other torments. As in death so in life, the vindicated, reborn soul proceeds on as a unified consciousness to become metamorphised as Osiris, resurrect, and live for eternity.

The only date in this chamber that we are able to correlate with historic events is 1844 AD. It highlights a time when the seed was germinated for collective humanity to awaken to a global awareness of itself as a single consciousness. The year marked the founding of the Baha'i faith in Persia (now Iran). The principles upon which this religion was based were ahead of their time, and included elimination of prejudice and extremes of wealth and poverty, religious unity, universal education, racial and sexual equality, an international secondary language within an egalitarian political context. Baha'u'llah established this faith for the express purpose of bringing in world government to the highest purpose. World government, as we shall see later, is a major aspect of the future toward which we are headed. In 1844, Samuel F. Morse sent the first telegraph message, bringing a new era in human communication, like the initial synaptic awakening of the global brain.

The horizontal passage connecting the Queen's Chamber back to the Ascending Passage/Grand Gallery is called The Path of the Coming Forth of the Regenerated Soul. At the end of this passage, in the west wall just before it rejoins the Ascending Passage, is an irregular well shaft that the texts refer to as The Gate of the West. The Gate of the West was 'Amenta', place of the setting sun and entrance to the underworld. The well shaft leads to the same place as condemned souls – the entrance to the symbolic underworld – the Pit or Chamber of Central Fire. The ascent can now be continued in a more truly enlightened state.

THE GRAND GALLERY, also known as the Hall of Truth in Light, leads up to the Antechamber and King's Chamber. Researchers have identified the expanded width and height of the Gallery as representative of the expansion in consciousness that the Christian era brought. One side of the Gallery begins with the date 30 AD on one side (representing the year of the Crucifixion, consistent with the time difference noted in relation to Jesus' birth date). The other side of the Gallery emphasizes the year 1776 - the date of America's independence from the parental control of England, just as the rebirth of the judgment process releases the initiate from dependence upon the authority of organized religion. The Gallery ends with the date of the First World War, 1914.

There is also geometrical evidence that the two side walls of the Gallery each represent 180 degrees, symbolic of the 360 degrees of space, while the seven corbelled courses of stone comprising these side walls – and called 'the orbit' in the *Book of the Dead* – correlate with the seven known planets of the solar system as they existed at the time of the Pyramid's presumed construction.[8]

THE ANTECHAMBER leads to the King's Chamber. The Egyptian writings call this the Chamber of the Triple Veil, where penetrating the veils of illusion that obscure reality precedes initiation.

Immediately before this Antechamber is an eroded stone cube called the Great Step. Projected within the geometry of this step is a 'hidden step' to which is attributed the date 1933, to be discussed shortly. With the Great Step, the time scale chronology changes from inch/year to inch/month, symbolizing a 'great step' in the evolution of consciousness. Significantly, this step is exactly in the centre of the pyramid, on the east-west axis.

Just above the Great Step, where the ceiling of the Gallery drops to about three feet, the date 1909 is indicated. In this year, the expedition of Admiral Robert E. Peary reached the North Pole. Since external events have their analogue within human consciousness, one could interpret this accomplishment (in the same genre as humans waLking on the moon sixty years later) as significant of humanity's contacting the 'inner' North Pole – the all-inclusive consciousness of the crown *chakra* at the top of the head. Thus, in 1909, the newly contacted light of the crown *chakra* illumined the unplumbed depths of the human psyche, and psychologist Carl Gustav Jung made his momentous 'discovery' of the existence of the collective unconscious.[9] The founding of the National Association for the Advancement of Coloured People (NAACP) in the same year was also expressive of the all-inclusive impulse, bringing into public awareness the need for integration of all members of the human family. The Luminous Lodge, a European occult society (of which Hitler was an initiate) believed 1909 represented a critical turning point between a contractive and expansive cycle of cosmic rhythm affecting world history.[10]

Each side of the Antechamber is a small passage, low enough to oblige a person to crawl in and out of the chamber. The dates connoted at each end of the first low passage indicate times when civilization was 'brought low' or debased: August 4–5, 1914, and November 11, 1918. These dates cover the duration of World War I. January 31, 1917, is also shown in sequence, and is the exact date of the United States's entry into that war on behalf of the Allies. Meticulous research and the inspired vision of pyramidologist Michael Mooney also reveal that the date 1987 correlates with the beginning of the granite floor just inside the vestibule of the Antechamber. In 1987, the blue star of Hopi prophecy manifested and the Harmonic Convergence took place, inaugurating the final phase of the Maya calendar. And the 1987 Nuclear Arms Limitation Treaty certainly will be judged historically as one of the most significant steps toward world unity. Additionally, an underground tunnel (perhaps indicative of the hidden 'Hall of Records' that Edgar Cayce predicted would be discovered toward the end of the century) was detected in 1987 near the Great Pyramid.[11]

The space within the Antechamber itself spans a ten-year pause between hard times; (the 'period of intermission' according to the Egyptian texts) from November 11, 1918, the date on which the armistice was signed to end the First World War, to the commencement of the great economic depression on May 29, 1928. The year 1928 also marked the beginning of a major reversal of weather cycle frequency, and is thought to represent a 'period of intermission', or interval, in the evolutionary pulse associated with the creation of ice ages and the great geological divisions of time.[12]

It is within this Antechamber that the archeological features suggest the idea of the 'triple veil'. This appellation, found within various initiatory texts, refers to the 'veils' of illusion, or peceptual filters, which obscure the enlightened state. (Jesus said that we see 'as through a glass, darkly'.) Symbolic of these three veils, the Antechamber walls reveal three vertical recessed grooves, which look as though they might each have contained a portcullis-like granite slab to block access to the King's Chamber. For the aspirant on the path, the first three *chakras*, signifying money, sex, and power, must be purified. Negative use of these fundamental aspects must be transcended before the initiation of the heart – represented by the King's Chamber.

As one enters this Antechamber, there is barely enough space to stand upright before confronting a prominent stone slab (reminiscent of the top half of a barn door) referred to as the Granite Leaf. Its centre bears the date of September 17, 2001 AD. This is the final date offered within the Pyramid. (Later dates have been computed elsewhere in the Pyramid by some researchers, but there is a lack of agreement as to their validity.) It is not part of the time scale, but the terminal end of a geometrically projected line extending down through the Ascending Passage to a point beyond the base of the Pyramid where it converges with the projected outer arris edge – geometrically anchoring the beginning date of 3999 BC. Unfortunately, we do not know what historical event(s) may have occurred on that date. However, the best way to preview what events might be in store for the ending date is by astrological means. A natal chart for September 17, 2001 AD ends this chapter.

After the Antechamber, a second low passage, barely a meter in height but double the length of the first, bridges the years from the end of the 1928 depression to 1936. These were years of intense preparation for the Second World War, in which failing economies depended upon armaments' manufacture. Nazis, Fascists and Communists came into heavy conflict, and revolution in Spain erupted. Stalin began his purging activities and Hitler stomped into the Rheinland. The Egyptian texts describe this passage as a time of chaos and confusion in which spiritual values disappear.

Taken as a whole, the Antechamber, flanked on each side by the two low passageways, spans the years1914-2001 AD. Within this time frame, the Hopi prophecies state, three 'world purifiers' will bring severe global experiences to clear planetary karma. The 'hidden step', referred to earlier, marks the year 1933, and is the implied geometrical measurement beneath the Great Step where the Grand Gallery and horizontal passage to the King's Chamber intersect. The Maya calendar also identifies 1914-33 as a significant time in

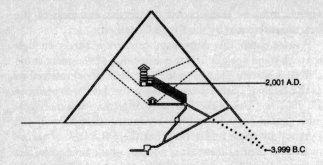

world history. The beginning of the horizontal passage with 1933 AD, to its end with 1953 AD at the far wall of the King's Chamber, represents a twenty year cycle, which the Maya calendar identifies as the 'Climax of Power',[13] and which seals the destiny of the world. The last veil to be lifted in the Antechamber was that of 'power'. The chasm between lower and higher consciousness is bridged when the purified aspects of lower awareness (money, sex, and power) serve a balance of love, wisdom and power in the heart. The intelligence of the heart then serves the higher centre of the Christ consciousness.

THE KING'S CHAMBER is where the initiation took place. This event represents the opening of the heart and the conquering of death by life; the victory of wisdom over ignorance. The Egyptian sources refer to it as the Chamber of the Open Tomb, and the Room of the Purification of the Nations. The nations are already being purified, and Hopi prophecy describes the third and final purification.

A red granite coffer, without a lid, is found in the chamber, and some sources consider it the onetime repository of the biblical Ark of the Covenant.[14] This is certainly an interesting possibility (with a wealth of implications for ancient 'high tech' applications associated with the planetary grid, pyramid energy and consciousness), since the coffer measurements correlate with the biblical dimensions of the Ark.

The King's Chamber bears the date 1936 at its entry, and ends with August 19–20, 1953, at the far wall – the same date

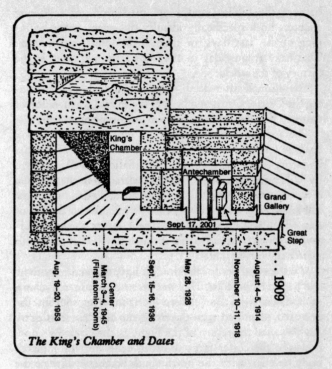

Aug. 19-20, 1953 | Center March 3-4, 1945 (First atomic bomb) | Sept. 15-16, 1936 | May 28, 1928 | November 10-11, 1918 | August 4-5, 1914 | ... 1909

King's Chamber

Antechamber

Grand Gallery

Great Step

Sept. 17, 2001

The King's Chamber and Dates

as the end of the blind passage in the Pit. As above, so below: whether a person ascends toward the light or regresses into darkness and ignorance, s/he is affected by the same deadline. In 1953, the Korean War ended. In 1953, DNA was discovered – that minutest part of human being-ness that resonates in synchronization with the great movements of the galaxy. Also of chronological significance is the midpoint date of this chamber: 1945. In this year, the Dead Sea Scrolls were discovered. On March 4–5, 1945, successful laboratory experiments were conducted with the atomic bomb, serving as the basis for the first experimental detonation at Alamagordo in July of that year. The first atomic bomb was subsequently exploded over Hiroshima in August 1945. This is a particularly powerful prophecy, because the biblical and Hopi predictions of following chapters both specifically identify this event as the beginning of the 'last days' or time of the 'great purification'. That hazy August day in 1945 was a turning point in the history of the world.

The ultimate after-death experience was that of 'becoming the Osiris'. Osiris symbolizes the eternal regeneration of nature. He is the ancient Egyptian prototype of rebirth.

The applicant, having mastered and purified the lower *chakras* (i.e., the lower nature) was now prepared for the initiatory experience. The goal of initiation is well expressed by William Kingsland as 'the full realization of the essential *divine nature of man*, the recovery by the individual of the full knowledge and powers of his divine spiritual nature, of that which was his source and origin, but to the *consciousness* of which he is now dead through the 'Fall of Man' into matter and physical life."[15]

It was customary for the dead of Egyptian antiquity to be laid to rest facing East. This was because the sun was reborn each dawn from the eastern horizon. The soul of the deceased, identified with the rising sun as it 'came forth by day', awaited the return of the Light. In the Great Pyramid, however, the coffer faces south in order for the initiate's body to align with the north-south magnetic flow of the Earth and to align the spirit with Kesil, the constellation of Orion, which the Egyptians associated with Osiris.

In discussing the energies focused during initiation within the greatest edifice of all time, we must emphasize to the reader that the Great Pyramid is the *primary* sacred site of the world, on the *master* node of the planetary grid. Primal energies, gestating deep within the Earth's core, emerge at this site up through the Pyramid's apex. Simultaneously, cosmic energies from the deep space, the galactic core, and pole star are channelled down through the apex and penetrate deep within the Earth into the energy grid that sustains the planet's health and equilibrium. Just imagine how it must have been to receive those energy vectors throughout one's own bodymindspirit!

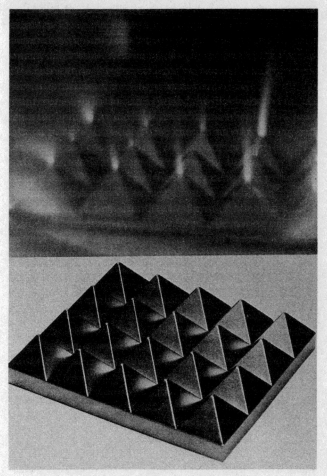

Kirlian photograph of pyramid energy

Initiates are said to have lain in a state of trance or deep meditation within the coffer for three days. During this state the initiate's awareness left the body to consciously travel the spiritual realms as it would after death. Hindus and Shabd Yogis call this ability 'soul travel'. The apostle

Paul was also acquainted with this facility when he said that he died daily, and that both physical and spiritual bodies exist, each with distinct functions (see Corinthians 1:26 – 58). Like the awakening of Osiris himself, regenerating from the hibernation of death to begin the ascent from the underworld toward the light, the initiate was deeply and profoundly transformed.

The word 'pyramid' comes from the Greek 'pyra,' meaning fire or flame, and 'mid' meaning middle or centre – 'fire in the middle'. This is clearly demonstrated in the Kirlian photograph showing a plume of etheric fire (light energy) being drawn through the pyramid's apex. The shape of a pyramid and its ability to both receive and radiate energy assisted the initiate to (with characteristic Egyptian appreciation of puns) 'pyramid' – that is, to 'peer amid' (look within), and to contact that force of universal energy which catalyzed the transformation of consciousness. According to researcher Mary Hardy, the energy emitted from the top of the pyramid is a standing columnar wave, a double helix, generated by the sides of the pyramid bending light and creating a vortex. Such is the energy that runs the Universe.[16]

The ancient symbol of a flame in a triangle is familiar to many spiritual traditions. Christianity sees it as the Trinity with the flame of life within. In the Hebrew Kabala, the flame is actually the glyph 'Yod' – the active creative principle translated as 'force'. We are reminded that it was from the primeval mound (of which the pyramid is but a representation) that Atum, the Egyptian God of Creation and archetype of the principle of light, first erupted. In the mystery traditions, this symbol is the power of the 'flame within' or 'fire in the middle' of the pyramid, and the mind when aligned with the higher forces of transformation.

From 17th century
Alchemical Treatise

*There is a way of manipulating matter and energy so as to
produce a 'field of force'. This field acts upon the observer, putting
him/her in a privileged position vis-á-vis the universe. From this
position the observer has access to the realities which are
ordinarily hidden from us by time and space, matter and energy.*[17]

The alchemical law is that when you change the energy you
change the manifestation of the mass. 'The manipulation of
fire,' say the alchemists, 'makes possible not only the transmutation of metals, but the transformation of the experi-
menter himself. The latter, under the influence of the forces
emitted by the crucible, i.e., radiations emitted by nuclei
undergoing changes in structure (as within Pyramid initiations) enters himself into a new state. Mutations take place
within him. His intelligence and his powers of perception are
raised to a higher level. He passes to another stage of being,
attains a higher degree of consciousness.'[18] The elements,
instead of being manipulated by the practitioner, as in alchemy, act *upon* and *within* the initiate to the same effect.

Humanity is currently undergoing a process, similar to
that of the initiate or alchemist. As mentioned earlier, as
Earth draws closer to the spiritual aura of the Great Central

Sun, the spirit of fire is awakened to resonance the light within matter, just as the return of the light at the time of the winter solstice brings a new awakening of all life. Those who are ready have felt its quickening warmth within as their inner being responds involuntarily to the impulse of increasing light. In this regard, the study of the interrelationship of wave forms and matter, known as cymatics, illustrates that the Pyramid's connection to the Central Sun is very old. A tonoscope is a metal disk sprinkled with a fine layer of sand which, when vibrated by sound, transforms that sound into its visual representation. For example, 'OM,' the universal sound, resonates the sand on the disk into a circle as the 'O' is uttered. By the time the 'M' fades away the circle has become filled with concentric pyramidal shapes, identical to the centre of the ancient Hindu Sri Yantra Mantra, meditation upon which is said to produce the visual afterimage of the Great Central Sun.[19]

Sri Yantra Mantra

In *Rhythms of Vision* Lawrence Blair writes about the study of the interrelationship between wave-forms and matter called 'Cymatics'. The late Hans Jenny built a tonoscope to transform sounds into their visual representation and apparently the universal sound 'OM' produces a circle with the correct utterance of the 'O'. By the time the 'M' fades away the circle has become filled with concentric triangular shapes, identical to the centre of the Sri Yantra Mantra, meditation upon which is said to produce the visual after image of the Central Sun.

The events and times prophesied within the stone chronology of the Great Pyramid describe the time of the collective awakening of the regenerative principle, 'the Osiris' within humanity. As the 'New Age melting pot', America has a particular role in the unfolding drama of world history. The early founding fathers were Freemasons, outer circle members of an arcane world 'brotherhood'. Benjamin Franklin initiated the symbol of the Grand Pyramid onto the Great Seal of the United States. Americans glance at it daily on the reverse of their dollar bills. The inscription beneath the Pyramid on the Great Seal says 'Novus Ordo Seclorum', and translates appropriately as 'A New Order of the Ages'. The eagle on the Seal's reverse side is the symbol of the nation and the esoteric symbol of the initiate in the world's great mystery traditions. Do you remember, during the first moon landing in 1969, those words flashed back to Earth: 'The Eagle has landed!'?

Contemporary pyramid research has revealed some promising future pyramid applications. These could be used in areas that currently pose a threat to civilization:

Food Scarcity – through seed germination, increased plant growth and food preservation.

Pollution – tests show that pyramid space can purify water, air and soil.

Energy Sources – through generation or enhancement of known and unknown energy fields.

War – peace is dependent upon humanity's greater understanding and elevation of consciousness. The **Pyramid**

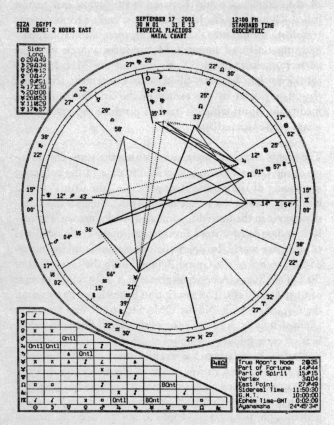

shows promise of serving as an initiator of higher levels of awareness.[20]

It is significant that, in spite of the Pyramid's real potential for limitless energy, increased food production, and combating pollution, it is not the government that is giving attention to researching these possibilities. It is ordinary individuals and groups with a shared vision and aligned consciousness who are bringing to light a profound body of knowledge that will make all the difference in the world to the unfolding of humanity toward – we are awed at the thought – planetary initiation. We shall determine our own destiny; it cannot be written for us.

In order to chart accurately the motion of the cosmic tides prevailing on September 17, 2001 AD, the last predictive date of the Great Pyramid, a computerized natal chart was drawn up for 12:00 noon on that day, according to the tropical placidian system. Three themes emerged from the chart: indications that this date is the time set for magnetic changes in our relationship to the sun, the final stages of karmic retribution – and the possibility of planetary initiation.

The chart shows the sun and new moon in the midheaven (symbolizing a new beginning). If you employ sidereal astrology (where the planets are in the sky astronomically rather than symbolically) the sun/moon then conjunct on the Leo/Virgo cusp – Leo represents the will aspect of the creative force and Virgo is a symbol of purification and initiation. In alchemical texts, the sun is depicted as the heart and the moon as the pineal gland, or 'third eye'. For the ancient Egyptians, it meant that sun and moon as the two eyes of Horus, 'lord of the sky,' were focused, projecting perfection and protection of the Earth. (When placed together, hieroglyphs representing sun and moon translate as 'eon' or 'millennium'.) In this chart they conjunct in the midheaven above the Sphinx.

With reference to initiation, the chart shows a grand trine between Mercury, Saturn and Uranus, in air – a configuration that Theosophical co-founder Alice Bailey associated with specific energies affecting the three higher *chakras* at the time of initiation.[21] It also represents individuation, in the Jungian sense, with the help of the Masters. However, such attainment appears hampered by certain emotional Martian energy that has not been spiritualized – possibly in the form of war and/or the complete purging of all back-karma.

A six year process culminating in 2001 AD suggests the possibility of a transformation in our relationship to the sun in areas of magnetism. This is indicated by Venus, reflecting the polarity of Uranus, the planet of magnetism. The opposites of sun and moon, quincunx Uranus, brings about radical change and transformation and indicates a possible adjustment of the Earth's position with respect to the sun whereby the magnetosphere and magnetic poles would also be changed in direction and intensity. Mercury is conjunct twenty-three degrees to Arcturus, which represents calamities and physical catastrophes. Edgar Cayce has prophesied that in the year 2000 or 2001, the poles would shift. This event certainly would 'transform our relationship to the sun'.

The configuration of Venus in twenty-six degrees of Leo epitomizes the law of 'As above, So Below'. Rudhyar's *An Astrological Mandala* (which can be likened to an astrological *I Ching*) fittingly describes this degree and sign with the image 'After the heavy storm a rainbow,' and relates the linking of heaven and Earth to the covenant with one's divine nature and promise of immortality. We are reminded that in the Bible, God gave the rainbow as the sign of His covenant with Noah after the Flood at the cataclysmic end of the last cycle of history. Hinduism also describes the *antakarana*, which is the 'rainbow bridge' whereby awareness is transferred from the heart to the head. It represents the complete uniting of the human and divine aspects of consciousness as well as left/right brain integration, which enables the harmony of cosmic law to manifest in perfection upon the Earth and within humanity. We have here an astrological configuration that encompasses this complete process, above and below, for the planet and for us.

Another reference to magnetism as it relates to radiation appears with Neptune placed between six degrees and seven degrees Aquarius. At six degrees, people are seen assuming individual responsibility for helping to draw into the mass consciousness releases of transpersonal energy in order to make the hitherto instinctual aspects of consciousness fully accessible. This faculty is the necessary preparation to the 'emergence of new mutations according to the great rhythms of the cosmos'. We're referring to the beginnings of the sixth root race, which will populate the New Age when it stabilizes. The *Astrological Mandala* shows the seven degrees symbolized by a child being born out of an egg – in other words, the cosmic egg out of which the universe is born, and the appearance in the Earth of new beings free of ancestral karma and the inertia of humanity's past patterns. It describes the new being as a product of evolution, expressing a fresh projection of the creative spirit of the cosmic whole and free of collective belief systems and cultural or racial influence.

Change in radiation is a key element in this chart for September 17, 2001 AD. The good news is that it could be good, and the bad news is that it could be bad. Depending on where each of us is at on our personal journey, the possibility of mutation versus transformation is implied. Although we have every reason for concern about the prodigious amounts of ultraviolet radiation admitted by the holes in the ozone layer, and the increasingly intense solar storms that release intense bursts of ultraviolet radiation, we are aware that ultraviolet radiation is the colour correlated to the sixth *chakra*, the seat of Christ consciousness.

We are divinely assured that changes in radiation will 'attune those who are His to that which He is'[22] – i.e., divinely improved mutants ('futants'?) or high frequency beings who are the product of revelation and transformation!

The *Astrological Mandala* reveals that in spite of the intense karmic retribution that the chart indicates, Pluto in thirteen degrees of Sagittarius shows that 'it is possible to joyously herald the dawn from high above the actual stresses of existence,' but that the New Age will have to deal with a residual of unfinished business from the world of today and the shadows of the past.

Jupiter in exact quintile (seventy-two degrees) to the Sun and Moon, shows that people who undergo severe trials in the name of purification as preliminaries to 'dropping the veils' before initiation, and who experience the energy of their higher consciousness with day-to-day consistency, will be protected and transformed by the intensity of the energies at work.

It is also noteworthy that it is America (whose Sun at thirteen degrees Cancer is conjunct Jupiter in this chart) where transformation of the creative forces will begin at the close of the old world order. The 'New Order of the Ages' will first take root on what is now known as the North American continent, and may be known in the future as the New Atlantis.

9

Meishu Sama and Johrei

In the frozen heart of winter, when the snowflakes swirl and settle in the bare branches of the plum tree, the sleeping centre of all natural things stirs with an inner knowing. At that moment in time, nature's unseen finger is turning the Earth around in her elliptical journey, reminding her of cherry blossoms and butterflies, and she allows herself to be drawn once again back to that eternal source of green things, warmth and light.

On such a day, in 1882, Mokichi Okada was born in a Tokyo slum. It was December 23; the first day after the winter solstice, when the daylight lingers to incubate the summer.

The importance and relevance of this very process in our lives is what Mokichi Okada (later known by his spiritual name of Meishu Sama) came to reveal through his life's work and teachings. Just as winter gives way to summer at the time of the solstice, the frequency at which matter vibrates is increasing as the Earth now enters again the aura of the Central Sun, becoming transformed by its special energies and passing from the old age of darkness into the New Age of light and harmony. 'God created the universe in perfect harmony,' Meishu Sama said, 'with law and order pervading it. Discord of any kind is man-made, and its cause is to be found in the violation of the laws of creation, of nature. If man will only discover and obey these laws which actually govern our existence, will learn to live in harmony with them, everything in this world will go well.' And it was at dawn on the summit of Mt. Nokogiri near Tokyo that Meishu Sama received the revelation that that very day, June 15, 1931, was the actual beginning, within the spiritual realm, of the New Age of light. The following spring, Edgar Cayce similarly declared that the New Age had just begun.

Meishu Sama apparently had been purified and prepared for his life's work by working off intense amounts of negative karma in his early life. He experienced a long history of chronic ill health, personal bereavements, and fiscal disasters (significantly, he was the inventor of the artificial 'morning sun' diamond) so crushing that a man possessed of less endurance and character would have been totally overwhelmed by them. It was not until the death of his wife and third child that he turned from atheism and began his spiritual quest for the meaning behind the extreme hardships in his life. He spent a number of years in intense religious enquiry and finally became affiliated with a Shinto sect, but was never fully satisfied.

In 1926, at the age of forty-five, he entered a state of receptiveness to divine revelation which lasted three months and in which was disclosed to him God's divine' plan for the New Age. He was told how he would be used as an instrument for the releasing of divine light, to dispel negative conditions, and for the full revelation of truth in order to prepare humanity for the New Age. 'Seeing truth means to penetrate into the very core of matter ... To see truth is, as it were, to climb to the top of the pyramid. The higher we climb, the wider our field of vision becomes and the more we can see.' Meishu Sama learned in his revelation that the Earth is going to face 'a mighty upheaval, the greatest cataclysm in all history'. He declared that at the event, considered as the biblical 'last judgment' a great cataclysmic action will take place in the spiritual realm followed by a similar counter-event in the physical world that will karmically rectify the mistakes of civilization throughout the centuries.[1] It was revealed to him that humanity is standing at the threshold of a great transitional period, a turning point from the old age of darkness to the New Age of light. Divine light is now being released, the tremendous spiritual vibration of which is overwhelming to the negative state that exists in the world today. He was told that only as people become attuned to this higher vibration will they change their attitudes and be better able to pass through the coming period of flux. However, to accomplish this, people must be purified both spiritually and physically. It is for this purpose that divine light is being released at this time, so that as many as possible may be awakened to higher knowledge and truth.

'Not only the purification of the human body, but a worldwide purification in every field is impending,' said Meishu Sama. 'This means a general house-cleaning of the whole world and the obliteration of the clouds of negativity accumulated during thousands of years.' In his first volume of teachings, Meishu Sama declared that 'extreme changes of climate and weather are all man-made'. He explained that human actions and speech of a violent, destructive, or negative nature create clouds in the spiritual realms which gather near their source until (like rain) they are finally dissipated by natural law in the form of turbulent weather or disasters.

Only individuals with fewer clouds of negative karma who perform greater services in the establishment of the coming 'New Order of the Ages' will be spared in the upheavals. He said this purification is coming to pass according to natural and divine law in order to rid the world of discord, disease and poverty, and turn it into a paradise where the old conditions of life will be eclipsed by health, prosperity and peace. And that is what Meishu Sama set out to do – establish a prototype of paradise on Earth.

So, from this foundation of one man's vision has emerged one of the strongest forces of spiritual transformation on the planet: the Johrei Fellowship. The three cornerstone principles of this approach to spiritual, mental and physical purification are 1) Johrei – building the light body, purifying the spiritual, healing the physical, 2) a consciousness and appreciation of beauty, and 3) Nature Farming.

Meishu Sama taught that every individual has a certain amount of accumulated clouds of negative karma on the spiritual body, created through thoughts and actions contrary to universal law. Normally, they are only eliminated when some major purification occurs according to the natural course of events, such as sickness, accidents and various problems. Since these clouds are of a spiritual nature, they can only be removed by a spiritual power: the power of the Light. And this is the power released through Meishu Sama. It is called 'Johrei', which means 'purification of the spiritual body'.

In a typical Johrei session, the practitioner and the person wishing to receive Johrei sit facing each other. After a short prayer and a turning inward to link up with the source of divine Light, the practitioner raises his or her hand and channels Light to the receiver. The hand is used like a lens to focus the Light on various parts of the receiver's body.

When directed by one person to another, divine Light permeates the spiritual body, dispelling the negative clouds and further awakening the inner being to truth so that the errors which caused the accumulations may not be repeated. The light body is built by purifying the spirit, and physical healing can then occur. According to Meishu Sama, a person's mental attitude and health improve because the blood, which is the interface between matter and spirit, is purified.

Interesting corroboration of this concept regarding the building of the Light body is echoed in the teachings of the Academy of Future Science, *The Keys of Enoch,* wherein it is explained that the Hebrew-derived 'Men-Ha-Ada-Mah' represents 'the transformation of the blood crystals and the freeing of the human chemistry from the Earthbound dimension so that [it] can exist in the next step function of universal intelligence. According to Enoch, [it means] the 'purification and regenisis' of the blood ... so that man is able to exist in the next orbital level of the Universal Mind. In essence, [it means] regenesis of the blood circulatory system so that man is able to exist with the higher Adamic creations and serve YHWH. *This regenesis of blood involves the use of unique energy vibrations of Light ...'* (emphasis added).

After one has received Johrei a few times, physical purification may begin, usually as the elimination of toxins in some manner. From a contemporary viewpoint, Johrei is a means by which to link up with our dimensional light bodies – something interpreters of Maya calendric prophecy indicate we need to do in order to be ready for the next evolutionary phase in 2012 A.D. (culmination date of the Maya calendar).

Johrei is also used on seeds and plants. This is the Nature Farming aspect of Meishu Sama's wisdom. The basic purpose of this farming method is to bring out the natural energy of the Earth and to utilize the soil itself to its fullest potential. Research has shown that the products of Nature Farming are superior in quality and taste, and stay fresh longer than petrochemically grown food. Experimental farms were established throughout Japan in the 1950s, and

'Light' written by Meishu Sama

today more than 15,000 farmers and gardeners contribute nature-farmed produce to the growing demand for this kind of food. Robert Rodale, organic farming expert, and author and editor of *Organic Gardening and Farming*, wrote after his visit to Japan:

> 'Another strong force for improvement in growing methods in Japan is a remarkable [non-denominational] religion … which recommends that its million members eat food produced on what it calls 'nature farms'. No fertilizers or pesticides of any kind are used – even compost is frowned upon, but leaders are very sympathetic to the organic gardening and farming idea and say that organic food is preferable to chemically-grown produce. Although the idea of a spiritual approach to farming might seem strange to some Americans, the … programme is very popular in Japan and also in Brazil, Hawaii and California … [It] is an environmentally oriented concept, with particular pertinence to problems that are faced by the people of any highly industrialized society. The fact that this religion is thriving in Japan is an interesting commentary on the resourcefulness of the Japanese in seeking new and different ways to solve their most difficult environmental problems.'[2]

At the time of writing, the California Energy Commission has funded a Nature Farm research/demonstration project monitored by a multidisciplinary research team of university professors and professional farm advisors. The First International Conference on Nature Farming occurred in Thailand in 1989, as well as the first meeting (since the Organic Merchants [OM] movement of the early 1970s) of organic growers' associations from across the United States. Parenthetically, the reader should understand that although government studies have confirmed the cost effectiveness of organic farming,[3] agribusiness did not respond to the findings, because in the United States petrochemicals and agriculture are controlled by the same corporate entities. To preserve their interests, multinational corporations in the petrochemical, drug, seed, pesticide and fertilizer industries are buying up seed companies and collections of organic open-pollinated (nonhybrid) seeds throughout the world. Subsidiaries of these corporations breed hybrid, patentable, sterile plant varieties increasingly dependent upon artificial pesticides and fertilizers.

In the interests of providing some spiritually sound insight into the importance of our reconnecting with the Earth at the most fundamental level, the following information is offered. Meishu Sama's prophecies and Earth-centred wisdom take on immediate contemporary relevance when contrasted with the commercial food system's disregard for and damage to the land.

The U.N. Food and Agricultural Organization has estimated that three-fourths of all natural vegetable varieties grown and native to Europe have become extinct because (like the fast food chains) 'agriseed' cartels have invaded with massive advertising and PR, and taken over markets where the original, traditional varieties used to predominate. Just as certain popular herbs and healing plants have been supplanted by the patentable drugs of orthodox medicine, the agribusiness seed industry lobbied heavily for legislation which led to the legal patenting of major hybrid vegetable and fruit species – and experimental animal species. Legislative efforts began in the early 1980s for the U.S. government to join an international agency that coordinates plant patenting laws worldwide. In Europe, growing or selling the seeds of plants not contained in the Common Catalogue of the European Economic Community is illegal. In a deliberate attempt to clear the market as quickly as possible for the new patented varieties, sometimes hundreds of varieties a month are deleted from the Catalogue, and violators are prosecuted.

Modern agricultural technology seeks to make all crops as uniform as possible, eliminating the natural profusion of varieties found within each plant species. With the Green Revolution of the 1970s, farmers and growers all over the world began to plant the same narrow range of hybrid seeds produced by the major seed companies. People simply stopped growing their traditional seeds, an infinite number of which promptly became extinct. Intentional elimination of genetic diversity is the real threat to future world food supply, because infestation and climate change can wipe out in a single growing season not only an entire crop (the Great Plains grow sixty percent of the world's wheat, for instance) but also the possibility of replacing it with a more resistant traditional strain or breeding into it survival qualities from a related variety. As an example, the U.S. has only two types of peas, which comprise ninety-five percent of the total acreage devoted to that crop; only three types of millet account for one hundred percent of that crop, although there may have been thousands at one time, according to the Graham Centre Seed Directory. (Edgar Cayce had prophesied the loss of important food producing regions in the coming Earth changes.)

Now that global weather patterns are changing, we find that most of the basic grains from which the present hybrids were taken have not been saved by the United States Seed Bank in Golden, Colorado. If the traditional varieties are not saved by individuals and concerned organizations, it may not be possible to breed resistance back into the limited and uniform quality hybrids now dominating. Whoever controls the seed – the beginning of the food system – can control the entire system. The seeds of hybrid species are not resproutable. One does not need a computer to project that the outcome of such an unchecked global trend could virtually eliminate nature's infinite bounty as a free and self-perpetuating food source. It could be usurped in a comparatively short time by compulsory dependence upon expensive, sterile hybrids produced by multinational corporations.

Original (meaning indigenous plant strains that have evolved to successfully survive stress, climate variation, and pests) open-pollinated (nonhybrid, fertile, continuously resproutable seeds that can be saved, usually up to two years) varieties are still available from a handful of family-owned seed companies, collectives and old time growers. As a very real survival resource in terms of future food needs and also as a valuable instrument of barter in rough times, these original open-pollinated seeds have their place in every family's garden and food storage plan.

According to Meishu Sama, petrochemicals and synthetic fertilizers negatively polarize the soil. This, in the short term, produces apparently abundant growth; but, in the long term, depletes the soil, exhausts its natural growing capability, and produces weak, mineral deficient plants. Unbalanced plants attract bug and insect infestations – scavengers which naturally perform a purifying function. These 'pests' are specifically programmed by nature with a taste affinity for confused plants of negative frequency. It is the innate function of insects to feed off imperfection and keep the natural world in balance. Because the human race has failed so miserably as stewards of the Earth and created so much pollution and imbalance, not to mention topsoil depletion, the insect population has proliferated to keep up with the demand. We therefore call them pests and infestations and blame *them*. They will stop when we stop.

Meishu Sama taught that nature has the capacity to resolve negative soil conditions and, over time, use them in a positive manner. Because soil takes up to seven years to regain organic integrity after petrochemical husbandry, integrated pest management is one approach many farmers now employ to minimize crop loss during the transitional period. A healthy plant would, by definition, have been produced by completely natural means. Successful organic farmers can readily confirm Meishu Sama's statement that crop losses due to blight and insects are minimal when the natural purity of the soil is nurtured.

In developing this theme further, Meishu Sama taught that the visible world is surrounded by an invisible sea of ether, which we call the spiritual realm. This realm is permeated with a universal energy from which all living things draw their life energy. This universal energy is composed of elements that blend into a perfect harmony to produce the creative energy known as the Power of Nature. The air element is a carrier for the spiritual counterparts of the other elements – earth, fire and water, which synergize to become the vital power responsible for fertility and evolution.

The spiritual nature of soil, worked with in Nature Farming, is not yet recognized by science. Native peoples know about it. The traditional Hopi of Arizona successfully raise abundant and nutritious corn by working with this spiritual element of the soil – soil from arid reservation land, which the U.S. Department of Agriculture says receives less than half the annual rainfall necessary for corn growing.[4] And the Hopi rain dance is rooted in ancient Earth knowledge. Rain is seeded by the dust raised into the air during the prolonged pounding of the dancers' feet upon the ground. The spiritual counterpart of the nitrogen in the soil's dust alchemizes in the air to bring about the rain.

Meishu Sama explained this phenomenon in terms of the

Alchemy alludes to the Spirit which is at the heart of matter: 'Su'

breathing of the Earth. Exhalation, warm like that of humans, originates with increased ground heat percolating up from the Earth's core (estimated at 5,400 degrees Fahrenheit) to stimulate the spring growing cycle. He defined the *spiritual power* of this heat (like the heat of the light transmitted by Johrei) as *Doso*, a Japanese term describing the element of earth, with nitrogen as its physical aspect. In this natural cycle, the heat radiates out through Earth's crust, rising and filling the space between the planet and the stratosphere, where it collects and is then returned to Earth with the falling rain. This is how nitrogen fertilization occurs naturally. To take the nitrogen from the air and use it artificially as fertilizer will initially increase crop growth, but, gradually, through nitrogen addiction, the soil will become depleted. The Earth's inhalation begins after the midpoint of summer, when the cooling draws the life force back into a quiescent state within the Earth and the growing cycle declines.

A consciousness of beauty in nature, through art appreciation, environmental improvement, landscaping, and floral arrangement, was also encouraged by Meishu Sama. The magnificent art museum he established in Hakone, Japan, is one of the finest in the world, and there is a school for flower arrangement – the ancient art of ikebana. Today, practitioners of Johrei seek to develop their awareness of the countless beautiful things in everyday life, for every phase of beauty contributes to the expansion of spiritual upliftment and understanding. Floral arrangements are placed in hospitals and prisons to raise the vibration and touch people in that quiet interior place that responds to nature and beauty.

The turmoil and suffering of the Second World War left in its wake a traumatized and exhausted world psyche. In the postwar years of the 1940s and 1950s, the concept of a New Age hadn't crystallized within the dream-mind of the slumbering masses. And yet, there were a few quiet voices who whispered the inspired words and held the torch as they moved through the darkness. 'Wake up. Wake up.' Energy and Light gathered unto itself the awakened consciousness of the first early risers, and later, as the sun came up on a certain morning, it was somehow known and felt that a new dawn would bring a new light and a New Age. Like a future echo ... 'What *is* that?' Meishu Sama had seen the vision, known the Light, spoken the language: 'It is such an unprecedented change that it is difficult to grasp its full import. It is a turning point which none of our forefathers were privileged to experience. How fortunate are we who live at this time to even partially understand the real significance of the change and to have the means, through Johrei, of making the transition easier for everyone by serving God and humanity.'[5]

Is changing the world the impossible dream? The Utopian myth? Well, Meishu Sama settled back in his chair and looked at it this way. 'God's plan is very interesting for it is just like the seed of a fruit … the fruit is the world and the seed becomes the centre … and at the centre of the seed itself is its essence. Because of this, in order to change the world the smallest seed only need be changed. It is just like throwing a rock into a pond – it creates ripples. In this way, making this world into heaven, the very centre of the centre, the tiniest point – that's where the various changes are made. Make these changes and you create a paradise on Earth.'

Meishu Sama died in 1955. He did not live to see the establishment of paradise on Earth completed, but he did live long enough to accomplish his goal of creating its prototype.

And those transforming ripples continue – the beautiful sacred grounds of Atami and Hakone in Japan are the heritage and spiritual focus for hundreds of thousands who practise the techniques he brought for purification, and share his vision … We have beheld the dream. We have called it Paradise on Earth.

The process of transformation has begun …

10

The Hopi

The Hopi are a proud and peaceful nation. Since ancient times, they have farmed the land and cared for the Earth with diligence and love. Their forefathers knew the Great Spirit and lived in harmony with His laws. The Earth Mother and the Hopi were as one, and the land was productive in response to the care it received. Water, trees and rocks were alive in a special way for these 'peaceful ones', as they called themselves, and to them the Great Spirit entrusted a particular area of land for safekeeping, and for posterity. The Great Spirit said it was the spiritual centre of the continent, and the land was called Tukunavi – Black Mesa.

It was a primal trust that was bestowed, for the Mesa must be tended by its stewards with prayer, ritual and fasting in order that the balance of nature be preserved for the whole world. It was intended to be a sacred place, remaining undefiled until the time of the Great Purification, when all the good people would be protected there and the Great Spirit would return to His people once more.

In northern Arizona, atop the sacred mountain of the Hopis and Navajos, lies Black Mesa, an island in the sky of more than two million acres that rises 3300 feet from the desert floor. Today the traditional people of these tribes strive to continue living as their ancestors did, tending their land and growing crops of corn, beans, and squash, and grazing sheep and goats. It's a hard life, deeply ruptured by twentieth century politics and pollution. Planting is followed by prayer and hauling water. Only the indigenous native peoples of the Southwest have learned to cultivate and harmonize with this arid land, mostly rock and sand, hardly any trees. Using a minimum of technology and the intuitive flow with nature bestowed by their culture, they alone have understood the way of that land and come into creative agreement with its harshness.

Tracing the history of these quiet people and the mystery of their lore reveals that the living core of their existence and purpose is identification with their myth. It is lived by the traditional Hopis with fidelity and is preserved intact. The Hopi myth embraces the complete cycle of creation, from the beginning of their nation until the time of the Great Purification when the Great Spirit will return. It is very similar to the Christian expectation of the apocalyptic 'tribulation' and subsequent return of Christ.

We are told that in the beginning, the Great Spirit laid out ears of corn before the people who had just emerged into this new world through a reed, from underground ant caverns. They had been protected there during the destruction of the third created world, while the poles changed places. The survivors of the previous world were those who had not lost the use of their spiritual eye or the opening on top of their head. (The native American kiva, a circular underground ceremonial chamber, is accessed by a ladder through a small roof opening, symbolizing the 'opening on the top of the head' or crown *chakra*. In the floor, below the roof opening, is a representation of the 'sippapu', the point of emergence through which the survivors of the last world entered this one by climbing up a hollow reed – a motif that is found throughout the esoteric symbologies of the ancient world, particularly the Maya; this will be explained in the 'Maya' chapter.)

The leaders of the various groups were invited to select some ears of the corn for the long journey ahead. Because the Hopi waited until last and took the smallest ears, they became the chosen ones. The Hopi leader had two sons. The elder was light-skinned, an inventor, clever and powerful but lacking wisdom. The younger had skin 'the colour of the Earth'. He was endowed with an innate understanding of nature's ways, was wise, but somewhat clumsy. The late Grandfather David Monongye, clan keeper of the Hopi prophecy, described the qualities of these two brothers in terms similar to the left and right brain functions of humans. These hemispherical polarities must come into balance if we are to solve and survive the global problems our left-brain dominance has created. The Great Spirit gave the life plan for harmony and balance to these two brothers, and the instructions were carved on stone tablets.

The oral tradition of the Iroquois regarding the stone tablets is very similar to that of the Hopi. It tells of two stone tablets being given to the red, yellow, black and white races by the Creator before their original migrations throughout the world. Details of each race's unique gift and life plan were carved on the stones. As Cherokee healer Lee Brown tells it, peace on Earth will not be achieved until the four tablet holders, each representing one of the four directions, sit in the same peace circle. After World War I, the native peoples who asked to be represented at the League of Nations in 1920 were refused. This meant the Eastern sector of the peace circle was open, and the native peoples familiar with the prophecy knew that no lasting peace would result. Prophecy says that the tablet holders from the four directions will come together for the purpose of bringing out their stone tablets and sharing their teachings at the end of this cycle. The Great Spirit cautioned, however, that if these stones were ever cast on the ground, a whirlwind would start up and devour the whole Earth. In other words, if the life plan instructions were intentionally discarded, holocaust would result – as in Hopi and other end-time prophecies.

The keepers of one of the original ancient tablets are the Oraibi Fire clan[1] of the Hopi, on behalf of the red race (East); the Hopi believe the 'true white brother' will bring the other tablet with him when he returns. Tibetans hold tablets for the yellow race (South); the Kikuyu in Kenya,

Africa, for the black race (West); and the Swiss for the white race (North). The Creator said that if these people should become separated from their teachings and their unity with each other He would shake the Earth three times. The first two shakings would be with the left and right hands and the third one with *both* hands, to get their attention and remind everyone of their relatedness.

At the original encounter between the Great Spirit and the survivors of the previous world, the group was told that in the future, when the elder white brother returned to the country of the younger, it could be the beginning of the Great Purification leading to the end of the new fourth world if the life plan were not carried out faithfully. The Great Spirit said the white brother should be welcomed home if he came bearing the sacred symbol – the cross within the circle. If he should come with *only* the cross, the red brother must beware and know that the Great Purification was not far off. And so it came to pass that when the missionaries arrived, they brought only the cross – 'a hard cross to bear,' because they and the white brothers who followed brought only oppression. They knew nothing of the sacred circle.

The various groups were then given instructions about their different languages and foods and their particular form of worship, and directed to migrate to all parts of the world and to live according to their instructions. The Hopi journeyed to the place where the Great Spirit had lived, at the spiritual centre of the continent. In this sacred area they were to pray for balance and harmony and to live within the life plan that had been taught them.

This symbol, given the Hopi nation by the Great Spirit, means, 'Together with all nations we protect both land and life, and hold the world in balance.' The Hopi inhabited Black Mesa 'since the beginning', many ages before the area became known as the Four Corners Area, where the borders of Utah, Colorado, New Mexico and Arizona now converge. The cross represents the spiritual centre, the heart of the continent, formed by the intersection of the North-South and East-West migration routes of the Hopi, which

The Hopi shield symbol

are also the axes along which twin beings, mentioned earlier, controlled the rotation of the planet. The circles in the quadrants have several layers of meaning: the four ventricles of the human heart; the four sacred breathing mountains within the borders of each of the four states that affect the weather (to be discussed later); and the indigenous peoples of different continents keeping balance together.

Carved on a rock in the vicinity of Oraibi village is a petroglyph that conveys the Hopi life plan prophecy of the Great One. Starting at the lower left hand corner, and moving to the right, the petroglyph means roughly the

Petroglyph of the Hopi life plan

following: The bow and arrow are the tools given to the Hopi by the Great Spirit. He is holding the reed through which the people emerged into this world after sheltering in underground caverns at the end of the last cycle. The upper horizontal line signifies the materialistic life path; the lower line, the life path prescribed by the Great Spirit. The left vertical line joining the two paths represents the first contact between Hopi and white people. The figures on the materialistic path are said to be two whites and the Hopi who adopted white people's ways.

It is forbidden to photograph prophecy rock, so slightly different versions of the petroglyph circulate. They are basically the same except for the finer details. In this depiction, the heads of the people on the upper, materialistic path are detached from their bodies. In another rendition, the figures are headless. These are people who lack integration and whose heads and hearts (like the left, 'intellectual' hemisphere of the brain and the 'feeling nature' of the right brain) have become separated. In the headless version, the implication is that the heads become, or result in, the circles on the lower path representing the first two 'world purifications'. The first circle is World War I; the second, World War II. The line of the lower path goes through both circles, indicating the polarity of extremes: all intellect, or all emotion. The second vertical line is the opportunity to change paths before the third Great Purification – indicated by an undivided circle above the line a 'mystery egg' that brings necessary integration and wholeness – and that the Hopi feel we are now approaching. (Black Elk and Crazy Horse, the great Sioux chiefs, had also both prophesied that three great world wars would occur within four generations, or by the end of the twentieth century.) Notice how the materialistic path becomes erratic and finally fades away. The path in harmony with nature continues. Corn and water will be abundant, the Great Spirit will return, and all will be well.

This 'life plan' prophecy of the Hopis is very similar in theme to that of the Great Pyramid, with its choice between two paths. If the time for return to the natural life path is missed (the first vertical line), a second opportunity *is* possible, but only after great tragedy. Similarly, in the Great Pyramid, one could ignore the Ascending Passage and continue down into the Pit. The well shaft provides a better-late-than-never chance to get back up to the Ascending Passage of life, but it would be extremely rigorous and require superhuman effort.

In an interview with the Black Mesa Defence Fund, Hopi elder of the Badger Clan, the late John Lansa, spoke these words:

The Hopi prophecies are drawn on a rock in Black Mesa. The prophecy says there will come a time of much destruction. This is the time. The prophecy says there will be paths in the sky. The paths are airplanes [vapour trails and air lanes]. There will be cobwebs in the air. These are the power lines [giant transmission lines span the desert from Black Mesa to Los Angeles and Las Vegas].

'According to the prophecies, "a gourd of ashes" would be invented which, if dropped from the sky, would boil the oceans and burn the land, causing nothing to grow for many years. [When the atomic bomb was dropped, the Hopi knew it was the signal for certain teachings to be released to warn the world that the third and final event could bring an end to all life unless people correct themselves and their leaders in time. As you will read later, Jesus himself made an identical prediction, as does the chronology of the Great Pyramid.] The prophecy says men will travel to the moon and stars and this will cause disruption and the time of the Great Purification will be very near. It is bad that spacemen brought things back from the moon [In NASA experiments, three types of Earth bacteria died after exposure to an Apollo 11 core-tube soil sample from the moon. This resulted in quarantine procedures for astronauts[2]]. The Great Spirit says in the prophecy that man will not go any further when he builds a city in the sky. People are planning to build a space station.

The prophecy tells of the gradual devastation of the Earth's natural processes because of human interference. The Hopis are today concerned for the whole planet and fear that every living thing might be destroyed. They are very worried about the spiritual centre and for all people to heed the instructions of the Great Spirit, otherwise everything will go down. If the white man would stop trying to teach us Christianity and begin to listen to what the Great Spirit taught the Hopis, then everything would get back in harmony with nature. As it is the white man is destroying this country.'

The tribe pray that their system of ethics and vision will be utilized by the white culture in time to avert the complete breakdown in the energy systems which hold the Earth Mother together.

Foreknowledge of certain world events has been handed down in secret religious societies of the Hopi. Throughout each generation, Hopi initiates have especially watched for a series of three worldshaking events, each accompanied by a particular symbol. These symbols, the swastika, sun and the colour red, are inscribed upon a rock and on the sacred gourd rattle used in Hopi rituals. Microcosmically, the symbols represent primordial forces that govern all life; they are presented to individuals during clan initiation rites. Macrocosmically, the symbols are used in three 'world purifications' that bring about circumstances that shake the world to release negative planetary karma. The ceremonial shaking of the gourd rattle signifies the stirring of life forces as well as the shaking of the Earth itself. On the rattle, the swastika (an ancient symbol of the sun) represents the masculine principle and the spirals of force emanating into the four directions from the sprouting seed. The swastika is surrounded by a ring of red fire, depicting the feminine principle as it encircles with its deep warmth to germinate

the seed. Both principles will be integrated by the third
purifier, which brings balance.

From their earliest sacred teachings, the Hopi knew to
expect signs of each shaking or purification. The first, to be
preceded by a bug moving along a black ribbon, became
recognized in due course as an automobile travelling along a
road. It was prophesied that the first world shaking would
then toss the bug into the sky – the airplane. The Hopi knew
that out of the violence and destruction of each world-shak-
ing, the strongest elements would reemerge with a greater
force to produce the next event. World War II, therefore,
championed by Germany and its swastika, merged later
with Japan, 'land of the rising sun'. (Naziism and antisemitism are again becoming dark expressions of the 'shadow' for those who choose to align themselves with the
forces of hate and oppression.)

The third purifier is symbolized by the colour red (or
possibly a red hat and a red cloak), and will result in the
total rebirth or annihilation of all life, say the prophecies.

Some Hopi interpretations of this prophecy believe the
colour red is specific to people. They say, 'The red hat and
cloak people will have a huge population.' They will bring
ancient wisdom and sacred texts from the East. Buddhist
'Red Hat' sects have established centres in the U.S., and we
are reminded of the prophecy by Padmasambhava, the great
Vajrayana master of the original Red Hat sect in the eighth
century: 'When the iron bird flies, and horses run on
wheels, the Tibetan people will be scattered like ants across
the world. And the Dharma will come to the land of the red
man.' Clearly, the wisdom of the East is an important means
of assisting the West's transformation to a higher state of
consciousness so that our ignorance will not ultimately
destroy us.

In this regard, an event of historical importance (the
knowing of which gives us hope and optimism for the
future), is shared by John Kimmey, a student of Hopi
prophecy who spent much time with the late grandfather
David Monongye, keeper of the prophecy. In 1979 the head

lama of the Red Hat sect of Drepung Monastery in southern India travelled to the United States specifically to fulfill Padmasambhava's prophecy and to 'plant the seeds of the Dharma in the West.' Guided by Spirit, and the means by which spiritual connections are made, it became clear that the spiritual centre of the continent was the place for this mission to be accomplished – i.e., Hopi land. The Lama travelled to the American Southwest to visit with Hopi elders and, during four days of ritual and ceremony in Grandfather David's kiva, the seeds of the Dharma were indeed planted in the West.

If Western culture fails to assimilate the wisdom of the East, the Hopi say the negative aspects of the colour red will eventually manifest from the East in the form of an aerial invasion by men who will darken the sky 'like a swarm of locusts'. This sounds similar to the biblical Revelation's reference to the invasion by the Kings of the East and two hundred million soldiers, and the great red dragon who threatens the nations. The colour red and the red dragon are suggestive of communism and China.

Whatever form the third great purification takes, the prophecies say there will be several signs: trees everywhere will begin dying (yes, this is happening); people will build a house and throw it in the sky (surely, the space lab?); cold places will become hot, and hot places cold (global weather patterns have been changing drastically for many years); land sinking beneath the sea and rising above it from below (such changes, also prophesied by Edgar Cayce, have begun, and are discussed in the next chapter); and the appearance of a blue star, which (when I first heard about it in 1972) was said to be 'far off and as yet invisible but soon to make its appearance'. Blue stars are hotter than the sun and extremely rare. The appearance of the blue star is foretold in a song which was sung at the major ceremony of the Hopi annual cycle in 1914 and 1940 preceding the two world wars, and again in 1961, just prior to US involvement in the Vietnam war. 'When the "Blue Star" ceremonial Kachina dancer next dances in the plaza, it will come,' the prophecy said.

In 1987, a number of wonderful things happened, not the least of which was the grand appearance of a spectacular blue star. In the Greater Magellanic Cloud, a distant subgalaxy of our Milky Way, a hot blue supergiant erupted in majestic, violent death, making world history and becoming the celebrated and spectacular supernova, SN1987A. Previously, the only celestial bodies believed capable of going supernova were white dwarfs and red supergiants. This dazzling spot of turbulence in the southern sky was classified as one of the most significant scientific discoveries of the twentieth century. The brightest supernova in four centuries, it was two hundred million times brighter than the sun at the peak of its brilliance.

This occurred just prior to the signing of the Nuclear Arms Limitation Treaty, Harmonic Convergence, and completion of the Nine Hells cycle of the Maya calendar, which brought to a close the Maya Fifth World. As predicted in the Great Pyramid's chronology, 1987 was an extremely significant year in world history. The importance of this Blue Star supernova's strategic location and impact upon the Earth should not be underestimated, for it plays an astonishing part in the awesome gestalt of world prophecy. Just how profoundly it impacted us and what that means will be revealed in the ' "Our" Prophecy' chapter.

Through their vital communion with the unseen forces that hold nature in balance, the traditional Hopi play a central role in the survival of the human race and this delicate sphere upon which it lives. If they are unable to maintain their tradition according to their ancient religious knowledge and instructions, natural forces for the entire planet become weakened, because their land on the Mesa is the spiritual centre, the point of energy balance. Their burden is now heavy as this ability becomes increasingly difficult to maintain. The Hopi regard the conditions of their life as a reflection of the rest of the world and the world as a mirror of their life.

In 1991, the tablets given the Hopi by the Creator (after they completed their migration and settled at the sacred centre of the continent) were shown to the governor of New

Mexico. Hopi title to that land is contained on the tablets. Their custodian, an elder of the Fire Clan, communicated during the meeting that the Gulf conflict was 'disturbing the underground serpent'. The elder said it was known to the Hopi that if the cycle of destruction was not reversed, the serpent would create other disasters and crises and inflict upon the living universe repercussions that would be very severe. He carefully explained that the spiritual effects of the conflict could be offset if the United States officially clarified Hopi aboriginal title to the land at the spiritual centre. The implication was that reestablishing correct 'order' at the spiritual centre would enable the centre to function according to its divinely ordained purpose – as the axis that directs the periphery, and from which harmony of the natural world emanates. It was the Hopi intention to offer to the leaders of the modern world access to Hopi knowledge that might enable those who were concerned to solve the present crisis. The friend who was my source for this information had helped set up the meeting, and was present when it took place. He said that it was his distinct impression that the governor had no comprehension of what was being communicated, nor did he appear cooperative to the request for assistance regarding the issue of title.

We are interpreting here that the disturbance of 'the underground serpent' refers to the dynamics of the planetary grid. 'Fohat' is the cosmic electricity coiled at the centre of the Earth. It stores solar *kundalini* and moves in a serpentine path. The Chinese call the lines of magnetic force within the Earth 'dragon paths'. Disturbing this energy is very, very dangerous, because it regulates and interacts with the support systems of the living Earth and the creatures upon it. As we shall learn later, the Blue Star also influenced the 'underground serpent'.

The Hopi knew long ago from their prophecies that the Mesa was rich in resources, but the Great Spirit had specifically instructed that they not be removed until after the Great Purification. He said, the Earth's wealth otherwise would be used for selfish gain and evil purposes. And it has.

Today, the Hopi see the Earth Mother's heart being torn open. She is being raped and plundered, and they are powerless to protect her according to their trust.

Since 1970, the Hopi land on the Mesa has been torn apart and devastated by coal strip mining and digging for oil and uranium. The resource-rich sacred lands of the Hopi and Navajo have become a national sacrifice area.

When the author visited the area, the situation could be summed up in the poignant sight of a baby goat with a small tinkling bell around its neck. It stumbled, lost, through the sticky troughs of black strip-mined overburden, and when we returned down the mining road, alongside the fast-moving slurry line of coal, we again saw the small creature sheltering from the wind inside a huge drag shovel.

Strip mining irreversibly damages the terrain with 'scars and strips for ever'.

Attempts to reclaim the land produce pitiful results. For corporations, strip mining is economical, but for the environment, it makes as much sense as extracting teeth through the side of one's face. And, after all the years of environmental degradation, pollution controls for coal-fired generating plants still are inadequate. Air pollution is now so critical in the area that Shiprock, a spectacular outcropping originally visible for 125 miles across the desert before the power plants came, is now visible for less than a mile when the wind prevails from the Four Corners area.

Gouging the land for uranium and strip mining is, the Hopi say, tearing at the very heart of Mother Earth. When this happens, nothing can prevent her death throes and the ensuing Great Purification. This may sound like quaint superstition to some, but we are beginning to detect a factual basis for much of what was previously dismissed as myth or folklore. In *Magnetic Fields of the Human Body,* Dr David Cohen reports that the strongest electromagnetic frequencies emanate from the heart and lungs of the human body. Considering the notion that Hopi land is the heart of the Earth Mother, we read in Joan Price's monograph *Earth vibrating* that the Four Corners area supports the highest concentration of lightning phenomenon on the North American continent. Certainly, the author's brief experience of camping in the area was interesting, illuminated as it was throughout the July night by the lightning and thunder of an electrical storm so violent it resembled a Hollywood sound stage.

To expand the concept of the 'heart' of the continent further, the reader should understand that the largest energy-generating power grid in the entire world is located at the Four Corners area. It provides electrical power for urban centres such as Los Angeles, Las Vegas, Phoenix, Tucson, the Central Arizona Project and Japan. At the time of writing, a consortium of more than twenty-five power companies and several government agencies ensure energy for the development of those areas. The construction of six major and fifty smaller power plants is having a staggering impact upon the Southwestern wilderness, upon the Hopi and their Navajo neighbours. Standing there amidst the incredible din which seems to vibrate the very ground one stands on, with the black fly ash raining down, it is not hard to equate this power grid to a massive organ, a heart, pumping vital electrical life force over its arterial power lines to nerve centres in distant cities – a physical manifestation of malevolent subversion.

It is economically cheap to use water from the Colorado watershed and from deep wells in the Mesa to cool the power plants and to transport coal in the form of slurry hundreds of miles away, to Nevada and to California, for shipment to Japan. But water is ecologically valuable in this dry region, and the huge amounts required by the power plants have far-reaching environmental effects. Strip mine blasting has damaged wells that now drain out into the lower wells of the power companies. Natural springs have dried up; the water tables are becoming rapidly depleted; rainfall is sparse and Hopi access to some traditional watering spots has been cut off by the mining operations. The appropriate federal agencies have failed to exercise the supervision of the mining company's operations that is necessary to minimize destruction of Hopi land and traditional culture.

Readers may well wonder why the land is being used this way if it belongs to the Hopi. The answer is that the Hopi Tribal Council was responsible. The traditional Hopi do not recognize the Tribal Council, superimposed upon them by the US government. The Council, composed primarily of Mormon Hopis acculturated to American business and money values, serves the interests of the federal government, private sector energy interests, and the nontraditional Hopi 'progressives'. The Tribal Council operates in direct conflict with the Kikmongwi (eight hereditary chieftains and spiritual leaders of the various Hopi villages), who are the true chosen and traditional leaders of the Hopi. The Kikmongwi would never, under any circumstances, sell the land. Yet, that is exactly what they have been duped and forced into. The following is an excerpt from the Kikmongwis' 'Hopi Declaration of Peace':

> To us, it is unthinkable to give up control over our sacred land to non-Hopis. We have no way to express exchange of sacred lands for money. It is alien to our ways. The Hopis never gave authority and never will give authority to anyone to dispose of our lands and heritage and religion for any price. We received these lands from the Great Spirit and we must hold them for Him, as a steward, a caretaker, until He returns …

Leases for the strip mining were covertly signed in 1964 – six years before operations began. The Hopi people did not even know about the contract for a long time. By then, Peabody Coal (a subsidiary of Kennecott Copper) was already on Black Mesa with a thirty-five-year lease, which was later extended to 2023 AD. According to the *Arizona Republic*, 'People were told the coal would be used to produce electricity and understood it to mean they would be getting Johnny Carson at the hogan.' It didn't work that way.

According to elder John Lansa, 'The Hopi know that you can't treat nature the way Peabody is or something will happen. There will be a time of many earthquakes or droughts or floods. Many people will get sick and die. The Hopis know this because the Great Spirit told them. The Great Spirit said, "I was the first – I will be the last." ['I am Alpha and Omega, the first and the last.' (Revelation 1:11). The prophet John was then instructed to write what he saw in a vision regarding the 'great tribulation' – the biblical version of the great purification.]

Perhaps the real crux of the matter lies with the Federal Government. The Bureau of Reclamation and the Bureau of Indian Affairs were established for the protection of Native American interests, but they are branches of the Department of the Interior, which is committed to the development of the Southwest. For instance, the Bureau of Reclamation had partnership arrangements with the Navajo Plant (one of the six major plants mentioned earlier) for twenty-four percent of income from that plant. The Bureau needed sixty percent of the coal from Black Mesa to fire that plant and produce electricity for pumping water for its own Central Arizona Project. Thus, the Department of the Interior is a buyer of the coal and water from Black Mesa. But it is also trustee of the lands, which it advised the Tribal Council to lease, and of the very resources it buys! The Indian Law Resource Centre has researched an extensive report for the Hopi Kikmongwis thoroughly documenting a long history of conflict of interest and forked-tongue double dealings over Hopi and Navajo land interests.[3]

There are no government agencies that *actually* protect the interests of Native Americans. Cash settlements are sometimes awarded for lands usurped by the U.S. government. Land is never returned. On certain rare occasions, land may be 'held in trust' by the government for the use of tribes, and for a specific time period. The Hopi have been culturally undermined by this process. In 1951, without the knowledge or consent of the majority of Hopi or their religious leaders, the Tribal Council filed a cash settlement claim against the government for treaty violations whereby lands and resources were taken illegally. When the case reached its final stages in 1977, the Indian Claims Commission ignored the petition of the Hopi majority who rejected the idea of accepting money for the ripped-off lands.

The Black Mesa coal field is one of the largest in the world; it is also rich in oil and uranium. (The Hopi had always maintained that the Kachinas – spirit embodiments – lived beneath the San Francisco Peaks of Arizona. We now know that possibly the largest uranium deposits in the world are located at the base of these mountains!) So, for the U.S. government, the power companies and corporate energy interests, the five million dollar enforced settlement was cheap at the price, barring the Hopi, as it did, from asserting any 'rights, claims or demands against the US in any future action'. It legally extinguished Hopi aboriginal title to the land as an indigenous people. As mentioned earlier, in 1991, the sacred tablets were shown to the governor of New Mexico in order to reestablish that title.

Another governmental action (Public Law 93-531) related to resource development involves the forced relocation of sixteen thousand (primarily) Navajo and Hopi from their jointly held Big Mountain ancestral land, southwest of Black Mesa. The effects of this tragically mismanaged and protracted effort have been called genocide and 'the second longest walk' with good reason. A virtual media blackout on this relocation has prevailed for many years.

The traditional Hopi have no political 'clout,' but their communications of protest to the powers-that-be 'call it like it is', and reflect their commitment to spiritual values. An example is this excerpt from a 1985 letter to two state governors (signed by six initiated Hopi traditional and religious headmen on behalf of the hereditary Kikmongwis, with David Monongye, keeper of the prophecy, as spokesman):

'As initiated Hopi members of Wuwuchim and Kachina Religious Orders, knowing our ancient spiritual instructions, warnings and prophecies, we see this as merely a political conflict ... instigated and promoted by the

Bureau of Indian Affairs after they quickly set up the so-called Hopi Tribal Council and placed them in the hands of the Secretary of the Interior who in turn uses them as a tool to begin mineral resource development with the aid of the multinational corporations. The BIA pressured the so-called Hopi Tribal Council to hire Mormon attorneys to bring about leasing of Hopi and Navajo homelands for mineral resource development ...

'Our forefathers have strongly impressed upon us warning all people that some day we may find corruption and greed linked with extremely powerful technological developments involving precious minerals under Hopi lands. Grave effect will result from tampering with the natural elements in the sacred spiritual Centre ... of our homeland. If this is kept in a natural order this area will be a refuge for all survivors when something happens in the future outside of this Sacred Area ...'

In speaking of the preservation of the sacred centre, an old Hopi man says, 'There is a seeing of things that can't be explained. There are shrines out there in the spiritual centre which are markers for spiritual routes which extend in all four directions to the edge of the continent. Through our ceremonies it is possible to keep the natural forces together. From here ... our prayers go to all parts of the Earth. They are the balance that keeps all things well and healthy. This is the sacred place; it must not have anything wrong in it.'

Hopi traditional elders have been arrested for trying to prevent burial sites from being bulldozed. Many of the Hopi shrines, the sacred foci of their prayer and rituals, have been desecrated. The delicate network of power paths that radiates out over the Mesa land to keep the energies of the planet harmoniously stabilized as part of the planetary grid has been interrupted and irreparably damaged. The Hopi, and those knowledgeable in geomancy, believe the desecration of the grid in the Southwest will have a devastating impact upon the rest of the planet. Major nodes of the planetary grid are located in the Bermuda Triangle and Mount

Shasta, California. A major grid ley line connecting the two sites runs directly through Black Mesa.

The existence of the planetary grid is referred to in the Hopi creation myth. The Great Spirit created a being to administer the universe. He, in turn, created an assistant: Spider Woman. She was to be responsible for making the energy web, or matrix, that sustains the life force of the planet and its life forms. So Spider Woman created twin beings, one of whom was to keep the world rotating by means of a network of living sound, or vibration, and the other to ensure stability of the land and assist the Earth's rotation by appropriate wind and air movement. According to Frank Waters's *Book of the Hopi*, one twin traversed the Earth, sending out a special sound that caused all the vibratory centres along the Earth's axis to resonate with the sound of the Creator. This being then took up his position at the North Pole of the world axis. The other twin topographically tempered Earth's terrain to be hospitable to life, and then assumed his position at the South Pole. At the end of the first three worlds, the twins were instructed to leave their positions, and with no one to control the polar motion (i.e., the axial spin), the world plunged into chaos 'and rolled over twice', after which a new world was born.

Spider Woman's energy web work is quite apparent today in the Southwest. Dr Elizabeth Rauscher of the Stanford Research Institute informed the author that magnetometer research has detected intense geomagnetic anomalies beneath Black Mesa. Fifty miles southeast of the Mesa, in Canyon de Chelly National Monument, is an impressive natural rock formation. A sensitive person can see spirals of energy coming into the top of this majestic sentinel. Its name is 'Spider Woman'. Off to the southwest, one hundred miles away, is Sedona's Bell Rock and vortex area. These and other rock formations, like those fifteen miles north of Black Mesa in Monument Valley, all function as downshoot energizers into the Earth's grid system, bringing balance between the negatively charged Earth and the positively charged atmosphere.[4]

Now, you know something about the story of Black Mesa and the spiritual, human, and ecological values threatened by the desecration of that torn land. What is happening to the Southwest and its indigenous peoples is the supreme example of how far we have come in our delusion, confusion and lack of planning. The following words of associate Penfield Jensen strike at the core of our collective error and mismanagement of the Earth. They are quoted here because they sum up the situation with an eloquence hard to duplicate:

Black Mesa is the symbol of all that is terrible and intolerable about our world. The extraction of coal from the flesh of one of the world's last traditional lands ... is criminal when viewed against the backdrop of our global destruction of everything and anything which preaches harmony and integration with the land. What Peabody, the Bureau of Reclamation and Southwest Edison perpetrate against the Hopi, all our technology perpetrates against the species: the destruction of a landscape and a culture in order to create profits (and waste). The Masai, the Indios of Brazil, the Trobriand Islanders, the Bushmen – aren't they telling us something too? What they say is simple. The Earth is our Mother. Start with that. From this common sense of what is sacred can grow what must become the means of our survival: a sense of ourselves as totally integrated with the processes and necessities of the land.

11

Edgar Cayce

Edgar Cayce (1877-1945) was a modern American mystic. He has been referred to affectionately as 'the sleeping prophet' and as a prophet of the New Age. Today, his many readings constitute a massive cross-indexed source of psychic records and associated data, which have been compiled for the use of psychologists, students, researchers and anyone who wishes to investigate them.

The Association for Research and Enlightenment (ARE), in Virginia Beach, Virginia, was founded in 1932 to preserve these records, conduct investigations and experiments, and promote conferences and seminars. Information continues to be catalogued and indexed under the thousands of subject headings as trends and events in the world today confirm and reflect the prophecies of Edgar Cayce. Quotations in this chapter are taken from those indexed readings.

This remarkable man was born on a farm near Hopkinsville, Kentucky, and as a child his talents were pretty much unrecognized, being dismissed as overactive imagination. He did impress his parents, however, by developing a degree of photographic memory when he slept with his head on his school books. Much later, as a young stationery salesman, his voice was threatened by a gradual paralysis of the throat muscles. Doctors had failed to discover the cause of the problem, and hypnosis had given but temporary relief. Edgar recalled his childhood sleep-learning ability, and asked a friend to give him hypnotic suggestion, by which he was able to enter a self-induced trance. Much to his own surprise, he knew exactly what medication and therapy to prescribe for himself – and was soon cured.

A group of local doctors heard about his unusual ability, and before long, Edgar Cayce was diagnosing their patients for them. His trance abilities developed so rapidly that he was even able to prescribe and diagnose for a patient 'in absentia', by purely telepathic means, their name and address being all that he needed. News of Mr Cayce's skill soon spread, and after *The New York Times* carried a prominent story on him, people from all over the country began to seek his help.

Edgar Cayce was a devoted family man, Sunday-school teacher, and gifted professional photographer, yet, over a period of forty-three years, he managed to give over fourteen thousand telepathic/clairvoyant readings.

The changes that Edgar Cayce foresaw in the course of his many consultations were to come on all levels – science and international affairs, social conditions, future shock, humanity's spiritual growth and understanding of inner reality. All are especially relevant today. Many of the changes appear to have already occurred, and we are in a time period when conscious human action is intimately connected to the fulfillment, or bypass, of important aspects of Cayce prophecy.

The echoes are reaching us that a world food shortage is very close. Changing weather patterns and crop failures within the United States have amplified this possibility to the extent that it has become a daily news item. In 1943, a Norfolk, Virginia resident asked Cayce if the purchase of a farm was still advisable. The reply was, yes, 'because of hardships which have not begun yet in this country, so far as the supply and demand for food is concerned'. At another time he said, 'Anyone who can buy a farm is fortunate, and buy it, if you don't want to grow hungry in some days to come.' Another person was advised in a reading to hold his farm acreage, 'for that may be the basis for the extreme periods through which all portions of the country must pass ...'

Other references include advice for returning to the land. In a 1938 interview, he stated, 'All that is for the sustenance of life is produced from the soil. Then there must be a return to the soil. Every man must be in that position that he at least creates, by his activities, that which will sustain the body – from the soil; or where he is supplying same to those activities that bring such experience into the lives of all.'

A tremendous amount of information was given by him about rearrangements of the geography before the end of the century. This would add to the problems of food scarcity, he said, and he predicted that the Great Lakes would empty into the Gulf of Mexico in the future. This would appear to be by way of the Mississippi Valley. If this warning comes true, an important food producing region of the United States will be lost. (The Chapter on Meishu Sama addresses the issue of commercial centralized food crops and the wisdom of individuals acquiring open-pollinated organic seeds.) Cayce said, 'Saskatchewan, the Pampas areas of the Argentine ... portions of South Africa ... these rich areas, with some portions of Montana and Nevada, must feed the world!'

Cayce predicted that new lands will appear in the Atlantic and the Pacific; among them, Poseidon, apparently one of the five residual islands from submerged Atlantis. (In 1974, archaeological researchers discovered part of this island off one of the Bimini Islands in the Bahamas – exactly where Cayce had predicted.) Other lands, he said, will sink.

During a reading in 1932, somebody asked the sleeping prophet how soon the changes in the Earth's activity would begin to appear. His reply was, 'When there is the first breaking up of some conditions in the South Sea [South Pacific] and those as apparent in the sinking or rising of that that's almost opposite same, or in the Mediterranean, and the Etna area, then we may know it has begun.'

The area 'almost' opposite Etna, marked by 'the breaking up of conditions' is undoubtedly the huge subduction zone in the South Pacific where the Western boundary of the Pacific plate itself breaks up to form the southwestern curve of the Ring of Fire as it thrusts against the Indo-Australian plate. Here, the moving sea floor turns down at the trenches rimming this part of the Pacific and deep earthquake epicentres line that downward path where ocean floor material moves under land masses. In this area of Cayce's prediction we find the island groupings of Fiji, Tonga, Kermadec and Loyalty – all of which surround a primary node of the planetary grid, the South Fiji Basin.[1] Deep ocean trenches (the Vityas, New Hebrides, Kermadec and Tonga) busily intersect the separate sections of the Earth's submarine crust which form these island bases.

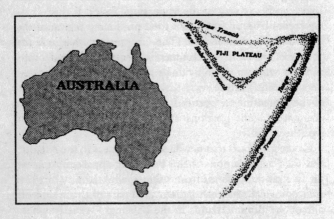

Tectonic subduction zone of South Pacific

The area of the Fiji Basin is one of the most seismically active locations in the world. As far as 'the breaking up of conditions' is concerned, in 1967, the Smithsonian Institution reported a seismic disturbance in the southwest Pacific so severe that a new island was thrust up for three months near Tonga. During 1977, in the Solomon Islands, northwest of Fiji, four quakes ranging between 7.2 and 8.1 also heaved up another temporary island. During 1978–79, three more 7.0 plus submarine eruptions in the same area produced additional land masses.[2] As noted above, Cayce had predicted that new lands would appear in the Pacific. Additional significant seismic activity has centred around the Kermadec Islands, with five 7.0 plus quakes, an 8.0 and an 8.3 between 1976 and 1986.

According to a scale based on long-term records, the National Earthquake Information Service says it is customary for one *great* quake (8.0 plus on the Richter scale) and eighteen *major* quakes (7.0–7.9) to occur in the world in any given year. Five of the eight great quakes recorded between 1976 and 1988 occurred in the Fiji Basin area of Cayce's prediction. During the same period, that area also received 11.33 percent of all the major quakes in the world.

Meanwhile (and this is not recent news by any means), there has been corresponding activity on the other side of the globe, which seems to have slipped by without any undue attention. As predicted, there has been violent activity within Mount Etna, on the Mediterranean Island of Sicily. During the 1970s, intense eruptions created fissures, new lava channels, and caused a new crater to explode on the northeast face.

Concerning Cayce's warning about the sinking or rising of an area opposite the South Pacific activity, as far back as 1959, a Reuters dispatch from Athens reported water levels in several Greek harbours had dropped, exposing the seabed in places and beaching craft in mud.[3] A more recent materialization concerns the water level of the Caspian Sea, which began sinking in 1975, leaving villages and port facilities high and dry and ruining the fish industry.

This problem aggravated difficulties within the Soviet Union. Under pressure from its water-needy Central Asian republics and Siberia, and shaken by repeated agricultural failures, the former Soviet Union sanctioned 'the grandest engineering project of all time'. This project, estimated to take fifty years to complete, would also compensate for the continuing water loss from the Caspian Sea by blasting a canal East of the Ural Mountains. The canal would connect with and reverse the flow of at least a dozen northbound rivers that run into the Barents Sea. Twenty percent of the fresh water normally destined for the Arctic Ocean would be drained south to increase irrigation and grain production. Some scientists cautioned that this purpose would be thwarted by a delay of the already brief growing season, because the spring thaw would be retarded by ice remaining in the new reservoirs beyond winter. Other scientists fear that, if not replenished by enough fresh water, the Arctic Ocean's warmer salt water would rise to the surface. This would induce the polar ice to melt and break up, intensifying global warming. Conversely, we are told that a reduction of warm water from the rivers' northward flow could *reduce* the Arctic Ocean temperature and cause an *expansion* of the ice cap (and, we would restate, further imbalance the geographic poles, with all the havoc that implies). There is one scientific point of agreement, however, and that is that the ice-covered Arctic is a key factor in establishing the Northern Hemisphere's climactic patterns. Therefore, reversing the flow of these rivers would drastically alter climate in the Northern Hemisphere, and possibly the entire world. However, since the dissolution of the Soviet Union, the future of this project is unknown.

As far as the actual 'breaking up' of the region of the Caspian Sea, all of northern Iran was shaken up by a 7.3 earthquake in mid-1990. More than one hundred towns and villages were devastated, and more than one hundred thousand deaths and casualties were reported.

Once the chain of geographical changes began, Cayce said, they would be followed by many others. He predicted that the greater portion of Japan (where the Pacific and Eurasian plates thrust together) would go into the sea, and that the upper portion of Europe would be 'changed as in the twinkling of an eye'. It should be noted, however, that Paul Solomon, a respected teacher known for his ability to contact the universal consciousness in much the same way as Edgar Cayce, has gone on record as stating that, owing to an increase in mass consciousness, this particular prediction no longer will need to happen. Cayce also declared that many of the battlefields of that time (1941) 'will become ocean, bays and lands over which the new order will carry on their trade one with another'. He also foresaw that the Earth would be broken up in many places. 'There will be open waters appearing in the northern portions of Greenland, and South America will be shaken up from the uppermost portion to the end.'

Of the United States, he said: 'The greater change will be in the North Atlantic Seaboard. Watch New York, Connecticut and the like. Many portions of the East Coast will be disturbed, as well as many portions of the West Coast, as well as the central portion of the United States. Los Angeles and San Francisco, most of all these will be among those that will be destroyed before New York, even. Portions of the now East Coast of New York or New York City itself, will in the main disappear.'

There was also a timely warning for West Coast residents – and one that presages many of the other major land changes. 'If there are the greater activities in the Vesuvius, of Pelée, then the South Coast of California – and the areas between Salt Lake and the Southern portions of Nevada – may expect within the three months following same, an inundation by the earthquakes. But these, as we find, are to be more in the Southern than in the Northern Hemisphere.' Stress along the San Andreas Fault (formed by the North American plate, edged by San Francisco, and the Pacific plate, supporting Los Angeles and areas south) is expected to be released any time by what scientists fear to be *the* overdue 'Big One'. For probably the first time in history, science and prophecy are in agreement.

The so-called Big One may in fact be what Gordon-Michael Scallion* defines as a 'Super-Mega quake' that the

---

* (Gordon-Michael Scallion forecasts Earth changes based on his intuitive insights. He publishes a survival guide for the nineties as a tool for increased awareness, and offers options for dealing with these changes as they affect personal and planetary consciousness.)'

Richter scale will not be able to measure. He amplifies Cayce's warning in updated terms, stating that the ultimate California quake will be preceded by serious quakes up the length of the West Coast. Scallion states that this catastrophe will not have a single epicentre, but rather, the land itself will displace its forces from North to South (i.e., Vancouver, Canada, to San Diego, California). He adds that, 'If an 8.0 plus Richter scale quake occurs in the Indian Ocean region – Sri Lanka should be watched carefully – then within days major earth changes shall occur in Japan, Alaska, Italy, Martinique and the Western United States and Canada.'

It is clear, however, that we appear to have had an undeniable period of grace regarding the fulfillment of negative prophecy. We hope it is grace that we have earned, so that events have not just been delayed, but short-circuited by a shift in the collective consciousness. The lesson seems to be one of hoping for the best and preparing for the worst.

For instance, with reference to Cayce's signs of the imminence of the West Coast catastrophe, there has been no stirring yet of Vesuvius in Italy, or of Pelée, on the Caribbean Windward Island of Martinique, but there has been a very close call. Eighty miles North of Mt. Pelée, La Soufrière volcano erupted with a reported 'atomic bomb intensity' on Guadeloupe Island in 1976, simultaneous to a 7.0 quake at an almost identical latitude on the opposite side of the globe, in the Philippines. To the South of Mt. Pelée, at a distance from it equal to that of La Soufrière, lies Soufrière. This similar-named smaller volcano also erupted a short while after its neighbour, La Soufrière. Cayce referred to the crucial location only as 'Pelée,' and the general assumption has been that he meant *Mount* Pelée. It erupted previously in 1902. However, 'Pelée' could refer to the *Island* Pele (pronounced the same as 'Pelée') which also just happens to be in the New Hebrides chain around the Fiji Basin grid node, mentioned above. A 7.0 quake was recorded there in 1976. This area should also be watched for a significant event or activity. Either way, it is noteworthy that scientists have classified volcanic eruptions into four major categories of intensity, the most powerful of which is 'Peléean.' This classification describes the most violent kinds of eruptions, with clouds of glowing ash and lava flows up to one hundred miles per hour. This is the likely magnitude of eruption Edgar Cayce predicted for Pelée.

In answer to some questions on historical perspective, Edgar Cayce tapped into the universal consciousness again to confirm that 'The extreme North portions [of the world] were then the Southern portions – or the polar regions were then turned to where they occupied more of the tropical and semi-tropical regions.' While discoursing on the phenomenon of the poles' displacement, we find that when he was speaking of the future of the Arctic and Antarctic regions, this information surfaced: 'There will be upheavals ... that will make for the eruptions of volcanoes in the torrid areas, and there will be the shifting then of the poles.' Cayce said this would occur around the year 2000–2001 AD. Also, the last date indicated within the Great Pyramid is 2001 AD, so we know an important event is in store for that time.

Fortunately, some far-sighted people questioned Cayce about which areas would be exempt from the upheavals he was announcing: 'Safety lands will be in the area around Norfolk, Virginia Beach, parts of Ohio, Indiana and Illinois and much of the southern portion of Canada and the East portion of Canada.' None of these locations have been free of earthquakes in the past. It would seem that we should be prepared to accept the unexpected in these matters, for another person was also told, 'Norfolk is to be a mighty good place, and a safe place when turmoils are to arise, though it may appear that it may be in the line of those areas to rise, while many a higher land will sink. This is a good area to stick to.'

Meishu Sama, the Japanese master, had pronounced in June 1931 that the New Age of Light had officially begun in that month. Although he and Cayce were unknown to each other, their perceptual acuity must have been very similar, because, in a 1932 reading, Cayce, too, said that the New Age had just officially begun.

Naturally, the people who consulted him on these subjects were anxious to know how they should regard the changes that were to come about. He gave a variety of responses on the subject, and a warning: 'What is needed most in the Earth today? That the sons of men be warned that the day of the Lord is near at hand, and that those who have been, and are, unfaithful must meet themselves in those things which come to pass in their experience.' When pressed to explain what he meant by 'the day of the Lord', he responded, 'That as has been promised through the prophets and the sages of old, the time and a half time [a biblical reference to the time approaching the tribulation] has been and is being fulfilled in this day and generation, and that soon there will again appear in the Earth that One through whom many will be called to meet those that are preparing the way for His day in the Earth. The Lord, then, will come, even as ye have seen Him go.' When asked how soon all this would be, Cayce, as recorded by his stenographer, answered, 'When those that are His have made the way clear, passable, for Him to come.' We are reminded of Jesus' response to the same question – that the Kingdom of God is within, so we would not know by observation (in the sense of where or when). Therefore, when enough people experience it within themselves, the Kingdom of God will become externalized on the planet. Those who have felt the inner spirit stirring *are* generally working for change, within themselves and society, to make a better world.

'There are those conditions that in the activity of individuals in line of thought and endeavour, oft keep many a city and many a land intact, through their application of the spiritual laws ...' Perhaps this is why, in Cayce's prophetic scheme of things, California has continued to survive, thus far, the ultimate seismic odds. However, the prophet did speak of 'tendencies in the hearts and souls of men' as being such that upheavals may be brought about in the Earth. These physical traumas will be due, he said, to the 'desires, the purposes and aims' of us all.

When things finally settle down, Cayce foresaw that emphasis will no longer be upon pure biological evolution, but sociological progress in the form of developing human mental attributes. Telepathic communication and full consciousness of the creative forces will enable future humanity to use these faculties as an addition to established science, in order to improve the quality of life. A 'new comprehension' and a 'new vision' will emerge from the hectic passage through the remaining years of the century.

'When there has been in the Earth those groups that have sufficiently desired and sought peace, peace will begin. It must be within self.' Mr Cayce's biographer, Mary Ellen Carter, points out that destiny is influenced by human will, but that there is also a time when it is rendered irreversible by human will.

12

The Bible

'For no prophecy of scriptures ever originated in the mind of man, but holy men of God spake as they were moved by the Holy Ghost.'

(II Peter 1:21)

The Bible contains many prophecies and references to 'the fullness of time,' 'the harvest', the 'latter' or 'last days', the 'purification of the nations' and the battle of Armageddon. God spoke clearly of these times (and sometimes not so clearly) through his prophets of the Old Testament, through the disciples who recorded the life and teachings of Jesus in the Gospels, and through John's vision of the Revelation. The various biblical prophecies present warnings to the reader of the signs to watch for before the finale, so that all who receive the message might prepare themselves, and be awakened to their spiritual identity and divine heritage. Again, we stress that it is not the end of the world that is predicted, but the end of the Piscean age and present world system. Preparation is needed to achieve sufficient faith, strength, understanding and purity to make the transition to that promised land of a highly evolved and truly righteous society of the Aquarian, Golden or New Age. It will usher in the final stage of the *Yuga*, the 26,000 year equinoctial cycle, and culminate in the evolution of humanity to a spiritual/fourth dimensional state of consciousness. The Bible records that it has always been God's way to provide ample time and forewarning before catastrophes or judgments. A renewal of religious interest and spiritual awakening are important signs of the predicted times, and this is happening today.

In the ancient world of the Hebrew prophets, villages and centres of trade and commerce were scattered over an arid landscape of relentless sunlight and hazy barren hills. The prophets who emerged to stir the pulse of conscience were a remarkable breed of men. Wandering between communities and royal cities, they would often appear out of the wilderness areas to warn or admonish, help, or advise. They were probably a thorn in the flesh of the populace, feared yet revered, as they spoke out against kings, corruption, and unGodliness. Through His prophets, God spoke directly in those days to people who would hear, and dealt just retribution to those who would not; or so it seemed. It was a simple affair, uncomplicated by the intricacies of technology and media.

A criticism often levelled at biblical prophecies is that they describe events of the prophets' own times. But this would not necessarily disqualify a prophecy from being true for our time, too. You can get a lot of mileage out of the major biblical prophecies because they deal with archetypal myths and images. While the perennial wisdom enables us to transcend the conditions of the world, it is the perennial ignorance that brings down the negative aspects of history that repeat in such predictable patterns. That is to say, failure to live according to natural law and divine will has consequences – returning karma. Biblical prophecy lets people know that God keeps His promises and covenants, and helps them understand more clearly God's will and the moral standards by which He judges, in order that people may harmonize their lives with them and thereby avoid suffering.

In the visions of the various Hebrew prophets, we see again and again events quite similar, if not identical, to those recorded in the annals of many ancient peoples, several of which are discussed in the chapter on Pole Shift. The prophets quoted below lived just prior to the great cosmic upheavals that appear to have accompanied the 'brief anomaly' of magnetic pole reversal around 860 B.C. If events that happened then are about to recur, the prophecy is still good. For example, the Book of Joel, from which the following quotes are excerpted, opens with Joel instructing the people to repeat to as many future generations as possible the prophecy he is about to give on the coming 'day of the Lord':

Joel, c. 820 BC: 'The Earth shall quake before them; the heavens shall tremble; the sun and moon shall be dark, and the stars shall withdraw their shining.' (2:10)

'And I will shew wonders in the heavens and in the earth, blood, and fire, and pillars of smoke. The sun shall be turned into darkness, and the moon into blood, before the great and the terrible day of the Lord come.' (2:30-32)

Amos, c. 800 BC: 'And it shall come to pass in that day, saith the Lord God, that I will cause the sun to go down at noon, and I will darken the Earth in the clear day.' (8:9)

Isaiah, c. 775 BC: 'For the stars of heaven and the constellations thereof shall not give their light: the sun shall be darkened in his going forth, and the moon shall not cause her light to shine ... Therefore I will shake the heavens, and the earth shall remove out of her place, in the wrath of the Lord of hosts, and in the day of his fierce anger.' (13:10 and 13:13)

Habakkuk, c. 628 BC: 'He stood, and measured the earth: he beheld, and drove asunder the nations; and the everlasting mountains were scattered, the perpetual hills did bow.' (3:6)

Many centuries later, the Gospels were written. They are accounts of the life and teachings of Jesus written by Matthew, Mark, Luke and John. These men also recorded in a firsthand and informal way very interesting information about the people and customs of two thousand years ago. The culture was still predominantly Greek, with Roman politics and Jewish religion. The political, social and moral attitudes of that time were quite corrupt, not so very different from our own, and the disciples who wrote the gospels originally were just plain folk from all walks of life. Matthew was a former tax collector, and Mark a scholar from a wealthy family. Luke had been a physician, and John (who also later wrote the Revelation) was a fisherman.

One day, on the Mount of Olives in the Judean hills, the disciples asked Jesus privately when the end would be, and what would be the signs of His coming again. Jesus spoke of wars and rumours of wars, of famines, pestilence, and earthquakes, and said that they would be but the beginning of troubles. He warned of religious persecution; false prophets and impostors claiming to be Christ himself, and performing such heavy miracles that even the wisest might be deceived. He said that unless God intervened, humanity would be wiped out entirely, but that for the sake of the 'elect' the time of trouble would be shortened.

In his discussion, Jesus also confirmed the visions of the Hebrew prophets. 'Men's hearts [will be] failing them for fear, and for looking after those things which are coming upon the earth: for *the powers of heaven shall be shaken*. And then shall they see the Son of man coming in a cloud with power and great glory' [emphasis added] (Luke 21:26-27). In this passage, the original Greek word for 'heavens' is 'ouranos' – the root word for uranium. One could read instead, 'The powers of *uranium* shall be shaken. And then shall they see (etc.) …' Uranium is shaken to produce atomic power. It is a matter of record and certainly a curious coincidence that the first nuclear experiments, detonated in the New Mexico desert at Jornado del Muerto (journey of the dead), was called 'Project Trinity.' When he beheld, on that fateful day, the awesome release of power wrought by their research, project director Robert Oppenheimer recalled the impact it had upon him. A passage from Sanskrit scripture echoed in his mind – Shiva, the destructive aspect of the Hindu trinity, saying 'I am become Death, destroyer of worlds ...' The result of that dynamic fusion, the bomb dropped on Hiroshima, was code named 'Baby Jesus'. This interpretation correlates with data from the King's Chamber in the Great Pyramid – for the date exactly in the centre, March 3-4, 1945, indicates the date of the first atomic bomb experiments. Also, the Hopi prophecies say the same thing. In a letter of appeal over the Black Mesa issue, the Hopi elders wrote to President Nixon, 'The Great Spirit said that if a gourd of ashes is dropped upon the Earth, many men will die and that the end of this way of life is near at hand.' Matthew, Mark and Luke each report Jesus as saying right after this, 'Verily, I say unto you, this generation shall not pass away until all be fulfilled.' And it looks verily possible.

'Watch therefore, and pray always, that you may be accounted worthy to escape all these things that shall come to pass, and to stand before the Son of man' (Luke 21:36). This was His last advice to the disciples on the subject, for He was speaking also of the events concerning the destruction of the Temple of Jerusalem, which came about in 70 AD, and which would have been witnessed by disciples still living at that time.

'And what I say unto you I say unto all, Watch.' (Mark 13:37)

St John the Divine was the youngest and most beloved disciple of Jesus. He had sat at Christ's side during the last supper, and it was to him that Jesus entrusted the care of His mother, Mary, during the crucifixion. We know that Jesus was aware that John had been chosen to receive the prophetic vision of the close of the Age, because John records at the end of his own gospel that, 'The saying spread abroad among the brethren that this disciple (John) was not to die; yet Jesus did not say to him that he was not to die, but 'If it is my will that he remain until I come, what is that to you?!' (John 21:23). After Christ's ascension, the Roman authorities put the finger on John. His preaching activities concerning the new Christian doctrine posed a threat to the establishment religion and the government arranged for him to be forcibly exiled for apostasy. John was banished to the island of Patmos in the Mediterranean, and it was during his later life that he had the vision recorded in the last book of the Bible as 'The Revelation'.

The Book of Revelation is an obvious account of some very real future shock, detailing signs of Christ's second coming and the events that presage the final judgment of humanity. Although interpretation has always been difficult and unsatisfactory, the veils of mystery are gradually lifting, as world events today shed light on much of the allegory. Many volumes would be necessary to explore fully all the aspects of John's amazing preview, but there are a few highly relevant trends forming today that relate to it.

The Revelation involves a series of happenings that occur in the spiritual world of the heavens. In the first part of the account, John sees a scroll with seven seals, each of which represents an aspect of retribution that must come to pass before the 'harvest is gathered', i.e. the last judgement when the 'sheep will be separated from the goats'. The seals are opened one at a time, and the first four release that famous quartet, the four horsemen of the apocalypse, bringing pestilence, war, famine and death upon the Earth. It is important to understand that the seven seals are allegorical to each of the seven *chakras* (energy centres, like valves between the etheric and physical bodies, which are related to the endocrine system) of the human body. With the opening of each seal comes 'revelation' and the opportunity to be purified and transformed by the particular energies released. The more successful we are in handling and transmuting within ourselves (i.e., within each *chakra*) the intense surge of purifying energy released by the opening of each seal, the less necessary it is for these releases to manifest in the external world as chaos and catastrophe.

The four horsemen are followed by a now familiar scenario: '... a great earthquake: and the sun became black as sackcloth of hair, and the moon became as blood; And the stars of heaven fell unto the earth, even as a fig tree casteth

CHAKRA CHART

Chakra No.	1st	2nd	3rd	4th	5th	6th	7th
Center Name	Base/Root	Prostatic	Solar Plexus	Heart	Throat	Brow or 3rd Eye	Crown
Yogic Name	Muladhara	Svad-histana	Manipura	Anahata	Vishuda	Ajna	Sahasrara
Color	Red	Orange	Yellow	Green	Blue	Ultra-Violet	---
Element	Earth	Water	Fire	Air	Ether	---	---
Planetary Influence	Saturn	Jupiter	Mars	Venus	Mercury	Sun & Moon	---
Emotional Influence	Suvival Security Racial Memory	Sex Physical Creativity	Fear Anger Power	Joy Compassion Grief	Communication Creative Expression	Ecstacy Direct Knowing	Bliss
Health	---	Prostate Ovarian	Ulcers Cancer	Angina Stroke Allergies	Thyroid Imbalances	Schizophrenia	Psychosis
Endocrine Influence	---	Gonads	Adrenals	Thymus	Thyroid	Pineal	Pituitary

her untimely figs, when she is shaken of a mighty wind. And the heaven departed as a scroll when it is rolled together: and every mountain and island were moved out of their places' (6:12-14). People from all strata of society are panicking and running frantically to the hills and mountains for protection. This would appear to be yet another vision of the shifting of the Earth's poles, accompanied by the meteor showers or the tektites that have been scientifically recorded during past geomagnetic reversals. In Revelation (16:18-21), when the kings of the Earth are gathered together for battle at a place called Armageddon (from the Hebrew, 'Hill of Megiddo', historic location of violent armed conflicts between Israel and her enemies), we read: 'And there were voices, and thunders, and lightnings; and there was a great earthquake, such as was not since men were upon the earth and the cities of the nations fell ... And every island fled away, and the mountains were not found ... there fell upon men a great hail out of heaven, every stone about the weight of a talent ... the plague thereof was exceeding great.' Now, the Hebrew talent weighed *seventy-five* pounds, so we know this was no ordinary hailstorm, but a frightening meteor shower.

Then, a dramatic silence falls upon the Earth as the winds are stilled and a mighty angel bearing the seal of the living God ascends from the East. The angel's voice echoes to the ends of the Earth, commanding, 'Hurt not the Earth,neither the sea, nor the trees till we have sealed the servants of our God in their foreheads.' The number of those so sealed is given as 144,000. The servants of God who are sealed in their foreheads are those whose third eye (pineal *chakra) is* active. They will have God's protection.

The sixth seal, or *chakra, is* related to the pineal gland. Physically, this light-sensitive gland orchestrates (among other things) the body's timing and its cyclical functions. Spiritually, it opens to the inner light and can be accessed through meditation. Jesus himself said, 'If therefore thine eye be single, thy whole body shall be full of light' (Matthew 6:22). Within this seal resides the 'I Am' presence – the actual consciousness and Light of the Christ. Becoming aware of our individual 'I Am' presence ultimately connects us to transcendent consciousness.

Jesus alluded to this reality when he described himself as the good shepherd who alone could lead the sheep out of their fold. He also said, 'I Am the *door;* if anyone enters through Me, he shall be saved, and shall go in and out, and find pasture' (emphasis added) (John 10:9). Jesus' parables contained outer meanings, clear to everyone, and inner meanings for 'those with ears to hear'.

Insight into the esoteric meaning of Jesus as the 'door' is found in the system of Jewish mysticism known as the Kabala. Daleth is the fourth letter of the Hebrew alphabet, meaning 'door'. (The Kabalistic Tree of Life is a map of how the universe was formed and manifested. It provides a context within which the gnosis is revealed so we can understand and explore how the forces, powers and energies of the universe manifest in each one of us.) In the Ari version, Daleth is the central pillar that runs from Tiferet (the heart), through the throat (the 'Mystic gateway of liberation' of yoga), through the sixth *chakra*, to Kether (the crown). The crown *chakra is* the seventh seal, or *chakra*, connecting one's awareness to pure cosmic consciousness. Within Kabalism, Daleth, the Door, is associated with the East, and, as noted above, the angel bearing the seal of the living God

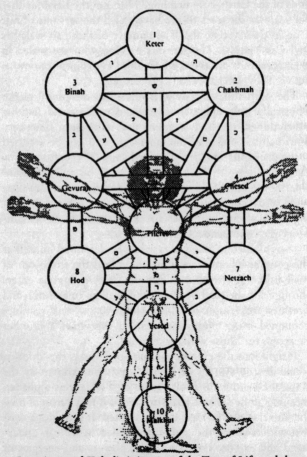

Superimposed Kabalistic images of the Tree of Life and the 'Adam Kadom' (the archetype of human perfection) show Daleth/the door at the sixth chakra.

(who performed the 'forehead sealing') ascended from the East. Jesus also said, 'I stand at the door, and knock; if anyone hears My voice and opens the door, I will come in to him, and will dine with him, and he with Me' (Rev 3:20). He wants to come in. Expressed here is the nature of the sixth *chakra* as the Door to higher consciousness, and of which Christ is both the Door itself *and* the Doorkeeper.

'I Am' (capital A) is one's higher Self, the Christed over-Self. 'I am' (lower case) is 'me,' the lower, human self. The words, and consciousness, 'I Am' express the covenant between the human and the divine self, and a knowing of one's true identity and destiny. As Jesus said, 'I Am in my father, and you in Me, and I in you' (John 14:20). When one attains enlightenment one becomes 'Christed.' However, Jesus is the Christ who embodies the *Office of the Christ,* an office encompassing the work of all Christed beings and Ascended Masters. These evolved beings are dedicated to the 'Great Work' of serving God's plan in order to purify and liberate the souls of this 'fallen' planet. As holder of the 'Office of the Christ', Jesus came to redeem our karma ('By Grace you are saved') and awaken the human race to Christhood – which is why He promised that we would ultimately do even greater things than He (John 14:12) – because we are also destined to become Christs! Jesus said,

I Am the way, and the truth, and the life.
No one comes to the Father but through Me.

(John 14:6)

Orthodox interpretation of that statement assumes the meaning that only through the person of the historical Jesus (and, by implication, Christianity) can one come to the Father (i.e., be saved from damnation, and get into heaven). *Misinterpretation* of this statement, more than any other in the Bible, is responsible for non-Christian realities being condemned as 'of the devil'. This statement by Jesus is the very *'lynchpin'* of Christian exclusivity (the nature of a linchpin being that without it the wheel falls off the axle).

And in defence of orthodox *interpretation* of this statement, millions of people have been tortured and killed throughout history. Indigenous native populations and entire cultures have been decimated and destroyed, and the world's great repositories of wisdom systematically destroyed with extreme prejudice.

And today, our cultural bias toward materialism has resulted in a fixation upon the historical Jesus of the past who won't be seen again until after Armageddon. In the meantime, the universal *Spirit* that He Is, is upon the land, alive and well, inspiring and illuminating individuals *primarily* (it would seem) *outside* of Christian orthodoxy! Christian mysteries do exist, of course, and the exoteric teachings of the Bible do contain esoteric meanings. It is therefore regrettable, to say the least, that while the Church (regarded as the 'body of Christ') is preoccupied with the physical body of the historical Jesus, the Christ Spirit appears to reside elsewhere.

According to Key 308 of *The Keys of Enoch* (one of the most significant contemporary adjuncts of the Western mystery tradition), the collective antichrist is the body of religious orthodoxies who withhold information on the true nature of the Christ, and faiths that do not evolve the soul. They understand scripture from the historical standpoint, but not the higher spiritual truths; they do not understand the *codes* within scripture that can transform ordinary consciousness into the consciousness of the living Light. The 'Key' (written in 1973) states that as a sign of the end, establishment religion will try to conceal and destroy interpretations of the scriptures which give people true spiritual liberation. (An example of this would be the recent discovery of the deception and collusion surrounding translations of the Dead Sea Scrolls. Text translations that were considered controversial or potentially heretical were suppressed. For forty-five years, to the vexation of the international community, the Vatican continued to defend its original choice of handpicked researchers. People whose whole lives had prepared them for reading these scrolls died without ever seeing the translations.¹ Now, thankfully, these texts are finally being published and made available.)

Stay with me now – If 'I' is the human-self, and 'I Am' is the Christed Self, a deeper meaning shines forth (i.e., is revealed) from Jesus' words:

> ... No one comes to the Father but through me
> becomes
> No one comes unto the Father but through *who I Am*.

Hence, 'I *Am* the way, the truth and the life. No one comes to the Father but through who I *Am* (the Christ within).' When we transcend our lower self, we can pass through the 'Door' of our 'I Am' presence (the sixth *chakra*) and merge with our Christed higher Self. The sixth seal, our third eye, is opened. The all-seeing eye above the Pyramid on the Great Seal of the United States is the symbol of the 'third eye'. By the time you get to use it, God and you behold each other through the same eye! Again, 'If thine eye be single, thine whole body shall be full of light', and 'I Am in my father, and ye in me, and I in you', said Christ (John 14:20). The universal force which is the radiant consciousness of the Christ guides the 'Way', reveals the 'Truth', and en'Light'ens our minds that we may fulfill our evolutionary destiny, become Christed, inherit the Kingdom. That is what the New Age is folks!

As described earlier, humanity is engaged in a collective shift from fear and separation to love and unity, from physical-human to spiritualized-human – Homo sapiens to Homo Christos. The personal and planetary challenges we face today are healing crises, rites of passage, to hasten our collective evolution toward enlightened consciousness.

In the original Hindu illustrations of the yogic *chakra* system ('yoga' means 'union' – of the human and the Divine), the sixth *chakra is* presented as a circle between two lotus petals (the pineal gland between the two hemispheres of the brain). Within the circle is the Sanskrit symbol of 'OM' (the 'Divine Word', the vibration that sources the universe) and an androgynous figure, half male and half female. This form symbolizes the 'divine marriage' of one's human and divine selves, as well as the synthesis within one's consciousness of all phenomenal polarities. When this exalted state is achieved, one transcends the world of duality and all opposites are reconciled. Individuation occurs. The Self is realized. And when our lower nature is transcended, our abilities become creatively expressed in service to personal and social transformation (see 'Resource' section at end). 'Not my will but Thy will be done.' When enough of us accomplish this, the Earth will again become Paradise.

It is important to remember that those with the 'seal' of the living God in their foreheads will be under divine protection in the future. We are also reminded of the astrological interpretation of the last date in the Great Pyramid, where it is made clear that those who have learned to consistently function from their higher consciousness will be protected and transformed by the energies at work. Hopi prophecy promises that the good people will be protected at Black Mesa when the time is right. And, from Revelation 3:16, we understand that it is necessary for one to make a stand in the matter: 'So then because thou art lukewarm, and neither cold nor hot, I will spue you out of my mouth.' A commitment is necessary, because a person is either 'on the path' or in the mass consciousness.

As the seventh seal is removed, John reports silence in heaven for half an hour before seven more tribulations are poured out, as a warning from God, to destroy a third of the Earth and its inhabitants: hail and fire mingled with blood burn up the vegetation, and 'a great mountain, burning with fire, was cast into the sea' so that a third of the sea and its creatures were turned to blood. Later when this plague returns again in full force, everything in the sea dies and the rivers and fountains become blood. Various historical accounts exist describing times when the rivers and seas turned to blood. The phenomenon appears to have been associated with the fall of ferruginous particles or other soluble pigment from meteorite dust when an errant meteor or

comet neared the Earth. Manuscript Quiche of the Maya
has recorded that the rivers turned to blood in the days of a
great cataclysm when the Earth quaked and the sun's path
was disturbed. The Egyptian Papyrus Ipuwer, which contains an account of the sun failing to rise, also mentions that
'the rivers were blood.'[2] Babylonians also recorded red rain
falling from the sky.[3] The Hopi prophecies state, 'The whole
world will shake and turn red ...' Nostradamus predicted
reddened water and (translations vary) reddened hailstones
or icy water covering the Earth. This would tend to corroborate that a cyclical phenomenon is being foreseen by John,
one that has actually happened before in historical times. He
may even have been clairvoyantly viewing the closing events
of a previous world epoch (the Akashic records). Meanwhile, back in the twentieth century, red mud has been
floating offshore along the Tuscan coast[4] and red rain has
repeatedly fallen in Florida due to airborne iron oxide dust
particles from African drought regions.[5]

'And the third angel sounded, and there fell a great star
from heaven, burning as it were a lamp, and it fell upon the
third part of the rivers ...' (8:10). 'And the fourth angel
sounded, and a third part of the sun was smitten, and the
third part of the moon, and the third part of the stars; so as
the third part of them was darkened, and the day shone not
for a third part of it, and the night likewise' (8:12).

Later, as the fifth angel sounds, 'I saw a star fall from heav-
en unto the earth; and to him was given the key of the bot-
tomless pit ... and there arose a smoke out of the pit, as the
smoke of a great furnace; and the sun and the air were darkened by reason of the smoke of the pit' (9:1-2). Locusts
swarmed out of this pit and tormented for five months all
who did not have God's seal of protection in their foreheads.
Although scholars put different interpretations upon this
scenario, we are personally reminded of the Hopi prophecy
concerning the people symbolized by the colour red who
invade 'like a swarm of locusts', darkening the sky with their
numbers. The national flag of Red China sports a huge 'master' star with its four satellites against a red background.

Could this be the time of a celestial body's collision with the Earth? Perhaps an immense nuclear event or Communist invasion is what the Prophet beheld. Nostradamus refers to a yellow race sweeping across Europe around the end of the century.

John says that the pain inflicted by the tails of the locusts was far worse than a scorpion sting; the torment would be so severe that many would try to commit suicide. We read that the shapes of the locusts were like horses prepared for battle, that they had men's faces and the hair of women. Their breastplates were iron and the noise of their wings was like many chariots running in battle. Modern interpreters compare this description and noise to Scorpion or Cobra helicopters, and the means of torment to a form of germ warfare or nerve gas.

Alternatively, if we go along with the premise that most of the catastrophic conditions prophesied are related to the Earth's imbalance and axial change, the reference to locusts or an insect pestilence could be quite literal (drought in Africa has already caused one of history's worst locust plagues). Atmospheric changes are the source of rapid proliferation of bacteria and insects. During the first few days of an electrically charged wind moving toward a low pressure centre, there are outbreaks of vermin and insect eruptions.[6] Scotland's Findhorn Community was advised by Paul Solomon (a respected teacher known for his ability to contact universal consciousness) to make friends with the local seagulls in order to receive their help in coping with severe insect infestations in the future. Massive electrical winds would be generated by shock waves from a celestial body colliding with, or passing close to, the Earth, which could account for an unusual and deadly plague. Many insect species have already assumed plague proportions because of ecological imbalances and increasing immunity to pesticides.

The first seven trials just mentioned are a taste of more intense ones to follow, and are a preview of what will happen if humanity does not change its present course, ignoring natural law and that which is spiritually appropriate. For

God says, 'As many as I love, I rebuke and chasten: be zeal-ous therefore, and repent' (Rev 3:19).

Then, later, 'there fell a noisome and grievous sore upon the men which had the mark of the beast ...' (16:2); and again, in verses 8 and 11, the sun is 'totally smitten,' scorch-ing people with fire and sores. This could well be related to the prediction by scientists that skin cancer will increase if the holes in the ozonosphere continue to deteriorate and leak in ultraviolet radiation—which they will, unless humans stop causing the pollution that degrades the protec-tive ozone layer. Also, with Earth's rotation slowing down, more intense ultraviolet will filter through the magnetos-phere. This, too, increases skin cancer. However, as men-tioned earlier, ultraviolet radiation affects the function of the pineal gland (ergo, the brow chakra). Mutations are the usual consequence – either through negative impacts on the human body which cause devolution, or positive impacts on the spiritual body which cause evolution.

At the beginning of the thirteenth chapter, John is stand-ing on the shore by the sea as a seven-headed beast with ten crowned horns rears its ugly heads from the depths. It is a composite of the same monsters recorded earlier by Daniel in his translation of the Babylonian king's dream. It receives authority and power from Satan.

As before, the parts of this beast symbolize the succession of worldly empires. Its ten horns, according to Daniel, rep-resent ten kingdoms over which the Beast will rule during the tribulation. It was originally tempting to identify this ten-horned beast with the ten-member European Economic Community (EEC). But, in 1986, the Community admitted two more members, comprising now a total population of 320 million (one third more people than the entire United States). The EEC anticipates a common currency through-out its member countries by the end of the 1990s, a political-ly united Europe, and shared military defence strategies. There can be no doubt that the EEC will change the power structure of the world and rise to immense importance in the near future.

It looks as though the world economic and political system is already consolidating in Belgium. In this politically neutral country, its capital, Brussels, is the seat of the European Economic Community, NATO, EFTS, SWIFT and IBRO. Brussels is where it's happening. The United Nations and the International Monetary Fund are committed to formation of a new international economic order, beginning with global economic development strategy as well as a single European parliament. This is the 'New World Order' promoted by ex-President Bush – not to be confused with the 'New Order of the Ages' envisioned on the Great Seal of the United States.

The world banking system's EFTS (Electronic Funds Transfer System) is committed to the eventual withdrawal of cash from society by means of the single debit/credit card now gaining popularity. This system is a cell in the body of a much larger, international electronic banking network called SWIFT – Society for Worldwide Interbank Financial Telecommunications, conceived by the progenitors of the Trilateral Commission. It represents the formal linking of the international banking community in order to realize more effective computer usage. SWIFT currently comprises more than thirty member countries who key in their own terminals to 'concentrator' centres in every member country. In the Western hemisphere, more than 1,200 banks are plugged into the SWIFT network. As a fast-emerging world power (hence the image of the beast arising out of the sea), the EEC will acquire an administrative structure which, irrespective of its political ideology, will be presided over by some kind of chief executive officer. From this centre of influence we may expect to see the seeding and growth of a future world government. IBRO (Inter Bank Research Organization) orchestrates the multibank network. A technology has already been established to facilitate the global economic system as the foundation of a future world government. Therefore, the issue becomes one of raising the mass consciousness of the planet – that is the task at hand. It is not world government that is to be feared, but the possibility of a deficit in spiritual awareness when it happens.

And, since eruption of renewed tensions in the Middle East, it has become clear that a ten-nation Arab Confederacy could also stand up as the real ten-horned beast of the future.

The great red dragon of 12:3 and the scarlet beast of 17:3 also have seven heads and ten horns and represent the modern 'Babylon' (corrupt world system). The horny beast will be represented by a powerful political leader, the antichrist, identified as Beast 666. He will temporarily solve many desperate world problems and gain tremendous popularity. However, he will be a vehicle of the negative force – a man with deceptive charisma, and a hidden agenda. Under his auspices, the Jews will rebuild their Temple. John tells us this antichrist will affiliate with an equally powerful false prophet or religious figurehead. We are told that, like the wolf in sheep's clothing, he will be exceedingly cunning and brilliant and attain enthusiastic acceptance by the masses when he begins to perform impressive miraculous feats in public. His ostentatious display of elaborate *siddhis* or powers, such as invoking fire down from the heavens, will lead many to the erroneous belief that he is the long-awaited Messiah. Around this time, the gospels warn us not to be deceived by any claiming to be Christ (i.e., Jesus reincarnated). At the instigation of this so-called prophet, an image (referred to as 'the abomination of desolation') will be made of the antichrist, to be worshipped in the new Jewish Temple. This will be the basis of a new and compulsory world religion. Nostradamus's clues to the identity of this antichrist are discussed in the 'Babylonian Prophecies' chapter.

Right now, a climate of acceptance is being prepared by religious leaders as the World Council of Churches works to accomplish religious amalgamation. If conditions are right, this will hasten world unity; if not, it will aid tyranny. 'And he had the power to give life unto the image of the beast, that the image of the beast should both speak, and cause that as many as would not worship the image of the beast should be killed' (13:15). Surely, George Orwell must have had this in mind when he wrote 1984, depicting Big Brother on television. Under his suppressive world government, the antichrist, Beast 666, will set things up for every person to bear his mark, his name or his number in their forehead or right hand, in order to buy or sell anything – including food and oil.

Under a world government (see also 'Astrological Predictions' chapter) it would seem reasonable for everyone to receive some kind of personal identification, such as the social security number used in the United States. Although most industrialized nations have developed legal codes to protect their citizens' privacy, computer technologies with a vast potential for misuse are being sold by the West to some third-world countries with histories of human-rights violations. By means of these technologies, governments are requiring their citizens to carry an identification card that makes surveillance and data compilation on any individual possible and easy. Behind these cards (which contain one's name, photograph, fingerprints, height, home address, parents' names, children's names, marital status, education, occupation, income, nationality, religion, family history and, possibly, tax-return information and any criminal record) lies sophisticated computer software linked to top-of the-line Control Data mainframes. Such systems are particularly attractive to governments disturbed by civilian unrest. The implications and ramifications of this subject were discussed in a Time magazine article of June 24, 1991, entitled 'Peddling Big Brother'.

As mentioned, the single debit/credit card now in use by the world's financial institutions is designed to replace cash (and, by implication, one's independence of 'the system'). Major credit-card corporations have begun service consolidation by merging with telephone and other service charge cards. The 'One World, One Card' advertised by MasterCard captures something of the flavour of the future.

One can well imagine the problems involved with people, especially in underdeveloped nations, dealing with or losing their identification or credit card. The problem of access to the system arises since cards can be lost or stolen. A number of theories have been advanced as to how this might be accomplished, including invisible laser tattoos that show up when scanned by ultraviolet light (similar to laser scanning of the universal product-code bars on merchandise at supermarket checkout stands). Chapter 14:9–10 gives specific warning that anyone who worships the image of the Beast 666 or the man himself, or receives his mark, shall lose God's protection.

A religious persecution and execution of those who will not comply is prophesied, but that those who resist in the name of Christ will live and reign with Him one thousand years at the end of the Age. Together, the dynamic duo of dictator and religious figurehead will rule with maniacal strength and charisma. Hitler and Himmler were amateurs compared to what we are told about these two!

For those who capitulate to the antichrist, a continuing purification of plagues reigns, the most noteworthy of which is a vial poured out over the Euphrates by an angel to dry up the river (see 'Babylonian Prophecy' chapter), so that the way of the Kings of the East (the Orient or the Middle East), whose army numbers two hundred million, might be prepared for the Battle of Armageddon. John compared the heads of the horsemen to those of lions as they spewed smoke, fire and brimstone (sulphur). He says their tails were like serpents with heads that had wounding power (cannons? missile launchers?).

It is important that we look beyond the immediate tumult of world events to the potential for resolution, rebalance, and healing. Inherent within the gestation period of prophecy is the tremendous power of intention and right action in *averting* it. Turmoil and confusion are integral parts of the equation today. Like leaking toxic waste, no longer containable below the threshold of awareness, today's chaos represents negativity, suppression, and denial becoming externalized into a conscious, combustive force. If we do not deal with problems before they escalate, we deal with them when they combust!

Finally, the demise of the last world system and its world government is described. (When John had his revelation about the end-times, the Babylonian empire was long gone. But because it had been the greatest empire in history up to his day, John uses the name as a metaphor in referring to the last world system.) We are told again that only a third of the world's population will survive, but that Satan will be bound for one thousand years. During this period, all who overcame the horrors of the tribulation and the persecution of the establishment will inherit the new heaven and the new Earth promised in Revelation 21:4. The dead, next, are resurrected and judged before the Throne of God, according to the Book of Life. Then, like the final curtain at a great cosmic drama, the New Jerusalem will descend from heaven, prepared for residence by the righteous, whose names were found written in the Book of Life. The twelve gates of this celestial abode are related to the twelve major power-points of the planetary grid acting as timewarp locks to raise physical existence to the new vibrational frequency of the next evolutionary phase. (See 'Our Prophecy' chapter.)

After the amazing and frightening implications of the above prophecies, it would seem appropriate to quote from Paul's gentle epistle to the Romans (8:28 and 15:4): 'We know that all things work together for good to those who love God, and to them who are the called according to His purpose ... For whatsoever things were written aforetime were written for our learning, that we, through patience and comfort of the scriptures, might have hope.'

Christ had said he would come again, descending in glory from the clouds. We are told that every eye shall see him, at the same time, all over the world. It seems unlikely that this means on TV, as media coverage surely will not be functional by that time, so another explanation must be possible. By the time Earth has been purified of all negative vibration, and the negative karma processed, those who survive will have attained much inner mastery ('The Kingdom of God is within' – Luke 17:21). When this occurs, humanity will have begun to enter into a new vibration related to the next evolutionary phase – the fourth dimension. Christ's second coming will, therefore, be seen by every person in the world, simultaneously, but *within an exalted state of consciousness,* by all who have made the transition to that level.

As the Revelation fades to a close in the last chapter of the Bible, the river of life is seen flowing in abundance from the Throne of God. Spanning the river is the magnificent Tree of Life bearing twelve kinds of fruit, and (as the zodiac) yielding its fruit every month. 'And the leaves of the tree are for the healing of the nations ...' As for the servants of God, the faithful, 'they shall see His face, and *His name shall be in their foreheads* ... and they shall reign for ever and ever ...'

Amen!

13

Babylonian Prophecy

'For we wrestle not against flesh and blood, but against principalities, against powers, against rulers of the darkness of this world, against spiritual wickedness in high places.'

– St. Paul (Ephesians 6:12)

The moving finger of destiny (no matter who was on the other end of it) has always pointed to the Middle East as the scene of the final world purification. The final world conflict called Armageddon is prophesied to take place in the Middle East. Armageddon is the ultimate gloom and doom prophecy, the one that brings up the fear levels, the one that shoots off the Richter scale. The fact that it did not materialize when so many of the prophetic conditions were present during the Gulf War could be interpreted as a sign that something had gone collectively right, that humanity had accomplished the ultimate, most challenging detour in all history. Many recognized it as great grace. Some called it a miracle. After all, the perfect prophecy is one that fails in the details but succeeds in purpose.

But several thousand years of Semitic turbulence were not extinguished by the Gulf War. As the euphoria of victory hung in the air with the smoke and burning oil, the troops came home to a swell of national pride. The President of the United States was assured a distinguished place in history, and America had demonstrated to the world in general, and to Iraq in particular, what the 'right stuff' was made of. Unfortunately, 'kicking ass good' is not the 'right stuff' for an Armageddon bypass. A flawed premise had once again been reinforced. And once again the watching world had learned that this is how conflicts are resolved.

The information presented here is offered because the research suggests so strongly that the Gulf War may have been the advance wave of an inexorably returning tide. Within the crucible of Babylonian history, a potent brew has bubbled throughout the centuries. An ancient fire has been lit and the ingredients need to be boiled down. Measuring the pace of prophecy against contemporary events of the Middle East enables us to observe what happens as the brew is stirred. When it started to boil, the Gulf War served to jam the lid shut. Whether this admixture will continue to stew into the consuming conflagration described by the prophetic recipe remains to be seen. They say 'A watched pot never boils'. Time will tell. But just how *close* it came to boiling over and the fact that it may do so again, is chronicled according to the prophecies that follow.

The Babylonian empire existed in the area we identify today as the Middle East. In the ancient world, it was centred in that fertile part of the Mesopotamian Valley through which the Tigris and Euphrates Rivers flow, corresponding to the southeast part of modern Iraq.

In historical times, Babylonia extended about thirty miles west of the Euphrates into the Arabian desert, until the blazing sun and aridity allowed it to penetrate no further. To the south lay the rich alluvial plain between the two rivers, which included Sumer and Chaldea, while in the southeast, the blue waters of the Persian Gulf lapped endlessly upon its busy shore. This was the commercial and spiritual centre of the civilized world. East of the Tigris, the empire was restrained by the natural boundary of the Persian hills and the contours of the Zagros Mountains beyond. The northern boundary was just beyond present-day Baghdad, capital of Iraq.

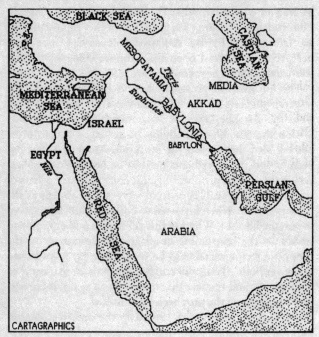

Ancient Middle East

Akkad, the first Semitic empire of the post-Flood period, was in the northern part of Babylonia (now Iraq).

Berössos is reported by Seneca to have learned that around 2300 BC, the priesthood of King Sargon of Akkad compiled a seventy-two volume astronomical treatise called the *Illumination of Bel*. Bel was the dominant god of the fertile crescent. In their work, the scholars predicted that 'when all the planets meet in Capricorn the world will be destroyed by fire.' But since such a configuration is considered to occur only once, at the end of each 'Great Year' or equinoctial cycle (that's right, once every 25,826 years!) need we really be concerned?[1] The answer, as we shall learn later in the chapter, is a resounding 'You bet!' Plato, in his *Timaeus* (verse 39d), says that the moment of the meeting of all the planets is that of 'perfect time' – that is, at the end of the Great Year or equinoctial cycle – and that the purpose of such a catastrophe is the purification of the human race (verse 22d).

Translation of this Akkadian prophecy comes down to us from the original language (cuneiform impressions upon baked clay tablets), through translation by Berossos into the Greek around 260 BC, to the English. However, worldviews and thought processes in the distant past, being pre-Cartesian, were basically subjective (i.e., lacking scientific 'objectivism') and quite different from our own. And many of the same words conveyed entirely different meanings then and now.

In the Greek translation, for instance, it was 'kosmos' that would be destroyed by fire. To the Greeks life was balanced between the forces of 'cosmos' and 'chaos'. 'Cosmos' meant 'world' or 'order' or 'world order,' all at the same time.[2] Cosmos was the ordering principle that brought coherence to the known world, outside of which was 'chaos'. Also, the alchemy of the four elements was very much a part of every-day life for educated Greeks, and although fire was certainly understood as combustion, inherent within its meaning was its primal association with spirit.

The understanding of how Capricorn (an earth sign) could be related to fire and to the demise of 'cosmos' also originated in Akkad. Akkadians conceptualized the Sun as sinking into the dark subterranean cave of the Earth during the winter. Then, on the first day after the winter solstice – the first day of Capricorn – the light began to return as the Sun emerged from the cave in the Earth. The Akkadians celebrated this day as 'the cave of the rising'. Later, in Hellenistic times, the followers of Plato maintained that when the soul was liberated at death, it ascended, like the sun rising at the solstice, through the sign of Capricorn, to join the gods in the realm of light. Therefore, Capricorn (like Babylon itself) was called 'the gate of the gods', just as its opposite sign, Cancer, was 'the gate of men' through which souls descended into physical incarnation in the world. To make one's transition during the December/January period of Capricorn was like exiting through the 'express lane'.

It is possible, therefore, that when the prophesied planetary involvement occurs, it will be in accordance with that ancient worldview; meaning that when the planets meet in Capricorn, certain influences will converge in such a way that the purifying effect of the returning light, spiritual fire *(ekpyrosis)*, will destroy the world, or the world system.

So what is it, exactly, that characterizes the present world system? Doesn't it have something to do with a petroleum-based, resource-dependent financial system, which, if not stopped, will fulfill the biblical prophecy of Daniel about the last world kingdom that will 'devour the whole earth and tread it down and break it in pieces'? The Hopi call a sorcerer who misuses his power by living off others or a rapacious plunderer and exploiter who creates and partakes of spoils *'powaqatsi'*. Indigenous people of the third world also know this entity – they call it 'capitalism'.

> *If the world*
> *were a global village of 100*
> *people, 70 of them would be unable*
> *to read, and only 1 would have a college*
> *education. Over 50 would be suffering from mal-*
> *nutrition, & over 80 would live in what we call sub-*
> *standard housing. If the world were a global village*
> *of 100 residents, 6 of them would be Americans. These 6*
> *would have half the village's entire income; and the*
> *other 94 would exist on the other half. How would the*
> *wealthy 6 live 'in peace' with their neighbours? Surely*
> *they would be driven to arm themselves against*
> *the other 94 ... perhaps even to spend, as we*
> *do, more per person on military defence*
> *than the total per person income*
> *of the others.*

The Hopi description of 'powaqatsi' matches the dictionary definition of 'spoliator'. The basest aspect of the eagle is that of a spoliator, but its loftiest is that of the initiate. It was because of this negative facet of the eagle that George Washington had objected to its adoption as America's national symbol.

Capricorn is the sign of political economy and major organizational power structures. Such a conjunction as the one prophesied bodes epochal change for the world! Esoteric astrology identifies Capricorn as the 'sign of the initiate,' because the light it releases penetrates the darkness, terminating undesirable conditions, bringing transformational beginnings, and positive mutation in forms of collective power.

A conjunction of five planets in Capricorn was chronicled in China during the year 1449 BC, according to the French astronomer Flammarion. We can't say exactly what happened in the world that year, except that the date does correlate with the beginning of the sixth dynasty in ancient Egypt – a period when the power of the pharaohs weakened and they became feudal lords, eclipsed by hereditary provincial governors.

OK, so when *do* the planets meet in Capricorn?

They already did. On January 15, 1991, a grand conjunction of six planets occurred in Capricorn, plus Venus, Jupiter and Pluto heavily aspected in Capricorn and in tension with each other, together with a very potent annular solar eclipse (meaning the moon covered all but a bright ring around the circumference of the sun), thus setting the world stage for a major, cosmic, transformational jolt. What a day!

Significantly, this very date was the one selected by the United States as the deadline for Iraq's withdrawal from Kuwait. In Washington, D.C., as the eclipse occurred, Venus (planet of potential peace) was setting in Aquarius. At the same time, on the other side of the globe, for Kuwait and Iran, Mars (war) was setting in the seventh house of open enemies. (The concentration of Capricorn energy at this particular time in history is another component of the evolutionary 'return of the light' described in the 'Evolution/ Involution' chapter.)

The opportunity was abundantly present and very real for both the literal and the figurative fulfillment of the ancient prophecy. Would the world ultimately be destroyed by the real conflagration of a third world war, or a metaphorical destruction of 'cosmos,' the world financial system?

The Akkadian priesthood of the first world empire, therefore, was predicting the demise of the last. Not only that, but when the circumstances of the prophecy manifested fifty-four centuries later, they came full circle and occurred in their very own backyard. And the instrument of that demise, as it turned out, looked like a man who saw himself as the reincarnation of Nebuchadnezzar, the ancient king of Babylon – Saddam Hussein. As the great cycle of history comes full circle, were we, perhaps, witnessing on the world scene an echo from the ancient past that continues to ricochet ominously, seeking completion? This Akkadian prophecy opens up pathways of inquiry that can best be examined within the context of other prophecies originating in, and concerning, the Middle East.

As a sacred city of enormous religious influence, Babylon was regarded as the meeting point of heaven and Earth presided over by Bel, god of heaven and Earth. The historical city of Babel ('Bab-el' – Gate of God), site of the famed Tower of Babel, was rebuilt and expanded under Nebuchadnezzar II sometime between 624 and 518 BC, and renamed Babylon ('Bab-ilani' – Gate of the Gods).[3]

Under Nebuchadnezzar, Babylon achieved its greatest glory, becoming an opulent and vital metropolis of world trade and spiritual influence. The priests were also the teachers of the youth and promoters of learning and research. They ran schools, workshops and observatories that were connected with the temples. Babylonia, cradle of civilization, was the source and nursery of ancient wisdom and knowledge, pioneer of civilization in Western Asia, proprietor and educator of Syria and Palestine for thousands of years before Israel became a nation.[4] People from nations to the east and west poured in to Babylon by land and sea. Her fleet of three thousand ships plied internal waterways and the great Tigris and Euphrates Rivers, giving access to the Persian Gulf and seas far beyond. The marvellous hanging gardens of Babylon, a great structure of lush, vaulted archways with tier upon tier of exotic blooms, vibrant colour, and cool shade, was a work of such splendour that it became one of Seven Wonders of the World.

The prophet Jeremiah had warned the people of Israel that unless they returned to God, they would be chastened through Nebuchadnezzar as the instrument of God's judgment. Barely two years into his reign, Nebuchadnezzar sought divinatory counsel about his military priorities, and promptly laid siege to Jerusalem, during which time fifty thousand Jews were forced into exile. Subsequently, he destroyed Jerusalem. The Temple was burned, its treasures appropriated, the buildings razed. Nebuchadnezzar was interested in taking as captives primarily those Jews who were 'skillful in all wisdom, shrewd in knowledge, and understanding in science'. Among them was Daniel the prophet.

It is said, 'Uneasy rests the head that wears the crown', and this was certainly true of Nebuchadnezzar's. Shortly after his conquest of Jerusalem, Nebuchadnezzar had a dream that eluded him when he awoke but left him with a prolonged anxiety attack. Outraged that none of his own metaphysicians or priestly advisors were prepared to interpret a dream the content of which was unknown, he ordered the execution of the empire's entire population of wise men. But the order was revoked when the Jewish prophet Daniel, who described his God as a 'revealer of secrets', was able to interpret the dream. (It is at this point that prophecies reported in the Bible also have application to what was going on in Babylon.)

Daniel reminded the king that his dream had been about a 'bright and terrible image' composed of various metals. One can imagine the king mopping his brow in relief, 'Ah, yes, that's right ...' Daniel said that the gold head of the image symbolized the Babylonian empire. The silver chest, brass hips, iron legs, and feet of iron mixed with clay represented the worldly kingdoms that would eventually succeed Babylon: Medo-Persia, Greece and Rome. It is believed that the fourth kingdom, the present era, passed from military Rome to Papal Rome, and that, symbolically, it continues today. In the dream, the image was destroyed by a stone unmade by human hands, which smashed the feet and crumbled the image ... and the pieces blew away like dust in the wind. Daniel said that this stone that brought down the last world kingdom, crushing history, would absorb all the kingdoms of the Earth into itself and become the 'Stone Kingdom' that would last forever and never be destroyed. Was it coincidence that during the prewar standoff in 1990, a syndicated columnist for *The New York Times* wrote that Iraq's newest missile had been named 'the Stone' by Saddam Hussein?[5]

In attempting to elucidate the significance of the dream stone as an important prophecy for *our* time (the civilization symbolized by the feet of the image) we digress briefly to examine an important ambiguity. When the stone smashed the feet, was the image *'knocked* off its feet' (an expression associated with negative surprises) or *'swept off* its feet'? (suggesting something rapturous). We are told that the pieces blew away in the wind – meaning that the results of the stone's impact would 'blow us away' – a phrase which describes something intense, powerful, and/or profound – either positive or negative.

On the negative side, could the archetype of the dream stone have been the asteroid believed to have careened into the Earth sixty-five million years ago, causing global extinctions and jolting our planet from one geologic age to another? Perhaps John had previewed a similar catastrophe of the future when he reported, in Revelation 8:8-11, that two-thirds of life on Earth perished after an object, 'like a burning mountain' was thrown into the sea, and a great star (called Wormwood) fell from heaven 'like a burning torch'. Could Nostradamus have been viewing the same phenomenon when he too prophesied that in 1999 'the great king of terror' would descend from the sky?

On the positive side, the apostle Paul had something important to say about a time in the future when the beloved of God would be, quite literally, 'swept off their feet'? in an event called 'the rapture'. In a letter from Athens to the early Christian group at Thessalonia, Paul wrote of the post-tribulation period: 'Then we which are alive and remain shall be caught up together with them in clouds, to meet the Lord in the air; and so shall we ever be with the Lord' (I Thessalonias 4:16-17). A modern variation on this theme is the expectation of mass evacuations by the space brotherhood, and other forms of 'ascension'.

There is something spiritually significant for us in being able to embrace both versions – and wisdom for the soul in Carl Jung's insight that mythic, archetypal themes and events repeat through time, and synchronize both inner and outer realities. Therefore, any shock of 'Earthshaking' dimensions, intense enough to 'knock' or 'sweep' us off our feet and 'blow us away' would represent a profound harmonic converging of the collective *outer* and *inner* experience. It is in such a space that the literal and the figurative, the physical and the spiritual, the drama of time and the bliss of eternity, become realized as a singularity. (As the 'Astronomical Predictions' chapter explains, astronomy and astrology synchronize in 1999 to bring about just such a phenomenon!)

Additional writings of the prophet Daniel give insight into the future. We are struck by his humility and the fact that he projects to us, through his account (Daniel 7), a sense of himself as a sincere and true servant of the light. He was quite elderly when he experienced this mystical 'night vision'. We are told it troubled him greatly and that he became ill for several days.

In the vision, four surreal beasts arose from the sea. (Interestingly, the first one fits the description of the griffin in a Nostradamus prophecy later in this chapter.) All we are told about the fourth beast is that it had great iron teeth, nails of brass and ten horns. Apparently, it was 'exceedingly terrible and strong', and, as in the dream of Nebuchadnezzar, signified the four Earthly kingdoms – the last of which is our own. Daniel wrote that it 'will devour the whole earth and shall tread it down and break it in pieces'. This is what our present civilization is in the process of perpetrating with military and ecological destruction on a scale unequalled in all history.

The ten horns of the strange monster were declared by Daniel to be ten kingdoms. Later, this same beast (with some modifications, but always with the ten horns) rears its ugly head many times in the Book of Revelation. The important role played by this symbolism in our future should not be overlooked, then, since it is emphasized so strongly. During the course of Daniel's dream, the ten horns were joined by another, which had 'eyes like a man and spoke great things'. We are told it/he made war with the saints. Here is the world leader prophesied in Revelation to arise and govern as the antichrist characterized as the personification of evil. Daniel declared he 'will change times and laws', and all authority will be given into his hands. In a subsequent text the prophet had another premonition about him: 'In the last days of those Kingdoms, when their sin is at its height, a king shall appear, harsh and grim, a master of stratagems. His power shall be great, he shall work havoc untold; he shall wreak havoc among great nations and upon a holy people ...' Could Daniel have been portraying a modern leader who began to make his intentions clear prior to the Gulf War?

Late in the first century AD, during his exile on the Greek Island of Patmos, St John also had a vision, its content and meaning similar to Daniel's. John tells us in Revelation 17:12 that the ten horns of the beast are ten kings without a kingdom; they have one mind, and give their power and strength to the antichrist. When one considers how strongly the prophecies of Nostradamus allude to an impressive federation of Arab nations, it seems possible that the volatile and shifting alliances between the Arab nations could stabilize into a ten-nation federation that will fulfill this biblical prophecy and champion a powerful leader, the final antichrist.

In his *Jerusalem Trilogy*, Murshid Samuel Lewis discusses those men of destiny, 'purifiers' who have arisen throughout history as the archetype of the 'madman'. Hitler, with his 'new world order,' was the most obvious 'madman'. In the second century BC, Antioches Epiphanes of the Seleucid dynasty sacked Jerusalem and desecrated the Temple in an attempt to force Greek culture and religion upon the Jews. The Egyptian pharaoh of the exodus in Moses' time was also considered a classic 'madman', as was Nebuchadnezzar.

According to Daniel, Nebuchadnezzar's madness came upon him just as he was boasting, 'Is this not great Babylon, that I have built for the house of the kingdom of the might of my power, and for the honour of my majesty?' (4:30). That Saddam Hussein defied the imperialist West, did violent and bizarre things (not so shocking in a fundamentalist culture that routinely castrates and dismembers criminals), and wasted a lot of expensive oil, was basically enough to make the media label of 'madman' stick. Or did the word 'madman' come trippingly to the tongue because he fit some kind of powerful historic archetype that recurrently gets to be called the 'madman'?

It is known that Hussein saw himself as a reincarnation of, or emulator of, Babylon's King Nebuchadnezzar, and that he also had an agenda to restore 'Babylon the Great'. Early on Hussein's agenda, like Nebuchadnezzar's, appeared to be the desire to destroy Israel. Plans to restore the historic ruins and rebuild the city of Babylon as well as the Tower of Babel began in 1978, and, in 1989, Hussein began recreating the Hanging Gardens of Babylon. Like the famous king before him who grandly rebuilt Babylon to the height of its glory, who conquered many nations, and who sought to rule the world, Saddam Hussein espoused similar aspirations.

It is important to understand here that (as has been pointed out by Jung and Eliade) in the ancient world, especially those civilizations of the Middle East, the worldview was predicated upon historical precedent. Like the symbol of the snake biting its own tail, history was perceived as eternally coiling around itself. Culture was modelled after the perfection of the 'first time' and how it was 'in the beginning'. Archaic cultures intuited that history was deeply rooted in the cycles of the celestial spheres, made sensible by gods, and executed by the founding king lines. Therefore, societies tended always to emulate the mythic past, the actions of the gods, and the illustrious exploits of their great historical rulers.

Accordingly, lives within those Middle Eastern cultures were focused within a prescribed blueprint, one that integrated human consciousness, and the rhythms of Earth and sky into a working harmony. It was a mode that, by the same token, also kept societies hidebound within tradition and enslaved to chronic conservatism. The achievements and policies of those who ruled were always oriented toward the compass of the past, so that each victory was a repetition of a previous triumph, each attainment an echo of an earlier accomplishment by a revered god or renowned monarch.

A concept of ancient Babylon (also found throughout other archaic cultures of the Middle East) was that of the divinity of the king whose ascendency to power inaugurated a new paradisiacal cycle or era of prosperity. Those who ruled were considered conduits for divine order, for the will of destiny and the gods. The person of the ruler himself was regarded as the source of abundant crops, good weather and fecund animals.

According to Eliade, Nebuchadnezzar believed himself to be a regenerator of 'cosmos', and said, 'A reign of abundance, years of exuberance in my country I cause to be.' For Saddam Hussein, enough of a cultural remnant remained to cast him in the part of the king who acts out a circumscribed role scripted by ancient historical imperatives. In modelling himself after Nebuchadnezzar, was the image of defiant indomitability that he presented to the world a vestige of the past, which allowed him to view himself as the destined regenerator of Babylon the Great – an empire that ruled the world – not one victimized by imperialism?

'Strong leadership means fulfillment of destiny'[6] declared the man who six months earlier had celebrated his fifty-third birthday with self-proclaiming banners, 'Your candles, Saddam, are the torches for all the Arabs' followed by a tableau depicting a baby Saddam rocking in a cradle in the marshes.' Did this mean that, like Moses, he saw himself as a messianic leader destined to liberate a unified Arab people from the bondage of Western imperialism into the promised state of a 'New Arab Order'? The scene was more likely symbolic of another, more ancient, leader: Sargon of Akkad himself. He was born in secrecy and placed in a wicker basket in the marshes of the Euphrates. Sargon's mother was an Akkadian priestess, and his father unknown. The river bore the wicker crib away, and a man named Akku found the little cargo washed ashore in the reeds and raised the child as his own. He grew up to be a gardener (which, note, is why Nebuchadnezzar later emulated this royal predecessor's gardening skill by landscaping the famous Hanging Gardens of Babylon). The story continues that Ishtar, consort of the Sun god, loved Sargon and saw to it that he became king. Another Middle Eastern myth of the same genre concerns the Egyptian sun god, Horus, who was hidden in a crib of rushes in the papyrus marshes of the Nile at his birth.

That is the personality profile of a person who sees himself as a man of destiny. There is only one man of destiny who is evoked in the prophecy for the Middle East, and that is the antichrist. Nostradamus prophesied three antichrists between his time in the sixteenth century and the end of the twentieth.[8] The last one, he predicted, would emerge from Mesopotamia – Iraq, at or toward the end of the twentieth century. Several Nostradamus experts have agreed that 1992–1999 are the years most likely for the antichrist to appear and for the final world conflict that he champions. The following references describe powerful leaders who may fulfill this role.

'This man will be called by a barbaric name that three sisters [the three fates of Greek mythology who spin, measure, and cut each person's lifeline] will receive from destiny' (1:76). The quatrain indicates that this man's name will include or give the key to his role and character, as a person destined to activate the world karma. Saddam, in Arabic means 'he who confronts'.'

Another provocative clue from Nostradamus appears as, 'To power will come a villain, wicked and infamous, tyrannizing over Mesopotamia'(VIII:7). An alternative translation renders the meaning that it is the countries who have struck alliances with the 'adulterous lady' (i.e., a veiled reference to Revelation's 'Babylon the whore' – the corrupt world system for which Babylon was a metaphor) who will be tyrannized. The quatrain ends by saying, 'The face of the land (will be rendered) horrible and black' – a fair description of an environment blackened by bombing and burning oil. Apart from the tragic results to the immediate environment and its creatures, these oil fires pose an apocalyptic threat in terms of aggravating the 'greenhouse effect' and increasing polar ice, changing the balance of the ice caps, and thus possibly affecting rotation of the planet. Nostradamus writes that the Arab prince who is the 'true serpent' will march almost a million men toward Iran, and that he will also invade Turkey and Egypt (V:25). The United States supported Saddam Hussein when Iraq invaded Iran with an army of almost a million men. Both Turkey and Egypt were part of the Arab coalition against Iraq, and Hussein threatened both countries – Turkey with missiles, and Egypt by assassination of its President. According to Nostradamus, then, an Arab leader described as the 'true serpent' is someone to be reckoned with.

An ancient myth concerning a serpent and an eagle originated in Akkad before the time of King Sargon. It told of the serpent and eagle who struck an alliance, each hunting up food for the other and its offspring, for mutual benefit. However, to gain advantage, the eagle planned treachery and devoured the family of the serpent. Distraught, the serpent appealed to the Sun god for retribution. He was advised to hide in the carcass of a dead animal, so that when the eagle came to feed, the serpent would be in a position to surprise him and tear off his wings and talons. This he did.

*Combat of the eagle and the serpent is represented on a
soapstone bas-relief from Nippur (Iraq) found in debris
near a shrine of Bur-sin of Ur (2400 BC)*

The myth is ancient but describes a perennial theme. It is one of
treachery, conflict and retribution. The ancients taught that
truth is contained in geometry, in symbols – and in myth. Just
how true this myth may be is indicated by the following. As
discussed in the 'Astrological Cycles' chapter, the 'home base'
of the constellation Aquila, the eagle, lies directly above the
United States. In the same way of reckoning, the celestial abode
of the constellation Orion is directly above that part of the
Middle East divided by a mountain range: Iraq and Iran.

The name 'Orion' is believed to have originated in the
Euphrates area of ancient Akkad, and is derived from the
Akkadian 'Uru-Anna' (light of heaven). Over time, the language corrupted to 'Aryan', which is what the ancient Per-
sians called themselves, and which became the modern
idiom, 'Iran'. Arab astronomer Al Babadur said the constellation was originally called the 'Strong One', but another,
Scaliger, affirmed the name was a corruption of the Arab 'Al
Shuja' (the Snake). In the early astronomical works of Bayer
and Chilmead, that word was translated as 'Asugia' – the
'madman'.[10]

Clearly, the antagonisms between the United States and the Middle East, past, present and future, are the visible fruit of hidden but powerful mythic roots. The placement of the Orion constellation, its origin, and name translations are synchronicities connecting the role of Iraq and the appellations of its military leader to a deeply mythic substructure.

What emerges from this research is a sense of the United States and the Middle East (specifically Iraq) as nations personifying archetypal forces: Eagle and Serpent engaged in a struggle for power. In its highest form, the serpent symbolizes wisdom and Earth energy; the eagle, transcendent consciousness. When the natural polarity between the two is resolved, they merge in union as that mythic hybrid, the 'plumed serpent'. The caduceus is a model for this process within the human body. The spiritual evolutionary impulse awakens the *kundalini* 'serpent power' from the base of the spine for its ascent. Conflict and personal chaos seem apparent as it uncoils and purifies its way up through the *chakras*. When it reaches the pineal gland nesting between the two 'wings' of the frontal lobes of the brain, enlightened consciousness occurs. What we witnessed playing itself out on the world scene in the form of the Gulf War was the identical, but macrocosmic, process just described.

With respect to the reconciliation between serpent and eagle, the time of greatest crisis is that of pre-breakthrough, when the power centre (third *chakra*) *is* disturbed by the serpent and must process its anger, fear and need for control in order for the awakened energies to pass the midpoint and stabilize at the heart. The Gulf War did not *process* any negativity, it suppressed it by force – which is why repercussions will continue to build and erupt until the resolution *is* accomplished and conflict resolved. Armageddon is what happens if it is not achieved.

Peace can not be achieved through power. But power can be achieved through peace. It's simply a matter of how one defines power. Environmental philosopher Gil Bailie put it this way, 'Maturity is the wisdom not to use all the power you have. Taboo is what to do while waiting on the wisdom.

It's not like law exactly. Laws are political; taboos religious. If a taboo is to work something has to be sacred.' So what does our culture hold sacred? An oil-dependent materialistic lifestyle?

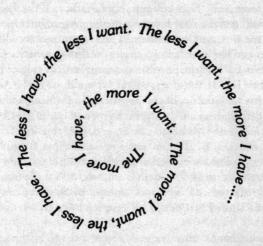

The less I have, the less I want. The less I want, the more I have.... The more I want, the less I have. The more I have, the more I want. The less I have...

Nostradamus had foreseen the decline of communism, an alliance with the West, and subsequent conflict – followed by a threat from the East. 'The law of More will be seen to decline, because of gifts from another nation and acceptance of a more appealing philosophy' (III:95). In one short sentence we have three prophecies, all of which appear to have come to pass. The 'law of More' refers to an early precursor of communism. The theory of 'all things common among friends' was propounded by English statesman Sir Thomas More in his *Utopia*. This work circulated in 1516, during Nostradamus's college days. The United States *did* provide the former Soviet Union with food and supplies for a very long time, and we did see the dissolution of the Soviet Union and the relinquishment of Eastern Europe. Quatrain IV:32 says that 'communal law will hold strongly the old ones, then removed from the midst, communism put far behind'. In other words, the old leaders will strongly support the system, but they will be removed from power.

The unexpected friendly alliance achieved between the United States and Soviet Union in 1989 also appears to have been forecast by Nostradamus, but he indicates that the rapport will not last long before something happens. 'One day two masters will be friends. Their great power will be increased. The new land [America] will then be at its peak. The bloody one [the possible antichrist] will be told of their number' (II:89). But then (VI:21), 'When those of the Arctic Pole [upper latitudes of the Northern hemisphere] are united together, there will be a great terror and fear in the Orient [East]. The newly elected one upheld, the 'great one' trembles. Rhodes, Byzantium [ancient areas close to modern Turkey] stained with barbarian blood' (VI:21). Could this have referred to ex-President Bush, who was at the time the 'newly elected one' who was 'upheld' by the US Congress and the United Nations in his decision to go to war against Iraq?

Nostradamus also warned about a large coalition of European and other Western forces who would take up positions next to Iraq. 'A large army of crusaders [nations of Christendom] will be arrayed in Mesopotamia ... and the enemy will hold his position ...' (III:61). This is a particularly germane prophecy, because the US was positioned in Mesopotamia (Iraq) and Iraqi forces did hold their position for six months during the prewar standoff. Also, in a 1991 interview, Saddam Hussein, in characteristic archaic parlance, pronounced the Gulf War as 'the last Crusading war'.

These are a few of Nostradamus's prophecies that appear to address aspects of the Gulf War and Saddam Hussein. It should be recognized, however, that we are currently embarked upon a process that will continue to move deeper into the realms of prophecy as the turn of the century approaches. Nostradamus referred in many other quatrains to the 'Great Arab' and the 'Arab Prince' and an Arab confederacy landing in Italy, moving through Turkey, the Balkans and Europe. These prophecies could portray possible repercussions of the Gulf War, or a subsequent and greater eruption from the Middle East, into an entire global theatre of war that also includes parts of southern Europe. And many more of Nostradamus's predictions can be expected to reveal their meaning as time elapses. Particular ones to watch for are a final round between Moslem fundamentalists and Europe, but culminating in the Middle East. While Saddam Hussein is down, he should not be considered out, and will feature at the fore of future dealings with the West. The keynote here seems to be 'Watch this space ...'

This particular chapter should be regarded as a work in progress, since affairs in the Middle East are kaleidoscopically dynamic, dangerous and volatile. What does seem clear is that Saddam Hussein probably was trying out for the role of antichrist. Like the rock musician who opens for the big act to follow, he may well have been the 'opener' for the real Beast. Hussein, as an unreligious Sunni, was not able to generate the right kind of mass support for a successful 'holy war'. The majority of Iraqis are Shiites who await a Mahdi (an Islamic messiah, a political and religious leader who, it is believed, will appear at the world's end and establish a reign of peace and righteousness). The rabid fundamentalism of the lmam (supreme) Mahdi, Ayatollah Khomeini, was able to mobilize the Iranian Shiites on such a basis. The reemergence of such a one would not be welcomed by the West.

The last quatrain of Nostradamus's to be quoted here is intriguing because it declares that the 'King of Europe will come like a griffin, accompanied by those of Aquilon, leading a great troop of red and white ones against the King of Babylon'. Classically, a griffin had the head and wings of an eagle or a man, and the body of a lion. And Henry Roberts, in his translation footnotes, says a griffin was supposed to guard the gold of Russia; so we assume that is who the King of Europe is. (Daniel the prophet also dreamed of a creature fitting the description of this griffin. It rose out of the sea and symbolized one of the four great civilizations of the Earth.) Aquilon describes the land of Aquila the eagle (the United States) or Western powers. The red and white colours attributed to the troops of America and Russia, above, also appear in the Native American prophecy given below.

This prophecy concerns a final war between three serpents. In a prophetic vision received by the great Iroquois teacher, Deganaweda, a red and white serpent sharing a single tail wrestled until they became exhausted. For a while, the white serpent accepted part of the red one, but the rapport ended in a heated argument and a fight. This implies that the alliance between the Soviet Union and the United States would only be temporary. The prophecy says the conflict will begin very slowly but eventually boil the Earth.

The prophecy, as told by Iroquois Mad Bear Anderson to the late Ojibwa shaman Sun Bear, continues: The two serpents will wrestle until the rivers boil and the fish in them die. Sun Bear said the interpretation given him by Spirit was that the two snakes shared the same tail because both sought the domination, control and conquest of humanity. They wrestled, supplying weapons to get other people to fight against each other. When they had exhausted almost all their resources they were in so much debt they couldn't afford to continue. He says the black serpent symbolizes the Moslem nations. The 'true serpent' was also identified as an Arab (Moslem) leader of almost a million men, according to Nostradamus.

Sun Bear pointed out that the black serpent had defeated the red and white snakes twice already (in Lebanon and Afghanistan), and that neither white nor red serpent knows how to battle the black one. He said that the Gulf War would affect all the nations of the world, and that it represented fulfillment of this prophecy. If the black serpent defeated the other two, he would look around for more people to fight with. Sun Bear said the black serpent would see the native people gathered in the hilly country along with others who seek to understand the spiritual ways of the Earth, but that at the last minute, 'the great light of Deganaweda will appear and frighten him away, never to bother the people again'.

In the chapter on 'Bible Prophecy' we explored the possibility of an antichrist emerging from a European confederacy of nations. Yet the prospect of such a person representing a Middle Eastern confederacy also exists. We seem to be talking here in a generic sense of 'East' and 'West'. Both regions are dependent upon the declining resources of an already depleted planet, the most important resource of which is their shared lifeblood – oil. The snakes of East and West may become embroiled 'to the death' over it. This is also how the two snakes described above are joined at the tail.

The axiom that no two things can exist at the same time in the same place is illustrated in the homeopathic principle whereby a little of what ails you is introduced into the body to cure what ails you. Like attracts like, and like cancels like. Therefore, if one accepts that at this time in history the light is increasing, exposing and displacing the darkness, it follows that light and darkness, 'good and evil' are polarizing in the process. So, rather than identifying the opposites as 'good and evil,' it would be more accurate to talk of that which is in harmony with the universe and that which is not.

People and conditions unaligned with the union of heaven and Earth are the ones that will fight to the death to maintain the world according to their model, their commercial and resource interests, and their oil. (Hence, the biblical condemnation and destruction of the 'corrupt' Babylon, because the *un*corrupt Babylon was the light of the ancient world. According to Mesopotamian tradition, Babylon was the holy city, the 'Bond of Heaven and Earth'.)' The battle of Armageddon, therefore, is much more likely to be the self-destruction of like attracting and cancelling out like. Armageddon is not a wrathful God striking everyone dead, but more like violent contestants striking each other dead.

It is not within the scope of this chapter to explore the historical, political, economic, or ideological complexities that divide East and West. The metaphors used here seek to address the substrata of the schism in symbolic terms.

Attitudes of adherence to outmoded tradition have kept large segments of Eastern cultures divided within themselves, stuck between the patterns of the past and the emergence into the twentieth century mainstream. No Arab ruler has ever come to power through genuine election. Male dominance through power is respected and permeates the cultural tradition. Women are treated as chattel. Brutal and archaic criminal penalties obtain for misdemeanors. Adapting to the needs of the time would mean the unthinkable – painful awakenings, looking up from the rutted roundtrack to see what else is real. To societies handicapped by the compulsory torsion of always looking backwards, asking 'What's new?' is dangerous talk.

Conversely, Western cultures do not relate to the cyclicalness of life, the great epochal tides and cycles of heaven and Earth that shape history and condition our future. We have lost our connection with the Earth and the guidance of the stars. In contrast to the polarized ways of the East, we tend to be culturally focused at a point somewhere in midstride – progressive, inventive, creative, very linear. We know little of the conserving principle of the circle, and so we consume all. Moving upon the tickertape of time, we gulp down the moment. We mine out the resources and move on. Life without a backward glance means no ballast restricts our freedoms – and wisdom has become disconnected from knowledge in the process. If we remain unwilling to change vectors, to 'de-material-ize', war may do it for us.

Life is the product of an interplay between two universal forces: the female, conserving principle of the circle, and the male, generative, principle of the line. Only in their balanced union is creation served and evolution fostered. The principles embodied in circle and line are encoded within the human psyche, governors of right and left brain function. They act to focalize into conscious awareness the true nature of the subtle rupture within the landscape of the deep mind. As polar opposites upon a single sphere, cultures of East and West reflect the macrocosmic realities of hemispherical imbalance – each separated by its own selective bias, yet bound by a shared biology. The division within ourselves becomes the division outside ourselves. Because we are overdue in healing this fundamental problem, we have collectively externalized the crisis enough to see it on the news, to have it preoccupy our waking consciousness, and even to kill people (both literally, and by psychological consensus) in order to preserve the illusion of our own needs and our separation. Every place in one's being that holds anger and fear is part of the overall conflict. Suffering and destruction will continue until we become accountable. The horrendous capabilities of nuclear, chemical and biological weapons have rendered war a totally inappropriate means of conflict resolution (if needed it ever was!). To believe otherwise hints at a Neanderthal mental process.

Can we/they ever change from a separative either/or mentality to a mutually inclusive one of both/and – and preserve the integrity of each? In the West, we see opposites as antagonistic. When fear and the need to dominate isolate those differences we feel separation and experience conflict. Ancient Eastern wisdom sees opposites as complementary. The intelligence of the heart seeks the harmony, focusing on the similarities. The founding fathers understood this when they inscribed 'E pluribus unum' ('Diversity within Unity') on the Great Seal of the United States. If we can realize that unity and tolerance within ourselves, we can experience the 'Novus Ordo Saeclorum' – the New Order of the Ages. If we can do that, we can get with the Programme! The Programme is our archetypal subscript, the cyclical pattern expressed through human consciousness that carries us toward wholeness. The Programme allows us to be fair and square in the moment and to access our higher Selves – the source of our highest mutual good and the repository of our highest collective wisdom.

ALLAHO AKBAR
'Peace is Power'[12]

14

Astrological Predictions

Perhaps the main stumbling block between astrology, the metaphysical abstraction, and astrology, the science, is the interpretive limitations of the astrologer. Astrology, like algebra, deals with symbolism rather than empiricism. As Michael Meyer states in his *Handbook for the Humanistic Astrologer*, 'Astrology is a functional application of the awareness of the active relationship existing between the microcosm and the macrocosm.'

Translating the forces and nuances of celestial influence into the specific and accurate life situations is rather like identifying culinary aromas as they waft from a kitchen. It would require a good nose and considerable gastronomical knowledge to be able to isolate from the many smells the specific foods being prepared. A much more subtle skill is required, however, to accurately predict what recipe will show up on the plate brought to the table.

Our individual astrology is a map of ourselves within the cosmic scheme of things. Emanations from the various planets exert a variety of influences on the Earth and its inhabitants. These influences or forces predispose; they impel, they do not compel. Thus, the unfolding of planetary and individual circumstances is coaxed into existence by that infinitely delicate combination of free will and unseen conduciveness. The latter, however, potentiated the free will part that over time became ego-driven, materially fixated and disconnected from the Earth. We became a dysfunctional planet.

As the prophecy chapters unequivocally set forth, it is the last decade of the century that will absorb the impact of cosmic shocks. As a buffer zone between the completion and inception of major historical cycles, the nineties represent the greatest challenge of history this time around. So it is the unseen conduciveness of celestial influence that must now impel human will to reharmonize with the evolutionary agenda. If we do not make the right conscious choices and courageous changes, the force of universal order will. That force is impersonal, direct and radical. Either way, the shocking and unexpected events in the future will undoubtedly bring out the best and the worst in us as we rise to meet, or resist, the challenges.

We can expect to witness unprecedented changes of epochal proportions, and events of a magnitude unimaginable by most people. We cannot doubt that our experiences of this 'interface' transitional period will be intense, extreme, powerful (both positive and negative) on all levels, because the real global crisis is one of consciousness and ideology. But help is on the way. Important astrological configurations are about to come on line which will prepare our consciousness to resonate with the appropriate frequencies for survival.

The three outer planets of our solar system – Uranus, Neptune and Pluto – are interpreted as being the planets of transformation, because they are outside the orbit of the finite boundaries of time and space represented by Saturn. Therefore, the outer planets are infinite and cosmic in their application to astrology. Their influence represents divine intention within the collective unconscious through the medium of finite form, as represented by Saturn and the other inner planets. An understanding of these three planets is important because they play such an important role in preparing us to move into the future with grace and equanimity. The study of the outer planets is really the study of cosmic wave functions, and we experience them in two primary ways: 1) the personal unconscious, arising from the collective unconscious, as archetypal symbology which communicates through dreams, inspiration, revelation, etc., and 2) in the world, through wave functions of social change and societal mass movements. Sensitive people respond to these energies. To the Greeks, the planets were the Gods. When the outer planets join in union (conjunction), there is a positive and powerful explosion of content from the unconscious mind into conscious awareness.

During the past two centuries, Earth's inhabitants have been receiving preparation for the very times that lie immediately ahead. Uranus, Neptune, and Pluto accelerate the growth of planetary consciousness. They were discovered at times appropriate to our evolution, bringing into conscious focus their specific offerings of energy and metamorphosis. All discoveries occur when the consciousness is ready to expand. Dane Rudhyar, one of the foremost astrological philosophers of our times, sees this challenge of quickened evolution as an opportunity for global initiation if humanity as a whole is able to respond positively and courageously to this downpour of galactic and divine energies. The Great Pyramid reflects a similar message. These three outer planets have played a very important role in shaping recent history, and during the coming years they will influence our collective destiny even more intensely.

Any discussion of the outer planets' role in prophecy should be prefaced by mention of the planetoid Chiron. In 1977 Chiron was discovered orbiting between Saturn and Uranus, i.e., between the inner and outer planets. In Greek mythology, Chiron was part-animal, part-human: a centaur. He instructed the greatest heroes of the age in wisdom teachings, medicine and art. Chiron, symbolized by this wise animal-man, represents the bridge between matter and spirit – the mundane world of animal-human awareness and the transcendent reality of human-divine consciousness.

At the time of Chiron's discovery in 1977, the counterculture of the sixties was in a process of reabsorption back into 'the system.' As young people matured and took their place in the world, the residual energy of sixties idealism and values was qualitatively transformed by Chiron's influence into a resurgence of transpersonal energy, stimulating a powerful opening up of mainstream consciousness. Chiron's energy began to define itself, coalescing into the collective totem of the so-called New Age movement. Now that we are in the described period of historical repolarization, Chiron assists the cultural and political shift into alignment with cosmic intention. Nowhere does the juxtaposition of cosmic intention and prophecy show up more clearly for our guidance than in the Maya calendar (discussed later).

Uranus was discovered in 1781, coincident with the French and American revolutions, allowing timely and conscious cognition of its unique forces. The birth chart for the United States shows Uranus in the sign of Gemini, and whenever this combination occurs there is always tremendous upheaval. Uranus's particular energy is ruthlessly revolutionary, paring away all stultifying and limiting beliefs and behaviour. It is the first planet of transformation beyond Saturn, and therefore, the first of spiritual awareness and attunement to the cosmos. It impatiently rips away the Saturnian mask of ego and limitation, crying impatiently, 'Enough of this self-centred, timorous myopia. Look out, look out toward the cosmos!' (or something like that).

Uranus replaces the past with a new vision, releasing original and unique evolutionary impulses within us to help our uncertain ascent. It nurtures genius and fervent enthusiasms. The American revolutionaries two hundred years ago experienced the power of Uranus's transformation, as do all who struggle against the hold of the past and against tyranny. However, it is really an externalization of the inner surge of renewal toward perfection that manifests. Uranus rules the sign of Aquarius, which presides over the beginning of the New Age. The 'New Order of the Ages' seeded by America's independence as a nation was symbolized by the discovery of Uranus, which will oversee the preparatory events leading up to the integration and anchoring of that new order globally.

From the nonsequitur of a great joke, sneeze, or surprise, to the great political events that suddenly tear down walls between nations, the kind of reality slippage that Uranus brings is radical, transformational, sometimes bizarre, and always *intense*. It was Uranus – ruler of electricity, the nervous system, and the unorthodox – that overlighted psychoactive substance exploration in the sixties. The view from inner space revealed and made conscious the true presence of a profound, numinous, and paradisiacal world, imbued with meaning and wonder – a reality terminally under siege and gasping for life. From a cosmic perspective, that sudden disruption of the familiar world, structured by powerful beliefs, group agreements and the preconceptions of other people's minds, was actually the input of energized originality from the deep psyche.

Neptune rules ideology, inspiration, dreams, etc. The attributes of this planet are mystical and its forms elusive, inasmuch as it embodies the *principle* of the unconscious (out of which Pluto, the pure *archetype* of the unconscious arises). Beyond Neptune's masculine identity as the mythic god of the sea, is the esoteric feminine domain of spirit or soul, the point of light within the mind – Psyche herself. So it was quite synchronous that in 1846, the year of Neptune's discovery, the first medical treatise on the unconscious was published. Carl Jung credits British physician C.G. Carus as the author of this book. It was called *Psyche*, meaning 'female soul' – which is exactly what the inner essence of Neptune represents. With Neptune's discovery the international influences of the industrial revolution and colonialism were introduced, but at the same time we saw the countervision of Thoreau and Marsh and rediscoveries of natural law.

Water is ruled by Neptune, and it is symbolic of the living spirit that can carry one beyond the existential illusion and delusion of the world. It works as a universal solvent to transform our limitations and fixed beliefs and to dissipate the remainder of what Uranus shattered (the Saturnian influences of ego and conceptual rigidity).

Pluto This planet is an escaped satellite of Neptune that became stabilized into its own orbit and was discovered in 1930, the same year as publication of Einstein's Unified Field Theory. Pluto represents the divine power within the unconscious, and was named after the Greek god of the underworld. Under Pluto's influence, unresolved matters are reduced to an undifferentiated state and finally are regenerated in a negative or positive form. Naturally, such random states, lacking initial cohesion and order, are susceptible to the influences of those most aware of the opportunity to take control. The discovery of Pluto coincided with the great Depression and the gestational years of dictatorships under Hitler in Germany and Mussolini in Italy, and the spreading of communism under Stalin. As pure archetype resonating deep within the core of the unconscious, Pluto stirs the dark reservoir of the collective mind and motivates the masses. So, it is not surprising that antisemitism under Naziism arose as a projection of the national 'shadow' in response to just such a collectively subconscious process.

The glyph of the phoenix is used to represent Pluto and to indicate the new birth arising from the ashes of the old. The refocalization of new forms, resulting from such disasters as major wars, can serve either to further negative and antiquated interests or to bring forth evolutionary change and the kind of radiant regenesis found throughout nature. Perhaps this is why Pluto also stands for the ultimate triumph of universal harmony with the human and the natural world. As the outermost planet, Pluto's changes are slow, its complete cyclical action affecting generations rather than individuals.

Astrological mapping of the years up to 2012 AD provides valuable insights into the nature of coming changes upon the planet.

The way in which we *respond* to the released celestial energies is crucial, because the up side of desperate circumstances will be accelerated flowering of the spirit amongst people who can relate positively to what is happening from the perspective of events working themselves out as part of an intense global healing crisis. Basically, what we are talking about with the other planet conjunctions is an initiation process for the whole of humanity.

In 1993 there occurred a rare and spiritually powerful astrological configuration. Astrologers with whom I consulted for the original edition of this book in 1975 agreed that this junction represented 'the turning point in the recorded story of this civilization'. In the 1980s, other professional astrologers considered the conjunction potentially 'empire-crumbling'. From a 1993 perspective, experienced astrologers everywhere were concerned and vocal on the subject, wanting to circulate advance notice about the profound magnitude of the changes this conjunction would bring. Noted political astrologer Graeme Jones considered it 'probably *the* most epoch-forming and astrologically potent phenomenon of the next two decades' – i.e., before the end of the present cycle in 2012 AD.

A conjunction of Uranus (the light bringer) and Neptune (soul receptivity) will be within eight degrees of each other until around the turn of the century, which means their immediate influence will be felt for a long time beyond the actual point of conjunction. Historically speaking, the changes that the conjunction set in motion will have a dynamic and lasting impact on the future. The union of these two planets can be understood as two infinite cosmic waves forming a harmonic that synthesizes Uranus's higher values of freedom and Neptune's expansive spiritual awareness. This harmonic union occurred under the auspices of Capricorn, sign of political economy and major organizational power structures. Very significant political and economic manifestations are implicated to stem from this conjunction, with the simultaneous stimulation of two separate cultural dimensions: namely, radical social/political transformations on the one hand, and enhancement of spiritual consciousness and culture on the other. Do not underestimate the quantum breakthroughs that can be achieved at this time in human rights, science, medicine, engineering, and our understanding of 'the mysteries'.

When there is a significant connection between the outer planets, impulses burst out of the collective unconscious in accordance with the cosmic evolutionary blueprint for Earth and its life forms. The reason we are in evolutionary crisis right now is because, as crew members of 'spaceship Earth', we have discarded our operator's manual and strayed dangerously off course. This also means we have become estranged from our own essential nature. Our detour from disaster, and survival itself, depends upon our ability to quickly realign with the evolutionary blueprint. Therefore, the spiritual intelligence projected by Neptune will facilitate that which is consistent with the blueprint, and guide Uranus's radical surgery of that which is not.

According to Dane Rudhyar, what is born at one conjunction develops through that cycle and fulfills itself in the next conjunction of those same planets.

What is created during a time of cosmic gestation has the potential of an enduring cultural/spiritual rebirth. Socialism was inspired in Russia during the last Uranus/Neptune conjunction of 1821. It was the time of the industrial revolution, a time during which the results of the French Revolution were being assimilated throughout Europe, where feudalism was replaced by the growth of industrial society. Believe it or not, Karl Marx's life and work is an articulation of the spiritual meaning of this cycle. The *Communist Manifesto,* written in the year of Neptune's discovery (1846), was published during a Pluto/Uranus conjunction in 1848 – a year in which revolutions broke out across the capitals of continental Europe. (Any conjunction between two of the three outer planets – Uranus, Neptune, Pluto – cosmically stimulates the forward movement of history. In this way, the Pluto/Uranus conjunction served to support the Uranus/Neptune conjunction.) From this one can infer that the *Communist Manifesto* was obviously a document of cosmic as well as historical significance. It anticipated the alchemical union of heaven and Earth in the mind of civilization within our social reality. Within this context, then, the Russian Revolution, which began around the midpoint of the cycle in 1905 and climaxed in 1917, presaged what will manifest from the 1993 Uranus/Neptune conjunction The collapse of the Soviet Union at the ending of the cycle, then, presages a major new economic-political expression, a hybrid that may somewhat fuse Marxism and capitalism, but actually surpasses the capabilities of both. It will embrace global economic concepts and realities toward the seeding of world government.

Now is the time to give conscious attention to what that means. Like the Fool in the Tarot stepping off the cliff, will we be borne up by angels or crash like a stone? If our collective consciousness is ready, everything will work out; if it isn't, it won't. Timing obviously is important, for we approach a critical period of eccentric activity and extremes. (One should bear in mind that this historical time period represents a battle between good and evil being played out on the physical plane.) We can allow, by default, a 'worst case' world government, or we consciously can intend and work to co-create world unity (something qualitatively quite different from a centrally administered monoculture called world government).

The seeds of a possible worst case were sown long before the average person ever considered the possibility of world government. The Trilateral Commission is a consortium of the world's wealthy power elite, established to foster economic and political cooperation between Germany, North America and Japan. In 1975, the Commission released a disquieting annual report, *The Crisis of Democracy*. The report, which presented a number of startling and controversial prognostications about the demise of democracy, also predicted that the postindustrial era, dominated by electronics, would 'evolve into new social structures' that would progress 'beyond traditional democratic forms'. A lot of people were not happy about that, yet the overall thrust of the report appeared not to be one of State Socialism (despite recommended 'improvements' that would broadly restrict Constitutional freedoms), but rather a global, computer-controlled technotronic mode. The 'New

World Order' espoused by ex-President Bush (a member of the Trilateral Commission), to be administered by the materially fixated, would not be a better place, no matter how efficient the political system.

As the 1990s progress – imagining a best case – just world government will be rendered realistic by an accelerated expansion of our worldview. Even though this is not apparent from our present vantage point, the 1993 Uranus/Neptune conjunction was charged to *make* it apparent as the decade progresses. Within the collective unconscious, Neptune subtly opens up people's spiritual Self-consciousness with an 'urge to merge', to blend head-on and heart-to-heart. With Uranus comes the wakeup call to mind-level awareness. So, the archetype of limitless spiritual feelings and emotion unifies with limitless conscious awareness. This is the nature of a cultural paradigm shift, or renaissance; and in this case, it is an extremely influential formula for the realization of a 'planetary culture of human completeness.'

The organic movement toward planetary unity – which Neptune deftly draws from the collective unconscious – fine-tunes one's inner sensing and impulses. This, then, is the nature of a graceful planetary unfolding, and we are reminded of the I *Ching's* wisdom regarding the 'Turning Point' – in this case the turning point of history,

> There is movement but it is not brought about by force. [It is] characterized by devotion; thus the movement is natural, arising spontaneously. For this reason the transformation of the old becomes easy … Societies of people sharing the same views are formed. But since these groups come together in full public knowledge and are *in harmony with the time,* all selfish separatist tendencies are excluded and no mistake is made.

The coming transition process leads to world unity on a spiritual basis of profoundly new principles. It births a new 'cosmos' or paradigm, the archetype of which is the core of our spiritual Self-awareness – it is the organizing principle of our present transformational process. According to astrologer Christopher Hedlund, who has explored the subject in depth, 'The same sort of breaking down and breaking through that we see in the outer world will be going on in our own psyches. For some this may be terrifying, for others it may be exhilarating. The issue is attachment versus opening to transformation and having the capacity to integrate the energies these planets generate.'[1]

Advances in progressive class and political revolution are often accompanied by cultural and spiritual advances. The rise of Goddess spirituality is an essential and progressive cultural ingredient that will initiate transformation processes on both political and spiritual levels. Crystallized patriarchal religious orthodoxies that want to preserve their dogmas do not welcome new interpretations or ideas. Patriarchal spirituality makes structures, while feminine spirituality uses chaos to reorganize them by transforming emotional realities. Carl Jung says, the Holy Spirit is to be feared because it is revolutionary in matters of religion. The Holy Spirit is the energy of the Goddess, the world of nature, and the creation, and the animating force within new life.

In the post-1993 years, the planetoid Chiron's spiritual, holistic, and healing influence translates through the mass consciousness as a spiritual awareness of the Self as executive organizer of action, rather than intellectual theory. Chiron mediates revolutionary political aspects brought into focus by Uranus. With this realization comes acknowledgement of a greater power than ourselves, and that it functions through us and for us. Experientially, this means that many geniuses and leaders will appear amongst those who can give up their ego and let the will of God and the visionary force transform them and the undertakings and causes they champion.

Pluto in Scorpio until 1996 (since 1984) represents philosophical application of a new physical awareness: the use of innovative biochemical research, and discovery of Earth resources to replace dwindling energy supplies. But, within the collective unconscious, deep, purifying, forces are at work. As the murky depths of the deep collective mind become clearer through this purifying process, we will begin to apprehend a new view of nature as being spirit-centred – the resacralization of the natural world. When we learn to refocus the lens of our perception to a holistic setting, the spirit within matter becomes apparent. As we all begin to understand the physical world as an alchemical union of spirit and matter, we will have another paradigm shift. This astrological influence is conducive to that shift_ the result of which is incompatible with a world economic/political system based upon exploitation and destruction of nature and indigenous peoples.

In December 1994, Pluto and Jupiter in the last degrees of Scorpio result in socialization of the transpersonal process. This means that our educational and religious institutions will begin to register important changes, so that our lives may begin to reflect, in practical terms, our highest ideals. Jupiter, sign of the higher mind and philosophies, will expand the general acceptance of new knowledge and truth. This period is the beginning of awareness that the chaos must run its course in preparation for a new epoch of sanity.

In 1995-2000 AD Uranus is in its own sign, Aquarius. Since Aquarius rules astrology, its reinstatement as an occult science can be expected, together with that of the other metaphysical disciplines. Aquarius rules the light, and intensification of the light during this decade will burn away many clouds of negative karma from the Earth plane. As Jupiter conjuncts Uranus in Aquarius during early 1997, sudden changes and worldwide upheavals serve to bring new concepts into focus and generate needed reevaluations.

At the beginning of 1998, there will be a major planetary conjunction when six planets (Sun, Moon, Mercury, Jupiter, Neptune and Uranus) converge in Aquarius. (We reiterate that what is born at one conjunction develops through the cycles and fulfills itself in the next conjunction.) This conjunction complements a 1962 preparatory cycle that set forces in motion with a similar alignment. This conjunction of inner and outer planets brings a major release of 'New Age' pro-evolutionary energy into the collective consciousness. The cosmic forces, focalized by the slower, more profound influences of the outer planets, become grounded and socially organized by the quickening function of the inner planets. This conjunction will assist us to achieve emotional mastery. And the emergence of new archetypes into conscious awareness will help us integrate our lower and higher natures. These are some of the definite, strong influences at work that will assist our individuation.

During 1999 AD, the solstices align with the galactic plane. In contemporary interpretation of Maya prophecy this phenomenon is explained as 'galactic synchronization'. It occurs at the midpoint of the last phase of the Maya calendar – right between the 1987 Harmonic Convergence and the end of the calendar in 2012 AD. This represents a matching of frequencies between the collective human psyche and the emanations from the Milky Way. In other words, this positioning brings us back into resonant connection with the rest of the universe in terms of being humanly attuned to the great evolutionary force this time around. Whatever it takes to reestablish that resonant connection can and will occur, negative or positive.

In September 1999, Mars conjuncts Pluto at seven degrees Sagittarius. Mars's raw ego and aggressive energy meet up with the transpersonal power of Pluto in the sign of Sagittarius, sign of the higher mind. Nostradamus had said that 'around July' 1999, 'Mars will reign for the good cause'. It looks as though a general uplifting and empowerment of consciousness is scheduled by the force of Mars's acting 'for the good cause'. Although anger is frequently regarded as a negative quality, we see here the righteous anger that brooks no opposition and forcefully sweeps obstacles aside as an instrument of the collective will toward good. New and worldwide codes of ethics may result. The nations, allied more truly than ever before, will share new healing techniques and natural resources made possible by research into the various energy fields from nondepletable sources.

In the last month of 1999, Mars moves assertively forward, crossing the Uranus/Neptune conjunction in Aquarius, and firming up the unifying growth initiated by their earlier conjunction in 1992–93. Mars infuses these three planets of transition with a rush of expanded aggressive energy. A greatly increased potential for spiritually based unity will be rendered by a growing perception within individuals that separations are illusion, and that survival of the human race depends upon seeing ourselves as a global family.

The potential is vividly apparent for people to experience a truly accepting and tolerant attitude toward all others, all races, and a dissolving of superficial differences. As Divine Mother, the Goddess, rises in her fullness, the presiding male force will move into true harmonic relationship with the feminine. From that union of equals will be reborn the divine child – the sacredness of life. Our collective and humanly biased perception of kindred species as commodities to be exploited *will* change. All creatures and growing things, from elephants to insects from rain forests to the tiniest weeds, will be recognized and revered as unique and equal expressions in the great chain of being.

And what of the end of the Maya calendar, December 21, 2012 AD? An astrological natal chart for that day says with great deliberation, 'This is a test!' It is an excellent chart for the spiritual reconstruction of planetary culture, a chart of extremes – of the 'mutate or die' genre. That is what such initiations are.

Basically, crisis and revolution will take up most of the 1990s, but against a backdrop of intense spiritual vibration. Emphasized are disruption; sudden change; grounded empowerment of subtle cosmic inspirations; extreme polarization between those who want to go forward and those who do not; awakening; a deepening of the sacred; expansion of spiritual work and awareness; possible collision of great political forces, likely to involve China; conscious people steering, in a transformative way, powerful tides in the heaving ocean of the collective unconscious.

Initiation is the practicum after all the theory has been absorbed. It is the 'trial by fire' whereby the acquired knowledge and wisdom are put to the test, in order to overcome.

Ceremony, ritual and 'initiatory' secret knowledge are disclosed when an aspirant undergoes degree-testing by an esoteric order. Inner experiences are also a part of many initiations. One treads the razor's edge over the abyss, as it were. For those who fail the advanced level, there is no second chance (not in the same body, at least), but for those who prove equal to the challenge, a profoundly new level of consciousness is attained. Many people who have undergone unstructured or involuntary 'mini-initiatory' experiences feel that the knowledge gained was not so much 'new stuff' as it was a newer, more profound, or more deeply insightful reperception. When intellectual knowledge is transformed to direct gnosis a shift is felt within the physical body itself.

The global initiation process is a deeply archetypal event, the dynamics of which include the breakdown of the collective ego's security and control patterns in order to produce an unanticipated 'deliverance' by the inner Self.

Could it be to this very end that every major nation in the world is experiencing the fact that there is no obvious solution to its serious problems? No nation has been capable of postulating even a reasonable theoretical solution. So be it. From a cosmic perspective, it is regrettably appropriate that the great power blocs of the world don't seem to have a clue about what they're doing. The dilemma, you see, contains within itself its own transcendent solution. Paradoxically, an articulable, believable formula or logical, reasonable strategy would be in our worst possible long-term interests. Such a *rational* approach, if it existed, would draw us deeper into the materialistic mind-field of deception that downplays the emergent truth of collective inner spiritual reality.

With all the lies and justifications stripped away, it is clear that the reality of First World financial karma is forcing a choice between 'globalism' – exploitation of the Earth and 'planetism', the recognition of and need for unity and interdependence with the Earth and each other.

The present cultural system is no longer appropriate to the true needs of the planet or most of its people. And for the species that we have not driven to extinction, life is no longer tolerable. What is really at stake is the life-styles of the rich and famous – that is, the countries of the First World (primarily the Northern hemisphere at the expense of the rest of the World. It is more than doubtful that the collision between capital and ecological survival will be resolved other than in the favour of Her, the Great Mother, Gaia – the Earth. Within our deepest spiritual knowing, we need to recognize that when the time of reckoning comes, as it will, there will be – can be – no fathomable problem-solving formula.

How *many* of nature's laws can be violated, for how long, before there is a problem? What constitutes a problem; for whom, and why? Is the problem 'significant'; and what constitutes significant, for whom? and why? How much of the natural world and how many of its life systems can be polluted, exploited, destroyed? Is there a threshold; and what constitutes a threshold? How do we know it has been reached? Whom does it affect, and why? How do you unscramble eggs? Because of these questions, short-term solutions such as pesticide use, chemicals, nuclear energy, etc., have become long-term problems, like an ever-expanding bubble about to burst. By the time everyone agrees that the bubble theoretically could burst, might burst, will in fact burst; that it's overdue, beginning to burst, is bursting ... *now* ...

That is an initiatory crisis.

It thrusts us, 'splat!' nose-to-mirror-snot-on-glass with our moment of truth, forcing us to realize a relationship with our individual and collective Centre, and compelling us to attune to what is growing inside and between us. The synergy of the collective Self is the source of our solutions. And it demands that we trust the process and the wisdom!

In *The Pentagon of Power,* Lewis Mumford describes the evolution of totalitarian political structures, saying that the only thing that can possibly save humanity is for God to rise up inside the human soul in the midst of great catastrophe. And that is exactly what many people will experience throughout the 1990s. With the poor and needy of the world already suffering beyond belief, catastrophe may be necessary to tear away the denials and delusions that insulate comfortable people and spoliational lifestyles. It certainly will induce a fertile psychic climate, one that traumatizes deeply enough to draw the liberating value of the hitherto dormant Self to the fore.

What Teilhard de Chardin calls a 'universal distress' is, in fact, the necessary turbulence to bring up the Christ-Self in the collective consciousness as the requisite resolution on a whole new level. But that could not happen if our rational minds knew we had the answer. Carl Jung addresses this phenomenon in very believable psychological terms – namely, that when the ego's sense of capability and security breaks down, it produces psychological turmoil, the resolution of which reconstellates according to the archetype of the Self.

That is basically what the initiation process is about. And it is the greatest possible initiation, because it is a sublime planetary process we will all experience as one humanity. What will be available to us by the year 2012 AD will be so rich and deep it is hard for us, this side of the century's turning, to fully conceptualize.

Planetary initiation is an event we can expect when physical conditions synchronize with the rhythms of the universe. It is a time when spiritual consciousness aligns with the appropriate dynamics of the cosmos, and the people of the Earth, the Earth itself, and the solar system experience a shift; an awesome, majestic, eschatalogical heave into the fourth-dimensional reality that awaits.

In summary, the astrological forecast for the near future is one of purification and growing unity. Externally, we are being prepared to become one people, a global family sharing a home planet under a political system of growing world unity. And internally? Internally, we are being prepared for planetary initiation!

As the millennium culminates, the fledgling Phoenix will preen the ashes of death and destruction from its beautiful feathers and fly off into the settling dust of a murky sunrise. A new culture *will* emerge. After all, who can hold back the dawn?

15

Maya Prophecy

'I implore Hunab Ku to help you understand what the
Maya knew and used so that the sacred symbols may
fulfill the purpose for which they were created.'
– Hunbatz Men, Daykeeper

When we look back into the receding wake of time, we usually prefer to see something solid, some archaeological
residue that lets us know the past really was there. Historical sites are well-regarded. Museum quality artifacts are
good. Records are good – hide, bark, reed, or mud tablets
that tell us something specific. Looking back further, an
unverifiable account by someone long since dead – that's
not so good. That is where the grey area sets in and squint-
ing begins. Then, there are the shapes and sounds that come
to us through the mist; we believe or feel that something was
there, but can't be sure. That is where myth and legend converge. It's a fascinating domain penetrable by fine-tuning
our intuitive faculties. Those who wish to explore beyond
that point do so without compass.

We can only answer questions like, 'Who were the
Maya?' or, 'Where did they come from?' by peering into
that grey area. The poetic response is that the Maya basically came out of the mist and returned into it. What happened in between was like an undulation of the back of the

Earth-serpent that arose around 2000 BC and majestically bore the Maya to great heights.

Archaeologists believe that the Maya, and other ancient peoples of the Americas, originated from Asia and crossed the Bering land bridge to Alaska about thirty thousand years ago. Vast numbers of small hunting bands are thought to have roamed south, following the migration routes of the great game herds. Then, about twelve thousand years ago, the glaciers melted. Sea levels rose, the land bridge became submerged, weather gradually changed, and the large game animals became extinct. Hunting was eventually replaced by gathering, and, as cultivation skills were developed, the Maya settled into the patterns that held them to the land. Their great civilization grew within the general area that ranged from the cool of Guatemala through the tropical lowlands of southern Mexico, Honduras, Belize, and on to the humid Yucatán peninsula of southeastern Mexico.[1]

But the prophet Edgar Cayce had a different perspective.[2] He said, the people who became known as the Maya were part of a massive exodus from Atlantis around 28,000 BC. He perceived that three great disturbances caused the breakup and subsequent submergence in stages of that great mid-Atlantic continent. The Cayce readings indicate that prior to the first inundation, the Earth's rotation around the sun had been different, revolving around the Pleiades and Arcturus. According to Cayce, representatives of that fated land mass fled in airships and watercraft and settled the Yucatan. The migrations fanned out to many parts of the world, but Mesoamerica and Egypt in particular. It is also significant that Cayce said the records of the Atlantean civilization (i.e., their highest knowledge and science) were all 'One' but divided into three repositories: Egypt, the Bimini area of the Caribbean (believed to have been the southwestern tip of Atlantis), and the Yucatan. The prophet declared in various readings that in the future, when the consciousness of the people reached the appropriate level of the initiate, each of these repositories would be discovered. He implied that this could occur by 1998.

The histories tell us that at the peak of Maya civilization, around 843 A.D., the powerful driving force that had sustained Maya culture lost its momentum and collapsed. Because it happened comparatively suddenly, at the interface between two great cycles of Maya calendric time, it is believed that a particular function had been served and that the Maya intentionally disincorporated their centres with great deliberation. Buildings under construction appear to have been left unfinished, their wall murals frozen in time, half completed. We can never know for sure why and how this happened, but it is known that major Maya cities were abandoned, that the population of several million people declined drastically, and that the jungle greenly enveloped the towering stone structures as if slowly to digest them. The Maya people continued, but their flourishing civilization did not. Toltec and Aztec empires followed close behind.

Olmec 1200 BC–600 AD. The earliest developed culture in Mexico, centred in La Venta.

Maya 2000–600 BC, preclassic era.
  300–843 AD, classic era, ended mysteriously.
  850–1400 AD, post-classic era.

Toltec 750–1250 AD. Mexican tribe who built an empire based at Tollan (now Tula, Hidalgo).

Aztec 1325–1525 AD. From Tenochtitlan, their empire dominated all Mexico until the Spanish conquerors perpetrated genocide upon them.

Mixtec 700–1525 AD. Inhabited southern Mexico. The last people dominated by the Aztecs.

Zapotec 100 BC–1525 AD. Inhabited southern coastal regions of Mexico.

Most of what is known today about the Maya results from the archaeological excavations that wrested the monuments from the jungle, from on-site restoration of the ceremonial complexes, and discovery of their function and purpose. The great volumes of fan-folded books that contained the records, wisdom, and science of these people were zealously destroyed by the Spanish missionaries. Three generations of scholars worked to decipher the precious writings of the few remaining codices and text fragments and to interpret Maya calendric information. We also owe a tremendous debt of gratitude to the vision of such modern interpreters of the ancient wisdom as Maya 'daykeeper' Hunbatz Men, Tony Shearer, Frank Waters, José Argüelles and Barbara Hand Clow.[3]

The Maya were a remarkable people – productive, industrious, creative. One has only to observe the intricacy of their complex hieroglyphic writing, highly stylized art, and the well-planned ceremonial and administrative centres of their cities, to appreciate their skill and attention to detail. With hard stone implements, they constructed steep stepped-stone pyramids, temple complexes, observatories, palaces and ceremonial centres. No wheeled vehicles or carts pulled their quarried stone, and no draft animals or beasts of burden assisted their building labour or agriculture, for horses and cattle were unknown to the Maya. They used an ingenious numbering system that enabled them to administer their huge city populations, and pioneered the mathematical concept of zero. Zero was written in the shape of the eye because, to the Maya, it also had spiritual implications and represented the Great Mystery. Maya shaman Hunbatz Men says the zero is linked to the symbol of the beginning, the Milky Way.

No Native American culture understood the heavens better than the Maya, or left such intricate records of its discoveries. Temple complexes and observatories were carefully designed by astronomer priests and geomancers. These buildings were erected in alignment with celestial bodies of practical and religious importance and keyed to the geomantic features of the land. And the astronomy they practised was so precise, it served as the basis for sophisticated understanding of a planetary world picture, the world's best calendar, and an unsurpassed system of time recording. Unlike most other early cultures, the Maya understood that 'the morning star' and 'evening star' were the same planet – Venus, in different positions. Without telescopes or precision instruments, the astronomer priests were also able to compile accurate tables to predict both solar and lunar eclipses as well as equinox and solstice times. They computed the distance of the Earth's revolution around the sun to an accuracy within a thousandth of a decimal point – but the Maya themselves did not use decimals.

To twentieth century minds, the Maya appear to have been a culture obsessively invested in the subject of time and its computation. What we are beginning to understand about them, in that respect, stems from the fact that enough evolved people are now interested in what the Maya were all about, and are beginning to decipher the language of meaning contained in the monuments, codices and calendars. The calendric information outlined below is in abbreviated form to convey a sense of the scope of Maya time and as a basis for understanding the prophetic calendric implications discussed later in the chapter. If figures fascinate you, read on. If not, be thankful you're not a Maya.

The calendar used throughout the early cultures of Mesoamerica, thought to be of great antiquity, was greatly improved and refined by the Maya. In this calendar, two separate kinds of year ran concurrently, the solar and the sacred. To the Maya, the mundane, solar calendar year was *Haab*. It was used for agricultural and practical purposes and consisted of 365.242129 days (thought to be more accurate than our Gregorian calendar of 365.242500 days). This year was comprised of eighteen months containing twenty days each, plus the five remaining 'unlucky' days added at the end. Each day had its own associations and omens.

The sacred year calendar, however, was used for ritual and ceremonial purposes, and lasted 260 days. It was called the

Tzolkin. This year represented the intermeshing of a small wheel with a number sequence 1-13 inside a larger wheel of 20 glyphs depicting individually named days. Each glyph projected a unique significance and quality to the day it represented. For instance, the calendar originally began with 'Alligator,' because the world was said to be created on the back of an alligator. 'Reed' synchronized calendric cycles and marked new beginnings. After the Spanish conquest, the calendar was changed to begin with the Reed glyph. 'Flower' was the last glyph, because the creation process ends in beauty. Using this system, a day with the same name and number could recur only once in each complete cycle of 260 days. The *Tzolkin* can also be regarded as a periodic table of galactic frequencies, because it is a fractal of the 'vague' count of the 26,000 year precession of the equinoxes.[4] The 26,000 year cycle of the sun's revolution around the Pleiades, the 26,000,000 year periodicity of extinctions reported in an extensive literature related to comet showers, and possible pole shift, as Earth recurrently passes through the Oort cloud,[5] and other celestial cycles related by periods of time, the factor of which is 260.[6] José Argüelles has named this calendar the 'Harmonic Module', because the 260 possible permutations of the 13 numbers and 20-day glyphs accommodate every possible computation of all the calendric measurements and movements. The

Tzolkin was also used as a means of divination and served as the basis of cultural knowledge.

When the *Haab* and *Tzolkin* calendars interfaced with each other in a complete 'calendar round' once every fifty-years, it was called 'the Binding of the Years'. Five such encounters completed one cycle of the 260-year *Tzolkin*. Therefore, a traditional Maya day always consisted of a combination of *Tzolkin* and *Haab* dates. The Maya cosmology held that there were thirteen heaven and nine hell realms. Therefore, calendar rounds were aggregated into alternating 'Heaven' and 'Hell' cycles. Thirteen of the fifty-two-year cycles (676 years) constituted a cycle of Thirteen Heavens; nine of them (468 years) comprised a Nine Hells cycle.

20 *Kin* (days) = 1 *Uinal* (20-day month)

18 *Uinal* (months) = 1 *Tun* (360 days); plus a *Vayeb* of five 'unlucky' days.

20 *Tun* = 1 *Katun* (7,200 days or 19 years, 73 days)

20 *Katun* = 1 *Baktun* (144,000 days or 394 years, 52 days)

20 *Baktun* = 1 *Pictun* (2,880,000 days or 7,890 years, 41 days)

20 *Pictun* = 1 *Calabtun* (57,600,000 days or 157,808 years, 21 days)

20 *Calabtun* = 1 *Kinchiltun* (1,152,000,000 days or 3,156,164 years)

20 *Kinchiltun* = 1 *Alautun* (23,040,000,000 days or 63,312,328 years)

The Maya 'long count', details of which are found in texts of the classic era, divided time into periods of thirteen *bak*tuns (144,000 days each) for a total of 5,125.40 years (in our reckoning). *This* is the figure that immediately concerns us. It is one-fifth the number of years in the exact Maya computation of the precession of the equinoxes – 25,627 years. Each of the 5,125.40 year segments constitutes a 'great cycle', an 'Age' or world epoch ruled by a different sun. We shall examine this concept more closely later in the chapter.

Beyond the *baktuns*, the higher time periods of *pictuns*, *calabtuns* and *kinchiltuns* were used primarily for rearview projection of time into expanses of history so vast they thrust uncomfortably against one's boggle threshold. One calibration at Quiriguá, Guatemala, known as the Mukul-mam glyph, records a date 10,240,000,000,000 years ago that José Argüelles (bless his heart) jokes is so far back, it's probably in the future! When one considers how the abstruse mathematics and astronomy of the Maya culture appear to have been integrated with metaphysical cosmology and mythology, it is nothing short of awesome. In Frank Waters' *Mexico Mystique* it is suggested that such an interweaving 'could have been a shorthand to describe a galactic type of science of a different dimension from the conventional physics we use to describe earthly phenomena'.[7] Other researchers also took up the challenge of that postulate, and by the time the global event called 'Harmonic Convergence' occurred in 1987, the full magnificence of what the Maya may *really* have been up to was beginning to dawn. Their elaborate record-keeping and calendric systems seem to have been an ingenious method by which they were able to plot and synchronize cycles of terrestrial and galactic significance within a 'master plan,' a clue to which had been preserved in the legends:[8]

> Thirteen Heavens of decreasing choice,
> Nine Hells of increasing doom,
> and the Tree of Life shall blossom with a fruit
> never before known in the creation.
> And that fruit shall be the New Spirit of Man.

The cycle of thirteen Heavens that followed this prophecy began in the year 843 A.D. This year is believed to have coincided with the end of the classic Maya era, a period marked by the mysterious abandonment of the Maya city centres described above.

The cultural mythos that informed the calendric cali-braons of Mesoamerica was related to a cosmo-magical con-

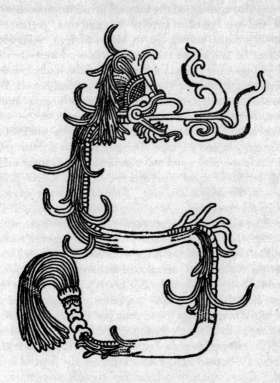

Feathered serpent

ception involving Quetzalcoatl – the feathered serpent. Quetzalcoatl was a god. He was also a mythic archetype of profound dimensions, as well as a human ruler, high priest, and culture hero who established an idyllic empire upon highly evolved principles. Although Quetzalcoatl was Zapotec, he became the prototype for the lineage of the Toltec ruling elite, at least nine of whom are known to have held the title of 'Quetzalcoatl'. To the Maya, he was known as 'Kukulcan'. Quetzalcoatl was many things to many cultures. Primarily, he was identified with the planet Venus, and as the god of wind from whom issued the breath of life.

He was also considered the cause of germination within the seed, and was linked to fertility. It is said that Quetzalcoatl brought unique knowledge to Mesoamerican civilization, and that he taught the early peoples how to measure time and arrange their calendars. He was also the lord of healing and magical herbs, the symbol of learning and beauty. But, above all, he was symbolic of the force of cosmic intelligence, the epitome of transcendent consciousness.

The name Quetzalcoatl is derived from the quetzal bird of Guatemala and Mexico. The quetzal had golden-green and scarlet plumage, and was considered the most beautiful of all birds. 'Quetzal' also means precious. 'Coatl' is serpent. In the Maya language, 'Kukulcan' means approximately the same thing. According to Hunbatz Men, 'Ku' is sacred, or God. 'Kul' is coccyx, the base of the spine, where latent spiritual energy resides. 'Can' means serpent. 'Kukulcan' therefore is synonymous with 'kundalini' – which is what the Kukulcan/Quetzalcoatl archetype is all about, of course. To be iconographically correct, however, the god Quetzalcoatl is not himself the feathered serpent, but the one who emerges from the serpent, just as the spirit emerges from the body through the top of the head, and the Morning Star emerges from the horizon.[9] Maya art is replete with motifs of a human head emanating from the jaws of a serpent.[10] Contemporary scholarship regards this emerging head as a symbol of enlightenment or transcendence.

Interestingly, the Aztec word 'coatl' means 'twin' as well as 'serpent'. Now, Venus as the morning star was Quetzalcoatl, Lord of the Dawn. Venus as the evening star was Xólotl, Quetzalcoatl's sinister twin, who, like the twin of our own dual nature, represents the darker side of human nature. Therefore, 'precious twin' is another interpretation of the name Quetzalcoatl.

Within the various surviving codices and texts of historic Mesoamerican cultures, there are a great many versions of the Quetzalcoatl myth. It is a vitally important myth, because it is essentially the story of the conflict between darkness and light, matter and spirit, order and chaos – the eternal struggle that rises to the fore at the end of every Age, and upon which our survival beyond the twentieth century depends. The generic rendering of the story, however, tells of Quetzalcoatl's mother, who swallowed an emerald and was impregnated by the power engendered by the spirit of the stone.' But, according to the *Codex Vienna*, she was a virgin impregnated by the deity. Similarities exist among many of the world's great spiritual archetypes, not the least of which is a virgin birth. Another account describes Quetzalcoatl as the offspring of parents who, like those of the Celtic King Arthur (an identical archetype, the major events of whose life mirror those of Quetzalcoatl), each belonged to opposing, warring factions.

This special child, named Topiltzin ('our Lord,' or 'our Prince') was born on the Maya date Ce Acatl, meaning 1-Reed, on the first day of the third Heaven related to the above prophecy, or 947 AD. The priests of the temple city of Monte Alban overlooking the Oaxaca Valley were keepers of the sacred tablets of the Order of Quetzalcoatl, and they had been expecting his birth. He reportedly lived fifty-two years (or one complete calendar round of the *Haab and Tzolkin*), and died as the year 1-Reed came around again, 999 AD, the first day of the fourth Heaven.

Under the instruction of the high gods, according to the *Codex Vindobonesis*, Quetzalcoatl introduced fasting and confession among the people, and created a magnificent sacred centre, which became the great city of Tula, or Tollan, in Hidalgo. It was at this place, the *Florentine Codex* says, that Topiltzin Quetzalcoatl first brought the true arts of civilization to his people. Both 'Tula' and 'Tollan' were derived from the word 'Toltecatl,' meaning 'reed' or 'place of reeds'. It also was from that word that the Toltecs derived their name, for it was descriptive of a refined person of great knowledge and artistic ability.[12]

Over time, Tula became the capital city of the Toltec empire, and flourished between 900 and 1100 AD. Like its founder, the city was historically real, yet archetypal in its design and function. Tula was regarded as the centre of the world, the opening toward the supernatural world of the vertical, as well as the pivot of the horizontal sociopolitical cosmos.[13] Like Babylon before it, and other great centres of empire in the past, Tula was cosmologically and geomantically harmonized with the energies of heaven, Earth, and the underworld. It was the sacred centre from which issued a way of life that perfectly integrated the rhythms of the cosmos and human affairs. The *Historia Tolteca-Chichimeca* describes Tula in terms of a highly organized city state of cosmobiological proportions, and allied with 'twenty other nations ... that represented its fingers and toes'. Like the temples of India and Egypt designed upon the proportions of the human body, and like Nebuchadnezzar's vision of an image whose feet with ten toes represented ten nations of the last world kingdom (ours!), Tula was also conceived and designed as a living body.

And, because the king embodied the principle of enlightened consciousness, he was the father image, and also the conduit through which cosmological order emanated into the surrounding environment of the perfect city, dedicated to peace and harmony. Tony Shearer's *Lord of the Dawn* says the people of Tula had learned that the secret of peace was the unity of all things. Quetzalcoatl performed many miracles and ruled with such purity of heart that his fame and influence fanned out like the rays of the sun. From him, the people of Tula learned the philosophy of the Tree of Life, sacred laws, and a way of life that entered into their inner hearts. He entrusted his secrets to an order of priests who were diviners and prophets, who practised the arts and sciences, healed the sick and administered the sacraments. In the religion of Quetzalcoatl, people learned not only how to raise kundalini, but how to open their heart to the light of the sun. In *The Serpent's Ascent*, William Irwin Thompson has written, 'the opening of the heart chakra to the light is one of the sublime religious experiences, and this image was, and still is today used by the Sufis as the insignium of their practice.' Opening one's heart means, at the very least, the willingness to feel. At best, it connects us, as Native

Americans would say, with 'all our relations' of the greater whole.

By all accounts, Quetzalcoatl looked different from his own native people in that he had a beard, and certain accounts say he was pale-skinned, like a white man. In this regard one should bear in mind that the place where myth and reality merge is usually in the region of synchronicity. A parallel appears to exist between the man, the myth, and the heavens, the connecting link of which appears to be the beard. As discussed in the 'Astrological Cycles' chapter, the sector of the heavens presiding over the area as far north as *Panuco* in Mexico and as far south as *Panama* is the constellation of Capricorn – associated with Pan, the bearded Greek nature god who was half goat and half man. Midway between Panuco and Panama is Maya*pan*, the capital of Yucatán, founded by the bearded Kukulcan, the Maya version of Quetzalcoatl. The constellation of Capricorn was called Capra, 'the Bearded One', by many ancient peoples, and Nuccu, 'the Beard', in Peru.[14] From the very earliest known times, the sun was considered to be reborn each year when it entered the sign of Capricorn immediately after the winter solstice. This celestial event has been celebrated in annual festivals throughout history by native peoples all over the world. In Peru it was known as 'the Festival of the Beard', and men wore bearded masks symbolizing masculinity and the seasonally renewed reproductive powers of the sun. The association of the bearded Quetzalcoatl/ Kukulcan with Capricorn, the Bearded One, as regenerator of the sun, would have been consistent with his function as God-king-priest, regenerator of Cosmos.

As 'the birthplace of the Sun', Capricorn was the 'sea-goat' hybrid whose fishtail enabled it to live in a cave beneath the ocean prior to the winter solstice. The goat part enabled it to climb (like a goat up a mountain) high into the sky after the solstice. The early Maya appear to have incorporated the symbols of their celestial counterpart within their mythos. Interestingly, Hunbatz Men says that according to the historian Berossus, 'The Maya descended in the form of fish, bringing their culture [to Chaldea].'[15] And Alberto Ruz Lhuillier, who in 1952 discovered the late seventh-century tomb of the illustrious Maya ruler Pacal beneath Palenque's Temple of Inscriptions, wrote in his journal that under the carved coffer lid was an inner stone cover, 'about seven feet long and thirty inches wide. It was of a peculiar curved outline, with one end flared like a fish-tail.'[16] And Temple's *The Sirius Mystery* documents many historical references to pre-Flood founders of civilization, fish-men who arrived from the stars. They were said to have descended into and arisen out of the sea in their craft, which no doubt gave rise to the idea of fish-folk or aquatic beings. All this bespeaks of Capricorn as intricately associated with the Maya, and of their possible origin from beyond the Earth. Although it is not within the scope of this chapter to develop this aspect of the Maya, it is, nevertheless, an integral part of the Maya mystique. The Dogon tribe of North Africa call the fish-men 'the Monitors'. And that is what the Maya did best – monitor and calibrate galactic time cycles for the planet.

Meanwhile, back at the Maya ranch so to speak, the story of Quetzalcoatl continues as trouble stirs in paradise. Enter Tezcatlipoca, Quetzalcoatl's brother, Lord of the Nine Hells. Like the biblical Lucifer and the Egyptian Set, Tez-catlipoca had not always been a negative entity, but became so over time, by popular demand, as an externalization of the human 'shadow'. It's an unpleasant job, but someone, or some god, always has had to do it. Consistent with his image as the polar opposite of Quetzalcoatl, Tezcatlipoca resided at the pole star region – which is why he was also called the Dark Lord of the North. He was the Jaguar God of the night sky, the demiurge who ruled the surface of the Earth-from the dark canopy of his lofty abode. As the deity of war, of magic (specifically black), and sacrifices (specifically human), Tezcatlipoca was both powerful and feared. And so it came about that Quetzalcoatl's adversary conspired to bring about the downfall of his righteous brother. Certain sorcerers under his direction sought to institute human sacrifice to the sun. But, as High Priest, Quetzalcoatl always rejected the idea outright, until finally his enemies came up with a scheme to entrap and discredit him.'[17]

A plan was devised to trick Quetzalcoatl into getting drunk on a potent potion of *pulque* at a religious festival. This was not easy, of course, but the brew was strong, and the terrible dark instinctive power from the unconscious that was the nature of Tezcatlipoca temporarily seized and overcame Quetzalcoatl. As High Priest, he was naturally celibate, pious and a role model for the people. A crisis of confidence in the ruler ensued when it was revealed that in his drunken stupor he had unwittingly had a 'romantic interlude' with a woman – who also happened to be his own sister! Another version points to the witch goddess as the decoy who laced the priest-king's drink with magic mushrooms, then seduced him into a depraved orgy. Either way, when Quetzalcoatl recovered and realized that he had broken the sacred traditions, he languished in terrible remorse.

The purpose of celibacy, of course, is to conserve sexual energy in order to raise the *kundalini*, sublimate (make sublime) the sexual energy into spirituality, and create enlightened awareness. By inducing Quetzalcoatl to sabotage the basis of his own spiritual evolvement by dissipating his sexual energy, Tezcatlipoca effectively pulled the plug on him. It appears that Quetzalcoatl felt constrained to abdicate his kingship and that he voluntarily prepared to go into exile.

When Quetzalcoatl, as the centre that controlled the periphery, 'fell from grace', so did the immediate environment. It is said that the people of Tula forgot the wisdom they had been taught, and that this was the secret work of Tezcatlipoca and the Jaguar societies. Essential order dissipated, and enemies invaded. Cosmos was again assailed by chaos. After the fall of Tula, at least six other cities are known to have integrated the social complexities of regional kingdoms, city states and empires around the traditions and meanings associated with Quetzalcoatl, but all fell short of the glory that was Tula.

It is known that after Tula fell, Chichén Itzá and Mayapan were founded and ruled by a king-priest known to the Maya as Kukulcan. It seems that he instituted human sacrifice to the sun at Chichén Itzá, leading one to believe that the Kukulcan lineage had become corrupt and that the title 'Kukulcan' no longer guided action but continued to sanctify authority.[18] Unfortunately, it wasn't very hard for Tezcatlipoca to corrupt the high teachings. Wherever there were those who refused to see beyond the tip of the finger that pointed to God, he encouraged their literalism. Thus, the sublime practice of opening one's heart *chakra* to the sun was replaced by the 'only' logical interpretation of the teachings – hearts being ritually torn out of chest cavities with flint knives and held, still beating, up to the sun. It was the fundamentalist version of 'giving your heart to God'.

As the story ends, Quetzalcoatl prepares to leave his beloved city, prophesying to his people that he will return in the future to establish a new order[19] at which time his doctrine would be received and his sons would be lords and owners of the lands, while they (the people of Tula) and their descendants would undergo many calamities and persecutions …'[20] He said he would come to close the last Heaven cycle and open the final Hell cycle of this, the fifth world. As he departed, Quetzalcoatl told the people that when he returned he would come from the East, like the Morning Star.

The *Anales de Cuauhtitlán* state that prior to his death,

Quetzalcoatl went into seclusion and made himself arrows. When he reappeared, the people were able to tell 'according to a sign' who the arrows would be used against, according to the day on which Quetzalcoatl returned to claim his kingdom. It was known that if he came on the date 1-Reed, he would strike down kings.

In the mythic version of his departure from Tula, the defeated king-priest sailed off into the Caribbean sunset on a raft of snakes, and as he neared the horizon his heart ignited and flew up to the heavens, where it became the morning star. The other account of Quetzalcoatl the enlightened one tells of him returning full circle to the Valley of his birth, where he lived and taught the philosophy of the Tree in the years preceding his death. He was buried beneath the 'Tree of Life,' the el Tule tree near Oaxaca. But that was not the ending of-the story, or of Quetzalcoatl.

Ten Heavens later, a bearded white man arrived from the East. The last time anyone had seen a bearded white man, it had been Quetzalcoatl! The Spanish explorer Hernán Cortés landed with his men at Tenochtitlán, now Vera Cruz. To him it was Good Friday, April 21, 1519 A.D. But for the Aztecs and their emperor, Montezuma, it was not a good Friday. It was Ce Acatl, day 1-Reed, year 1-Reed – the beginning of the nine Hells cycle and the prophesied date of Quetzalcoatl's return.

If the actions of Cortés on behalf of the Spanish crown and the Catholic faith smelled more like Tezcatlipoca than Quetzalcoatl, it was because the man beneath the armour was not the anticipated, messianic incarnation. It was Quetzalcoatl in his wrathful/purifying aspect, wearing the mask of his dreaded alterego; the dark Lord of the Nine Hells himself – Tezcatlipoca. In *Lord of the Dawn,* author Shearer writes that the native holy men, the 'keepers of the book', knew him to be a great master who wore a strange mask that he would remove by the end of the ninth Hell, and that everyone would be surprised to see who he really was.

The rest is history. The Hells began with a bang – the roar of cannon, screams, the clash of steel – death and disease awash in the mud of the Spanish army and their horses. In their wake, Christendom was established. Genocide was perpetrated upon the population. Montezuma was murdered. The Aztec empire was destroyed. Within the first 'Hell' period of fifty-two years from the arrival of the Spanish, an estimated population of twenty-five million people between the Isthmus of Tehuantepec and the Valley of Mexico had been reduced to less than one million. The Maya were among the fiercest resistors of the Spanish. But, ultimately, some two hundred million people of the Americas came under Spanish domination. The best anyone can make of the conquest is that it was a 'purification' that allowed the Christian ethos – similar, in its pure form, to that of Quetzalcoatl – to replace Aztec culture in fulfillment of the prophesy.

Insight into the nature of cyclical time is provided by Octavio Paz, who explains, 'Cyclic time is another way toward absorption, transformation, and sublimation. The date that recurs is a return of previous time, an immersion in a past which is at once that of each individual and that of the group. As the wheel of time revolves, it allows the society to recover buried or repressed psychic structures so as to reincorporate them in a present that is also a past.'[21] We are reminded that in psychoanalysis, the cure is often associated with recovery of a forgotten memory, but within cyclical time, it is not memory that calls up the past, but the past itself that returns for healing, completion and apotheosis.

It is with this concept in mind that we proceed to examine the five world Suns, or world Ages, of the Maya. For, as the wheels of Maya-based calendric time churn up the wake of history before us, we would do well to heed the *I Ching's* wisdom about 'Revolution' – that order and clarity appear in the apparently chaotic changes of the seasons if their regularity is noted by marking off the passages of time so that people are able to adjust themselves in advance to the demands of the different times.

The ancients were of the conviction that order, once established, had to be carefully maintained, for it was

Xochicalco   Xochimilco   Malinalco

Acalpixan   Tenochtitlan

always in imminent danger of being engulfed by chaos; which is why the Mesoamerican peoples took such pains in their calendric calibrations. According to their calendars, four previous Ages, each ruled by a different sun, had come and gone. And each of those Ages ended in a cataclysm that was symbolized by the calendar glyph that represented it: 4-Jaguar, 4-Wind, 4-Rain, 4-Water. Thus, jaguars, wind, rain, and water were the agents of each Age's destruction.

The Maya texts designate Quetzalcoatl as the postflood deity who established the present Age of the fifth Sun in 3113 BC. Historically, something important obviously was happening at that time. Within a few years of each other, cultures of antiquity were registering big change and new beginnings. As stated previously, each Age comprises a Maya 'great cycle' of 5,125.40 years, which means that our present Age of the fifth Sun is due to culminate with the graduation of the 'life wave', (described earlier in this book) by December 21, 2012 AD. The duration of our 5,125-year Age is the time it takes for Homo Christos to emerge (like the transcendent human heads emerging out of serpent's jaws) from Homo sapiens.

The four directions and the stability of the physical plane, geometricized as a square, crop up everywhere in the ancient world, and as the central motif of the Maya-based Aztec calendar. This calendar places our current and fifth world Age, the synthesis of the previous four, in the very centre. It is identified by the glyph 'Ollin', meaning 'movement', or 'shift'. At the centre of the calendar, all five Ages are incorporated within, and comprise, an Ollin/movement symbol. The Ollin glyph is really an ideograph (outlined for emphasis) shaped as a turtle. This particular glyph was central to other calendars of the Americas, and is, we surmise, contiguous with the Native American concept of the world as Turtle Island – a great turtle who would roll over on its back at the end of the Age. Once on its back, a turtle is helpless and cannot right itself without help. In the Maya mythology 'First Father' was reborn out of the turtle shell when it split apart (as in the 'Ollin' movement/shift of the turtle shell). He then set about establishing a new order between heaven, Earth, and the creation of a new time. This is the myth that is about to repeat – by the end of this Age – 2012 AD. The Ollin/movement glyph is number seventeen in the Aztec *Tzolkin*. The same number in the Maya *Tzolkin* is that of the head of a turtle called 'Caban', meaning 'Earth'. 'Planet

Earth', which appeared in some of the codices, is depicted by the same turtle head, and likely is the etymological root for the Maya word 'Bacab' of which Bishop Diego Landa wrote. In *Relación de las Cosas de Yucatan,* Landa reported that, according to his Maya sources, the Bacabs 'were four brothers whom God placed, when he created the world, at the four points of it, holding up the sky so that it should not fall. [In Egypt, the four sons of Horus performed the same function.] They also said of these Bacabs that they escaped when the world was destroyed by the deluge.' The Bacabs, the first of whom has a man-sized turtle shell upon his back, are depicted on a column at El Castillo, in the temple of Kukulcan at Chichén Itzá.

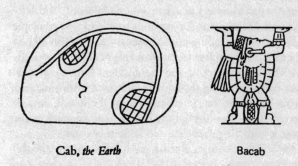

Cab, *the Earth*   Bacab

Indeed, the enigmatic egg-shaped 'omphalos' stones found throughout Central America were used as geodetic markers and are, in fact, representations of turtles. Iconography of India also shows the world supported on the back of a tortoise. All of this illustrates in a rather succinct way how well the archetypal images of macrocosm and microcosm match, and how, as Hermes Trismegistus had assured us: 'That which is above is like that which is below.'

It would be a mistake to presume that all peoples of antiquity believed the Earth was *literally* situated on the back of a turtle. Ancient wisdom was always symbolic and Earth-centred and, unlike our formulae, easy to remember indefinitely. Plato, who was an adherent of the Pythagorean school had said, 'The Earth, viewed from above, resembles a ball sown from twelve pieces of skin.' And so, the faceted turtle shell was an entirely reasonable facsimile of the Earth with its tectonic plates and geometric grid features.

Although traditional interpretation of Ollin/movement as 'earthquake' is supported by other prophecies as part of the Earth-cleansing process in the future, 'Ollin' should be understood *primarily* as movement in the sense of 'shift' – the energizing principle of which is Hunab Ku, translated as 'One, Giver of Movement and Measure'. He is the architect of the universe, as well as the operant creative principle symbolized in Maya art by a G-shaped spiral.[22] It is this spiral that describes the above five Ages. José Argüelles explains Hunab Ku as not just a name, but a description of purpose and activity as well. 'Movement corresponds to energy, the principles of life and all-pervading consciousness imminent in all phenomena. Measure refers to the principle of rhythm, periodicity, and form accounting for the different limiting qualities which energy assumes through its different transformations.' Hunab Ku is the centre of everything, be it cell, seed, or galaxy. Hunab Ku is the light within the human mind, within matter, within the galactic core and points beyond.

The 'Shift', of course, is what this book is about – the shift of human consciousness (the 'ol' of 'ollin' means 'consciousness'), the shift of Earth's geophysical poles, and the corresponding shift of our whole solar system into a new evolutionary phase with strong implications for a dimensional shift – one synchronized to the greater universal realities that lie beyond earthbound limitations. For this to happen, we must be open to the changes that are bringing about unified planetary consciousness. The esoteric purpose and function of the Maya calendar is to facilitate and track the requisite multiple shift.

When the atomic bomb was dropped in 1945, it brought down karma and prophecy along with the fallout. Subsequent underground testing disturbed the planetary grid; changes occurred in the Earth's weather and its rotation; we began shredding the web of life, basically to support profits; people began losing touch with the Earth and their instinctive knowingness. One senses the gathering storm and the chaos returning once more ... And it is here, at *this point*, that a Shift is occurring to realign us with what is real, important, necessary and without which the world will go to hell in the proverbial handbasket (although I have never met anyone who knows what a handbasket is, other than that it's something you go to hell in).

Amidst all the Twinkies and Ding Dongs, environmental degradation, MTV, broadcast commercials, rush-hour traffic, Dow Jones averages, crime in the streets, high cost of living, Ninja Turtles and nuclear warheads, something else is going on.

The 'People of Light' are being quickened.

Quickening is what happens when the embryo within the egg is enlivened and begins to stir in its becoming. The compelling force of the calendar's last *katun*, 1992–2012 AD, is not likely to be spent without accomplishing the transformation or disintegration of corruption within the traditional world order. For those who choose the old ways, it will be the end of their world. For those whose pledged allegiance to the sacredness of life and the planet, no matter what, the sound the old makes as it crumbles will be the sound of one egg cracking.

This point in time, even as you read this, is also where ancient and modern Maya cosmology is converging with the grand evolutionary Master Plan for planet Earth. It is clear that knowledge of this Plan and responsibility for its execution is shared by many of the world's major wisdom teachings.

In 1973, *The Keys of Enoch* were given, one Key of which was to catalyze a crucial part of the Master Plan by the end of the last Hell cycle.[23] These teachings of sixty-four Keys, on seven levels, were given for the quickening of the 'People of Light'. Enoch (synonymous with Thoth), the master initiator of Light, addressed the evolutionary implications of Earth's dilemma and need for a return to centre: Key 204 (numerologically reducible to 'six,' number of Return) gives the Key for the 'Great Return':

> If a global network of Spiritual humanity unites to draw upon these [spiritual] energies [of the Higher Self] and focus them with a unified purpose, towards the marriage of a consciousness evolution to a scientific evolution, the world will be One Planetary Mind that will fuse with other planetary worlds and understand how our planetary mind is One of Many thinking membranes between evolutionary systems.

The Key describes the transmission and imprinting of 'living energy codes of light' via our electromagnetic energy spectrum to raise the consciousness of our evolving species, and provide instructions for the new building blocks of life within the galactic Tree of Life.

In the interest of grounding this information, the reader should be aware that electromagnetic frequencies actually transmit information and interact with biological functioning, especially that of the DNA and the central nervous system. The pineal gland (sixth *chakra*) orchestrates the functioning of the human psyche by producing a host of psychoactive chemicals such as melatonin, dopamine, serotonin and others which affect consciousness. For psychophysical effects can be positive or negative, depending upon the frequency of the field.[24]

The Key, echoing the Maya concept of evolutionary mediation from the centre of the galaxy, also discloses that our local universe has at its centre 'a more developed pattern of astrochemical networks and reprogramming life syntheses known as the Higher Evolution'.

By 1987, the Maya factor, like water seeking its own level, had found and flowed into the hearts of its own. The shift in human consciousness was realized (made real) by an event directly attributable to the Maya calendar, a global phenomenon known as the Harmonic Convergence. This was the Maya calendar 'going public'.

Significantly, no multimedia campaign had coaxed this remarkable event into action; no T-shirts, posters, or mobilizing symbol touted it to planetary prominence, nor did it seem necessary. A true resonance fanned the spirit and intent of 'global linkup' right from the start. People all over the world pilgrimaged to sacred sites or went to their favourite places in nature. The event was understood as the beginning of a new energy, a new vibrational frequency being transmitted from the centre of the galaxy through the mediation of the sun. There was no real agenda other than for people to celebrate together, to be in the conscious awareness of 'one mind', and to experience the day in joy and unity. One cannot doubt that the morphogenetic field of our 'global brain' was profoundly influenced. From the gatherings of people who focused their energies at the sacred sites, nodes of the planetary grid, the reverberation hummed through the Earth mother's nervous system as well as (by that time) the exoteric nervous system of the planet's major communications media network.

One recalls the intense community organizing and networking, the personal challenge of spiritual preparation for attunement to the new energies, and the sense of conscious participation in a great transpersonal force moving us through history and toward an entirely new phase of human evolution. One recognized a wave of awesome dimensions approaching as a great, exuberant number of people embraced and rode its swell. Like the plumed serpent itself, it crested, brilliant and magnificent ... dawn, August 16, 1987, the last day of the final Nine Hells cycle of the Maya calendar. This date appears in the prophetic chronology of the Great Pyramid at the threshold of initiation known as the 'Great Step'. And rightly so, for this was the end of the final Hell cycle that had begun with Cortes's arrival in 1519 AD (nine cycles of fifty-two years = 468 years after the invasion).

The Harmonic Convergence was *the* pivotal event in terms of the Maya 'time schedule', for it shifted the Homo sapiens mind field of the Earth into harmonic resonance with Earth, the Sun, and the Centre of the Galaxy, Hunab Ku, 'One, Giver of Movement and Measure'. It is Hunab Ku as the galactic core that sources evolutionary change in synchronization with other universes. *The Mayan Factor* elucidates the Mayan 'galactic synchronization beam', a programme that paces evolution and human DNA in increments of 5,125-year 'worlds'. And the *Keys of Enoch* describe the Lords of Light who issue forth programmes of redemption and resurrection from the centre of the galaxy to evolve planetary populations.

With Cortés's arrival, Quetzalcoatl's prophesied return occurred. 'Thirteen Heavens of decreasing choice and nine Hells of increasing doom' had run their course. And by the end of those nine Hells, Tezcatlipoca, dark brother of Quetzalcoatl, indeed had removed his mask. Like children afraid of the dark and (literally) our own 'shadow', we *were* surprised to see who he really is. He is the externalization of our collective shadow and all for which we have not taken responsibility. Tezcatlipoca is our dark twin, our own separation from 'ourSelves,' which our psyches interpret as the separation 'out there.' He brings the gift of wholeness, as did the dark force personified by Darth Vader in *Star Wars*, who, at the end of the action, took off his mask – revealing himself as the hero's own father. Tezcatlipoca, for those who prefer *not* to see who he is, is still who they think he is – someone else! Ultimately, there is nothing outside of ourselves and we are all connected – to each other, and everything else.

The last part of the prophecy had referred to the Tree of Life that would 'blossom with a fruit never before known in the creation and that fruit shall be the New Spirit of Man'. The Tree of Life appears at the ending of all great cycles, and is a symbol of life arising from a lower to a higher state – which is why there is always a serpent coiling around its trunk, and a bird high in its branches. The last page of the Bible also ends with the Tree of Life, the fruit of which is for the healing of the nations. With its roots in the Earth and its branches in the heavens, the Tree of Life may well be the most ancient of all metaphors for the transcendent link between Earth and heaven. Like the Maya reed, the trunk facilitates the transition from one state of being to another. We are the tree, of course, earthbound, yet aspiring toward the sun. The trunk is our spine, around which the serpent of *kundalini* coils to reach the bird who sits quietly in the leaves, waiting, alert, to embrace the serpent with its outspread wings. When they meet, the tree silently blossoms. The serpent raises her head and smiles at the bird, who returns her gaze, as if to say, 'I've been waiting for you'. The bird gently picks up the glowing serpent in its golden beak. There is a rustle of feathers and softly beating wings as they rise together into the heavens, always toward the bright horizon as the dawn breaks, and always as the first rays burst forth.

On just such a morning, when all was hushed and still and the promise of a new day hung in the air like morning mist, an old Zapotec legend prophesied something wonderful would happen. *The Lord of the Dawn* describes the locus of the prophecy as the Tree of Life, the el Tule tree near Oaxaca beneath which Quetzalcoatl was buried. This tree is a magnificent towering presence, a Sabino, related to the Sequoia and one of the oldest living trees on the planet. The *Encyclopedia Brittanica* says the tree is two thousand years old, but the native people say it is more like five thousand years old. The prophecy, now fulfilled, said that as the first rays of the dawning sun of the new cycle warmed the Earth, billions of tiny spirit beings would burst from the heart of Quetzalcoatl. They would slowly rise through the trunk, through the limbs and branches, appearing as sparkles of light. Erupting from every leaf and shoot, these Light spirits would circle the globe and implant themselves as seeds of peace and love within the heart of each receptive human being. This was the Spirit of Quetzalcoatl ... come again ... on that special morning of Harmonic Convergence, August 16, 1987, the last day of the final Hell cycle. The Tree of Life did, indeed, blossom with a fruit never before known in the creation, and that fruit *was* the New Spirit of humanity.

The Maya identify the end of the current cycle of history with the glyphs for 'Storm,' followed by 'Sun' (1992-2012 AD) – which produces a rainbow. Again, we are reminded of the final date in the Great Pyramid, which shows September 17, 2001, with Venus at twenty-six degrees of Leo represented by the Sabian symbol 'After the Heavy Storm a Rainbow,' which links heaven and Earth to the covenant with one's divine nature. The Maya welcome the return of Light and the coming 'Solar Age' as a time when we move once more into resonant relationship with the Light, the full spectrum of which illumes all the *chakras* and bestows 'the mind of the Sun.' The Egyptian Thoth ('the mind of Ra', the Sun), Enoch, Quetzalcoatl, Arthur, Jesus, are all initiators of Light arising now within the human psyche from a central archetype because it is the appropriate historical time for them.

The final phase of the Maya calendar, code-named 'Time Shift', began on July 26, 1992. It inaugurated an evolutionary, global phenomenon again best expressed by the Red Queen when she said to Alice, 'It takes all the running you can do to keep in the same place. If you want to get somewhere else, you must run at least twice as fast as that!' In case anyone hadn't noticed – time is speeding up.

Time Shift is the final twenty-year *katun* of the calendar that deals with a shift; not only in the way we perceive time, but also in the timing frequencies that comprise the structure of time itself. That's a big one. This is because, as the Light on the planet increases, it refines the vibration of matter, which has a spiritualizing effect. As this occurs, duality decreases, and we move into greater Oneness. This means that time and space (or, more accurately, 'timespace,' because time and space are a continuum) also accelerate. Yogic texts confirm that as the duality of the physical plane diminishes, time speeds up, and by the time one is able totally to transcend duality, time ceases entirely and we become One with the All.[25] Anyway, the wonderful part is that as time accelerates, so does *synchronicity*. Synchronicity is the phenomenon of meaningful coincidences and things coming together in effortless harmony. It is what happens when we are 'in the flow', in the right place at the right time, or 'on the same wavelength' with others. Synchronicity is associated with the kind of sensitive resonance that we develop when we are really 'tuned in'. This is the state of mind where intuition and telepathy come into play, and which helps the synchronicity happen in the first place. In everyday terms, quicker creative manifestation occurs on the one hand, and/but more instant karma on the other. It's like anything in which one becomes proficient; if we move within the universal flow, responsive to the needs of the moment and the spirit of the times, becoming more compassionate, loving and Self-aware – increased synchronicity and harmony will result. For those unwilling to accommodate or adjust to these new energies, it will be a difficult time indeed, because the opposite of synchronicity is obstruction, frustration and confusion.

Thus, we will begin increasingly to experience the apparent separation between past and future, inner and outer, dreamtime and waking, self and other, as a semipermeable membrane allowing oneness with and flow between. As this occurs, the reductionist paradigm responsible for the left brain dominance of our culture will itself be reduced.

In exploring this phenomenon, Terence McKenna, inner space explorer and author of *The Archaic Revival*, believes, we are approaching the 'end of history', and are about to enter 'hyperspace'. In other words, a multidimensional, simulsensory reality is approaching that will transform, or engulf, the traditionally perceived time vector of history.

By the year 2012 AD, 'it', and we, will have 'broken through'. Indeed, tantalizing predictions by Nostradamus hint at major interdimensional breakthroughs occurring before the end of the century, with scientific, technological leaps through time and space.

In the meantime, clues about what the transitional, closing years of the 'Age' (1992-2012 AD) hold are contained in the currently dominant glyphs of the Maya calendar. Like zodiacal signs, the calendar glyphs act as lenses for consciousness. During the coming years, the destiny of the planet will be guided by 13-Reed and 20-Ahau.

13. Reed   20. AHAU

Thirteen Reed synchronizes cycles. In order to do this, it brings transformation and new beginnings by means of destruction or renewal, breakdown, or breakthrough. Just as the reed arises from the fertile darkness of the soil to break through the surface of the earth into the new light of day, 13-Reed is the time-tunnel to new dimensions. It is the instrument of quantum leaps. Planetary alignments and evolutionary shifts occur during 13-Reed periods. Thirteen-Reed catalyzes into our immediate experience the personal and planetary circumstances of the death or transformation aspect of judgment.

Twenty Ahau, as last glyph of the day calendar, and heart of the calendric system, unifies and completes all natural, cultural, religious, and prophetic time cycles. The tail end of the age of Pisces is upon us, as is the close of the Mesoamerican fifth world, and the Kali Yuga of the Hindus – all nested within the culminating revolution of the precessional Great Year. Ahau means 'Lord'. In this case, he is the Solar Lord who mediates the pulsations of evolutionary energy from the centre of the galaxy. He represents the transcendent intelligence of the Sun. Through his 'blowgun' tube, Ahau exhales the fecudating principle of the solar mind to the creation below, thus bringing the awakening and resurrection aspect of judgment.

It is not within the scope of this chapter to explain the Maya-Egyptian connection that forms the broader context for this time shift and its meaning for our time (the subject of a book in progress).[26] Nevertheless, we can say with assurance that beneath the surface of popular culture, rich foment and restructuring is in process. Today, the Maya temple complexes and sacred centres (and others all over the world) are being reactivated. It is the mandate of 20-Ahau that ancient wisdom from the beginning of the cycle be awakened to come full circle, to bless and enlighten those who are ready at this, the ending of the cycle. And, consistent with the function of 13-Reed, work is being done to synchronize at least thirteen of the Mesoamerican calendars.

The greatness of the Maya and their gift to the world is gradually becoming understood. Hunab Ku is calling his own. There is work to be done before the dawn.

PART FOUR
Destination

16

'Our' Prophecy

The dream you dream alone is only a dream.
But the dream we dream together is reality.

-Yoko Ono

In the fourth century BC, when Euripides, the great Greek dramatist, was encoding the world's wisdom into his plays, the word 'apocatastasis' was created. It described the restoration of being, or a being, to its natural state ('apo', reversal; 'apocatastasis', in classical tragedy, the intensified part of the action directly preceding the catastrophe). It is a word that also describes the process of 'shift' signified by the central symbolism of the Maya/Aztec calendar stone. As the prophecies examined in this work move toward their apotheosis, it becomes clear that the world is embarked upon its own apocatastic process. It is a process that the great rhythms of the cosmos and the forces of nature support. So, as James Thurber so wisely put it, 'Let us not look back in anger, nor forward in fear, but around in awareness.'

The prophetic Maya drama has not quite achieved its denouement, either. It continues to flow out from the past, resonating with our own, and in so doing carries us along on its momentum. This part of the Maya journey is also our own, and so the story continues.

On February 2, 1987 (six months before the Harmonic Convergence), eight persons on the initiatory path met at the Temple complex of Palenque, Mexico. José Argüelles, a decoder of the timing and meaning behind the Maya calendrics, was there, and also Barbara Hand Clow. She explained that understanding the Maya factor not only reawakens our hidden knowledge of ourselves in the universe, it also shows that we are to participate in the progression of events leading up to our emergence in the 'galactic society'.

The group had come together for the purpose of activating Earth energies to assist the shift in human consciousness and to reactivate the temple's energies. By performing sacred ceremony and ritual, their intent was to signal the higher intelligences about our readiness for the events about to occur in the final phase of the Maya calendar. The anticipated response to that signal was an activation of the movement pattern within the etheric body of the planet, resulting in the increased release to humanity of knowledge or energy patterns stored in the noosphere (planetary mind field).[1]

On the walls of the Temple of Inscriptions at Palenque are reliefs depicting the nine lords of the underworld who rule the Nine Hells. They represent the *Bolonti Ku* – '*the* roots of Hunab Ku, the only giver of movement and measure'. Daykeeper Hunbatz Men says this symbology can be paraphrased as 'the place which marks the sacred cycles of human beings in union with the Tree'.[2] Six months later, the end of the Nine Hells cycle would be globally celebrated with the Harmonic Convergence, and the roots of Hunab Ku and the 'Tree' would awaken as never before.

Solemn ritual was enacted by the eight people deep beneath the Temple in the tomb chamber, to effect an increase in the higher mind communications being released to the planet during the final Maya cycle of the Solar Mind (i.e., the quality of consciousness that operates in galactic accord) immediately prior to the Convergence. And in the court of the Nine Lords (the courtyard called The Palace), sacred ceremony was performed to activate Earth energies needed to assist the coming 'shift'.

Exactly twenty-one days later – at 7 hours, 35 minutes, and 41:37 seconds Universal Time, February 23, 1987 – a

seemingly miraculous, supracosmic, *unrecognized*, yet
nonetheless specific response signal of phenomenal proportions (superlatives fail) *was* received! It generated an evolutionary shockwave throughout the planet and its life forms
for the acceleration of human consciousness and activation
of 'root' energies deep within the Earth by means of the
planetary grid, throwing the switch on an entire field of
global resonance in readiness for alignment with the new
energies and the awakening of consciousness.

The signal itself had originated 170,000 years ago in the
Large Magellanic Cloud, a distant subgalaxy of our own
Milky Way. It travelled through time and space in accordance with the impeccable rhythms and inexplicable intelligence of the universe – *to synchronize the evolutionary pulse
of planet Earth with that of the galaxy* – right on schedule.

Those ceremonial evocations at the Palenque Temple
complex had expressed the nonlinear connection between
human consciousness and universal mind in attunement
with cosmic timing. The response signal received exactly
three weeks later was *precisely* the one anticipated by that
evolved and deeply privileged gathering at Palenque. It was
also the fulfillment of the prophecy, long awaited by the
Hopi, that would herald the beginning of the Great Purification. In short – it was the 'Blue Star'. With a brilliance two
hundred times greater than the sun, a hot blue supergiant
had erupted in to a **Supernova** making world history, and
front page news all over the world.

Within the first ten second of going supernova, an intense
blast of neutrinos – one hundred times more than the sun
will radiate in its entire ten billion year lifetime – raced
ahead of the shock wave. These subatomic, massless,
chargeless particles silently zoomed directly through the
Earth, north to south, along the corridor of Earth's magnetic force lines. The neutrino salvo preceded a flash volume of
ultraviolet and infrared radiation, X-rays and gamma rays.
Reports said the radiation released in the first few seconds
was as much as that from all the stars and galaxies in the visible universe combined. We got the lot!

Ancient civilizations watched the sky for omens the way we watch it for weather forecasts. They believed that moving celestial bodies, like comets and supernovas, were powerful omens of important events on Earth. And this is true of our auspicious supernova. The 'big bang' of its luminous genesis was the sound of prophecy being fulfilled. It heralded the inauguration of galactic events relating to a major evolutionary shift, and the Hopi Great Purification. On the first day of the Persian Gulf War, a luminous 'ring' around this supernova was photographed by the Hubble space telescope. The photograph was circulated by the Associated Press, and also published in *The New York Times*.

Escalation of the Gulf War to the ground war phase began on February 23, 1991 – the fourth anniversary of the supernova's explosive birth. The Blue Star was on target and fulfilling its role! It remains to be seen whether the scientists' prediction of a brilliant recrudescence of the supernova at the end of the century[3] will coincide with Nostradamus's prediction for the same period.

'The relationship of supernovas to the evolution of life on Earth is straightforward,' says science writer Donald Goldsmith. 'Supernovas make cosmic ray particles; cosmic ray particle impacts produce mutations; mutations drive evolution ... Far from being an isolated event, far distant from Earth and incapable of having an effect on us, SN1987A- [the 1987 supernova] can be seen as the latest in the chain of events that shaped our solar system, our Earth, and ourselves.'[4] 'In a very literal sense,' says University of Illinois astrophysicist Larry Smarr, 'we are the grandchildren of supernovas.'

Scientists were excited that new elements were indeed synthesized in the explosion, especially radioactive nickel, which decays to cobalt and then iron. Iron seeds probably grew into progressively heavier elements. Neutrinos are released by the sun; there are several kinds. But neutrinos from an exploding star had never been seen before. Supernova explosions are known to produce gold, lead, and uranium. 'In fact, the explosions achieve the ancient alchemist's nightmare of turning gold into lead!' joked Harvard's Professor of Astronomy, Robert Kirshner, who says that generations of supernovas created the elements we take for granted – the ink in this book, the oxygen you breathe as you read it, the calcium in your bones, and the iron in your blood are products of the stars. This grand idea that we are literally made of starstuff, is reflected in the popular song 'Woodstock', by Joni Mitchell (written in the Woodstock year of 1969, the year of the Blue Star's original discovery): 'We are star dust, we are golden, we are billion-year-old carbon.' The death of stars is part of the origin of life.[5]

Estimates as to how many people the neutrino hail passed through that morning vary from five million to 'each person on Earth'.[6] Unquestionably, our subtle, or etheric, bodies were influenced, our DNA, our psyches – as, therefore, was the core of Earth that generates the magnetic field which energizes the planetary grid! Living organisms sense the Earth's geomagnetic field and derive vital information from it, as well as adapting behaviours to its changes.

A visionary scientist, the late Walter Russell, had described radioactive particles as spirit in the process of becoming matter, and as spirit penetrating the interface of matter. Mythically speaking, neutrinos can be appreciated as the spirit force of the stars, the babies, the seeds of light. Could these neutrinos have been the 'living energy codes of light' – referred to in the Keys of Enoch and described in the previous chapter – for the quickening of humanity?

The ancient alchemists may have been describing these seeds of light when they wrote of the 'scintillae,' the infinitesimal sparks of light contained in the 'arcane substance' (basically, mud). These scintillae were regarded as the quintessence of the four elements, and they emanated from the spirit of God in the form of the World Soul. Although the scintillae have generally been interpreted as the light within nature, there may yet be a deeper, more complete, meaning.

According to the Gnostic doctrine of the Seeds of Light harvested by the Virgin of Light, the psychic nature of these luminosities was as 'seeds of light broadcast in the chaos', (the seedplot of the world to come).[7] In using descriptions similar to those expressed by the scientists quoted above. the alchemists wrote of the scintillae as 'seed ideas of nature; the origin of species', and considered them to be 'entelechia' – the vital force urging organisms toward completion.

Pursuing this line of thought, Jung elucidated the relationship between the archetypes of the unconscious and the phenomenon of time, which link our inner and outer realities and point to the synchronicity of archetypal events.[8] He addressed the importance of alchemical ideas in the psychology of the unconscious, and, impressed by the alchemical insights of Paracelsus (the fifteenth century Swiss alchemist and physician) wrote that it struck him as significant that the characteristic alchemical vision of sparks scintillating in the blackness of the arcane substance should change into the 'interior firmament and its stars'. Paracelsus beheld the darksome psyche as a starstrewn night sky whose planets and fixed constellations represented, according to Jung, the archetypes in all their luminosity and numinosity.[9] The psychological meaning of these seeds of light is clear. They are the germinal luminosities emanating from the darkness of the unconscious itself as well as the external seeds of light-life from supernovas in the darkness of deep space. Consistent with supernova as metaphor, we even speak in the superlatives of a 'flash' of inspiration, or of profound insight 'blowing one's mind'.

Examining more closely the idea of neutrinos as the seeds of life, coverage of the supernova in *Scientific American* was prefaced by the statement, 'Supernovas are more than distant spectacles: they make and expel the seeds of life.'[10] The previous Maya *baktun* (1224–1618 AD) has been called the 'Baktun of the Hidden Seed,' the 'hidden seed' being interpreted (correctly, I believe), as the archetypes of the sacred world view during an expansive civilizational cycle.[11] Indeed, texts quoted by Carl Jung also equate the scintillae with the 'archetypes stored up in a supracelestial space'.[12] In a more literal sense, however, 'the hidden seed' sandwiched the *baktun* within a matrix of evolutionary energy. The beginning and ending of the *baktun* were both literally 'highlighted' by supernovas: one in 1230 AD, and Kepler's supernova in 1604 AD. – the last one visible to the naked eye. Both supernovas appeared in the constellation Ophiuchus (the Serpent Holder).[13] Naturally, this is significant, because Ophiuchus is the Latin name of Asclepius, the Greek healer who became deified, whose worship is associated with snakes as symbols of wisdom and healing. More importantly, though, in Mesoamerican mythology, Ophiuchus is none other than Quetzalcoatl – the agent of cosmic intelligence and the germinator of life within the seed. At a particular juncture in the Maya calendar, the heart of Quetzalcoatl was prophesied to burst open in a blaze of light, disbursing small spirit beings as sparkles of light for the renewal of all life on Earth. That historic date, code-named Harmonic Convergence, arrived six months after the prophesied blue star burst forth its own seeds of light as Supernova SN-1987A. We are reminded of Jung's insight that 'The starry vault of heaven is in truth the open book of cosmic projection in which are myths and archetypes. In this vision astrology and alchemy, the two classic functionaries of the psychology of the collective unconscious, join hands.'[14] This illustrates, once again, that the arcane wisdom, far from being 'old stuff', is the perennial wisdom, encompassing great truths that can never become outdated. The real fact of the matter is that we're only beginning to catch up with the wisdom of the past.

Neutrinos, cosmic rays and radiation from the birth of the supernova blasted out spherically, of course, through the universe. However, the alignment of constellations distributed throughout space between the supernova and the Earth was very specific! The vector of neutrinos and radiation that directly impacted the Earth (illustrated overleaf, although not to scale) transited the tip of Sagittarius's arrow, which points to the centre of the galaxy. Sagittarius is the closest to the galactic core of all the zodiacal constellations, and it relates to the higher Self. The neutrinos, like those other seeds of life exploding forth and exuberating their way to a

SUPERNOVA VECTOR

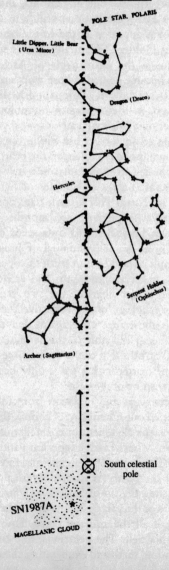

date with destiny and an ovum, journeyed on through the tail of the Ophiuchus, the Serpent Holder, described above. Almost at the speed of light, they continued Earthwards, through the thigh of past pole star Hercules ... through the head and sinuous body of past pole star Draco the dragon ... through Polaris, our current pole star ... and beyond.

What is significant about all this is that the two supernovas of the previous Maya *baktun* and the Blue Star Supernova of 1987 were events activating the Serpent Holder's specific energies – *kundalini!* Also, during the Harmonic Convergence of the same year, Uranus (radical newness) was on the foot and aligned with the head (Ras Alhague) of the Serpent Holder who is stepping into the Milky Way toward the centre of the galaxy, the celestial region associated with the higher mind and the destination of the *kundalini* serpent.[15] The symbolism spread out here is, of course, more than coincidentally connected to the Quetzalcoatl energies

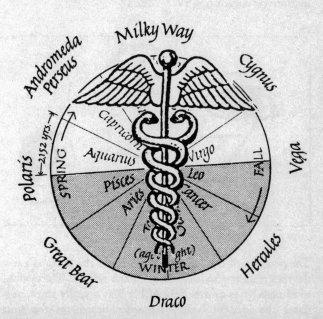

and the associated jolt of evolutionary force characteristic of ascending serpent energy – especially since the radiation and neutrino path also crossed Draco, constellation of the Dragon, and our current pole star, Polaris.

Consistent with the idea of pole shift and the Mesoamerican prophecy of the present world culminating in a 'shift', one should bear in mind that spiritual causes precede physical effects. The supernova disbursed the mysterious contents of the Blue Star's ripe seed pod throughout the universe, preparing Earth and her gene pool for an evolutionary sequence. That sequence aligned the magnetic core of the Earth, and the compass of human consciousness with the centre of the galaxy – attuning them to the galactic haronic. It was a sequence that prefigured an extraordinary synchronization prophesied by the Maya calendar – the Harmonic Convergence, the celebration of which created an incremental resonant shift, in preparation for more transformational events during 1992–2012 AD.

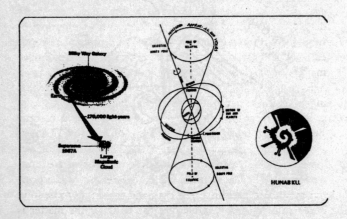

The position of the supernova relative to the Earth is a few degrees from the South Pole of Earth's ecliptic. The symbol of Hunab Ku as centre of the Milky Way visually accommodates the idea of 'shift'. Arguelles designates the four 'blades' as pulsation streams from the galactic core that emanate spirals of spin/counterspin (like DNA) to inform the life code. We are employing the symbol to also illustrate the means by which the SE/NW vector of the neutrinos functioned to 'shift' the life code a notch, thus repolarizing the field.

Because of the precession of the equinoxes, the North celestial pole describes a circle around the pole of the ecliptic, which is fixed in Draco. And Draco coils around our pole star, just as the serpent of ancient texts coils around the cosmic egg. It is important to remember that, as discussed earlier, the pole star profoundly influences the collective consciousness. Therefore, we see that the predominant symbology here is related to serpents and higher consciousness (while Polaris, our pole star, polarizes consciousness – toward the light/or not – because this Age is humanity's graduation time).

As a mythic form of the serpent, the dragon has played a major role in the ancient lore of most world cultures. And even when this does not appear to be the case, if one peers deeply enough into the obscure crevices of the tunnel of time, there is often within the darkness a dim glow of hooded eyes, the guttural echo of distant thunder, a warm hint of marsh gas and dragon breath.

In the West, where the serpent is responsible for promoting wisdom, or tempting Eve (depending on how you look at it), but certainly instigating the 'Fall', where St George slew the dragon and drove the snakes (read 'Druids') out of Ireland, where the antagonist in the fairy stories of our impressionable years often was a dragon, dragons are 'controversial'. The fact that this maligned creature was a positive symbol in past historical eras, and continues to be so in other cultures today, is because the truth of the matter is that the mythic slithery one is a symbol of the *life principle*.

The entwined strands of DNA reveal the pattern of the life principle. The entwined strands of the pranic nerve channels of *kundalini* are of the same pattern and represent the same principle. It is not the life principle that is 'good or bad,' or the symbols that represent it, but the way it is expressed – by people.

Characterizing our three evolutionary brains, psychologist Jean Houston says, 'The striving and territorial protectiveness of the reptile, the nurturing and family orientation of the early mammal, the symbolic and linguistic capacities of the neocortex may multiply our damnation or grace our salvation.' It is the unconscious and instinctive drives of our own reptilian brain that animate the deadly reptile of materialism, separation, self-interest and the misuse of anger, power and sex residing within our own lower natures. The second brain is the paleomammalian 'fight or flight' brain of emotion. As we aspire to transcend the lower nature, the interaction of the sympathetic and parasympathetic nerve currents causes the 'serpent power' of *kundalini* to ascend the tree of the spinal column. The third, neocortex, brain is the bird, the creature of the higher realms of consciousness where love, wisdom, and power are synthesized and creatively expressed in service and enlightened awareness. The feathered serpent materializes when the Self realizes who it really is. Pay close attention to the myths, for beneath the masks, within the mists, throughout the fables, it is our own story that unfolds.

Historically speaking, the dragon's most meaningful relationship is probably with China, because the home base (or home summit?) of the dragon constellation resides directly over that country (see 'Astrological Cycles' chapter). In China, the symbol of imperial sovereignty was an ascending dragon with an egg or a sphere that, historians assert, is being belched forth by the dragon. However, the image likely depicts an aspect of the celestial dragon breathing its energy into the Earth. Identification of the dragon with the person of the Emperor may date back as far as five thousand years, to the time when Draco as pole star delineated true North, and cosmic energies flowed into the Earth grid through the North Pole. At the Temple of Heaven in Beijing, nodally oriented north-south, the Emperor traditionally faced north to ceremonially draw down the 'dragon power' unto himself for the nation and into the 'dragon paths' of the planetary grid. Assertions in Chinese mythology that dragons visited mortals in some of the temple complexes can be understood as geomantic metaphor.

The lines of magnetic force in the Earth that we call ley lines, and which comprise the planetary grid, were known in China as 'lung mei' – paths of the dragon, along which flowed the dragon current. They were divined by practitioners of 'feng-shui' – wind and water, meaning 'that which cannot be seen or grasped'. *Feng-shui is* the geomantic art of harmonizing the *chi* (life force) of the atmosphere and the *chi* of the land with that of humanity for mutual benefit.

In this way, human consciousness was influenced by the architecture (the shape of a structure), geographic placement and celestial alignment of certain buildings and cities. There were two kinds of dragon paths: those of the Blue Dragon were yang (positive/male) energies that arched over ranges of mountains and hills, and along highland ridges. Paths of the White Tiger were yin (negative/female) energies coursing along rivers and subterranean channels, following lowland geographical features. Individual lines were associated with one of the five planets known to the ancient world, and corresponded to the five elements of fire, water, earth, wood and metal. By thus interpreting the geographic energies of a region, geomancers could create and utilize environments that enfolded humans, the Earth, and the heavenly bodies in one harmonious pattern.

Owing to the assiduous work of many researchers, particularly the Global Mapping Project at Governors State University in Illinois and the Dragon Project in Britain, it is now recognized that practically *all* sacred sites, settlements, cities, pyramids, obelisks, temples, and monuments of antiquity were grid-oriented, user-friendly and cosmos-related. According to Dragon Project co-founder Paul Devereux, 'The Earth is drawing us back to the ancient sacred sites to teach us more about living on her body. That information is now being taken and put into the collective consciousness where it is being developed and explored. It is

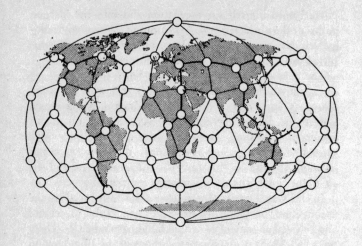

Planetary Grid

being put into this huge telecommunications "cortex" [the global brain of electronic media], so that we can in-put what the planet is telling us on a global scale.'

Clearly, the global infrastructure of the Earth grid was understood and coherently utilized throughout the entire ancient world. On a very profound level, it provided access to the source and nature of human consciousness and the knowledge that the Earth, like the universe, is alive, dependent upon, and informed by currents of magnetic energy, which are, in turn, influenced by cosmic forces from the planets and stars.

As mentioned above, supernova explosions are known to produce uranium – and uranium deposits are known to be located along grid lines above which grow long, straight, expanses of sagebrush. According to two quite dissimilar sources, Walter Russell's *Atomic Suicide?* and Australian Aboriginal shaman Gooboy Ted Thomas, uranium in its natural, undisturbed state has beneficial properties, but it becomes harmful when disturbed and removed from the ground.

The currents of 'dragon power' were considered to draw in their wake vitalizing energies that fertilized the living body of the Earth, that balanced and healed her life forms, and elevated human consciousness, attuning it to the greater whole. A function of monolithic stone placement, therefore, was to modify the grid currents, 'acupuncturing' them for specific purposes. Many of the standing stone henges were oriented for predictive readouts of solstices, equinoxes and other celestial events. According to geomancy expert John Michell, this was important because during eclipses, the magnetic field of the Earth and, therefore, the energy of the grid, diminishes greatly, and certain phases of the sun and moon, as well as sunspots and solar storms, also cause changes in its strength and direction.

By the time we began to rediscover the grid's existence and its purpose, the whole system that enables the planet to function and which depend upon the grid, was so impaired by human ignorance and abuse that prophecies about coming 'Earth changes' began to make uncomfortable sense.

In order to get spiritual understanding out to the people before his passing in 1972, Hopi spiritual leader Kikmongwi Dan Katchongva wrote a wonderful little book, *From the Beginning of Life to the Day of Purification*.[16] Danaqyumptewa, now a Hopi elder, was the book's translator. He emphasizes Dan's understanding of the Great Purification as a 'mystery egg' that would hatch something 'mysterious' in global consciousness after the appearance of the auspicious Blue Star. This insight appears to have presaged accurately the true nature of things to come, for the supernova itself, and the events surrounding it, appear very much associated with the idea of an egg.

In a moving account of his experience at the el Tule tree in Oaxaca, Richard Leviton writes in *The Emerald Modem* about the prophesied release of spirits of light from the buried heart of Quetzalcoatl. 'A cordon of angels make an enveloping fence of light around the huge tree which seems to sit like a mother bird on a precious egg of light. Inside the egg are a million crystalline facets ... I realize this radiant crystalline egg is the heart of Quetzalcoatl, poised for a glorious hatching.' Leviton then predicted that when the egg burst open (as it was said to have done in 1987), it would require skilled geomancers to channel the released energy through themselves, anchoring it into the Earth at el Tule, then allowing it to move, as if through sluice gates, out in a flash of heavenly radiation through the web of world energy channels.

Most astonishing of all is the fact that, astronomically, the supernova occurred at seven [plus] degrees of Aquarius.[17] The symbol for seven degrees, according to *An Astrological Mandala*, is 'A Child is Seen Being Born out of an Egg'. If this image, the keynote of which is given as 'the emergence of new mutations according to the great rhythms of the cosmos' seems familiar, the reader will recall that it is also associated with September 17, 2001 AD, the last prophesied date in the Great Pyramid, with Neptune at seven degrees of Aquarius. This repetition makes doubly significant the supernova's placement at this degree, for it spiritually resonates the collective unconscious around the principle of this symbol of the child emerging from the cosmic egg. This means that in 2001 AD, we can expect *an energizing of the core spiritual process* that began in 1987 with the Blue Star supernova in the same degree and sign. The cosmic activation of the symbolic child emerging from an egg is extremely appropriate for the birth of the new, divine, complete humanity in the twenty-first century. We are further told in *An Astrological Mandala* that this child is a new product of evolution, that s/he constitutes a fresh projection of the creative Spirit emanating from the planetary whole, and that the power of the whole focused within this child is free from racial or cultural tradition.

As far as the archetype of the child is concerned, it represents the beginning of life and that which is instinctive. The future and its potential also reside in the 'child'. It is, therefore, a motif that, in uniting the opposites, becomes a mediator, a bringer of healing – that is, one who makes whole.'[18] The majority of therapists and an informed public are now quite familiar with the psychological value of reclaiming and healing the 'inner child', and a great deal of work is currently being done at this level.

According to Jung, the more outwardly directed and differentiated consciousness becomes, the greater of severance from its root condition of connectedness with the 'child'. If the childhood state of the collective psyche is repressed to the point of exclusion, the unconscious content overwhelms the conscious aim and sabotages, even destroys, its realization. Our link with the primal inner child of the original, unconscious, instinctive state (our little reptilian self, if you will) must be honoured, or we end up doing things that threaten or destroy its embodiments – small children, the species, rainforests, the natural systems of the great Mother. Western culture has done this, and more. And we now face the consequences, as our collective 'karmuppance' comes down with the fulfillment of prophecy.

So, at the wisdom level where 'everything furthers,' it becomes apparent that the problems the world reflects back to us match the parts of ourselves that created the problems, the parts that lack wisdom and harmony, the parts experienced as separate from the whole, and that need healing. 'World crisis' is both challenge and opportunity. This turning point is our collective initiation test – because karma comes from unlearned lessons *and* enough people have now begun to experience a shift in their lives toward love and unity and away from fear and separation. This is the primary challenge of our time.

Lao Tsu said, 'The purpose of contracting is served by expanding.' And, as T. S. Eliot might have said, '… the end of all our exploring will be to arrive where we first started, and know ourSelf for the first time.' Out here on the leading edge of the evolutionary spiral, the One has become as many as it possibly could. Seeking knowledge, it ended up cerebralized, analyzing and naming everything down to the last quantum particle. But analysis and fragmentation ultimately devolve into disunity, and obscure the Self. When the Self is unknown, conflict between its disparate parts ranges from loneliness to war. The Self is the central arche-type of the collective unconscious, and the organizing prin-ciple of the psyche and its wholeness. It folds our awareness in upon itself, so that all errors are mirrored back to us by karma as lessons keeping us accountable, until we under-stand that balance is restored by synthesis and cohesion, which ultimately evolve into unity; and revelation of the Self. The mind analyzes – the heart synthesizes. The turning point is where the heart is awakened. Historically speaking, we are at this juncture. America's motto, inscribed on the banner in the beak of the eagle of the Great Seal, reminds us that America was founded on the principle of 'E Pluribus Unum' – 'Out of the Many, One'.

A similar process exists in the shamanic tradition of the world's native peoples. The initiatory experience is consis-tently one of extreme crisis, fragmentation, a brush with death, etc. Dreams, trances, rituals evoke themes of dismem-berment and death. These are initiatory purifications that serve to break the mould of the old non-Self. The pieces are then reconstituted, resurrected, and (like the phoenix rising from its own ashes) reconstellated according to the arche-type of the Self. The 'new' mould is then an appropriate repository of higher consciousness, and exceptional psychic and healing powers. The shaman serves humanity. (Christ's resurrection, and the dismemberment and reassembly of Osiris, the Egyptian mythic archetype, are classic exam-ples.) In the worst possible way we have been 'going to pieces' and are now in the process of 'pulling ourselves together'. This is the process that the world itself is now embarked upon. Ophiuchus, the Serpent Holder, is impor-tant for the same reason. He is the constellational 'lens' through which significant cosmic energies have recently projected to Earth. As Asclepius, he is also credited with the shamanic skill of restoring the dead to life. King James I of England wrote of the death of Hippolytus, 'After his mem-bers were drawn in sunder by foure horses, Esclepius at Neptun's request glewed them together and revived him.' In a remarkably complete way, Ophiuchus focuses the process of transformation for humanity, from the awakening of *kundalini* to the restoration of the Self.

What seems clear is that the mighty labour now begun is actually our Self-birthing project, or – in the shamanic sense – our rebirth. The most important thing with a birth is to simply let go and release into the process. Fear, addictions, ego and alienation are but passing shadows, contractions, as we prepare to deliver that which has been gestating within us. The new being is consciously 'remembered' and resurrected by its connection to Spirit. Spirit is source, umbilicus. It is the tie that binds us to the universe and the Light that nourishes.

The body of prophecy presented here is no longer a long-term speculation to be dismissed or feared. There is no longer any distance between us and it. We are already past the midpoint of prophecy and coming into the home stretch. As we prepare for our 're-memberance', the world can neither look away from its problems, nor assume that it can survive endless assaults on its collective being. The real world needs remedial measures. Our focus here, however, is not upon the 'figure' of darkness that we all recognize, but upon the emergent 'ground' of Light. The paradigm shift is where figure and ground reverse. That is what we are interested in – and attunement to a building, creative Presence. There are no immediate answers, but there is *process*. When the intelligence of the heart is awakened, it sensitizes us to the issues in the right way. Right action springs from combining the intelligence of the heart with the knowledge of the head. It is a place from which to start. (For ideas and direction to right action, refer to the 'Twelve Steps and Resources' at the end of this book.)

Chaos theory talks about attractors, patterns, and processes, and demonstrates how a small incremental increase in just one variable can lead to extensive change in the resulting pattern ... A butterfly flutters its wings, and a hurricane is born. 'The butterfly effect' refers to a small action that initiates the evolution of a major system. Our individual actions have an inestimable but certain effect upon the world. And, like the butterfly, we are emerging from the chrysalis of history. There is no owner's manual on emergence, wing drying, or flight. Butterflies just do it. For us, the flight part might take a leap of faith.

The celebratory theme of the future as a new birth reminds us to 'lighten up'. With succinct wisdom phrases worthy of one's best dress T-shirt, Werner Erhardt used to say, 'Now is when it is. Here is where it is. You are what it is. Celebrate!'

In *Starseed,* Ken Carey also articulates the heart of wisdom, 'All are invited to remember their essence, their purpose, their reason for being here, and to bring through into this age of transformation the sense of celebration that invariably accompanies such remembrance.'

Many, many evolved beings throughout the years have spoken of this moment. As if it were today, 'The Mother' who served with Sri Aurobindo in India during the 1930s wrote in her characteristically matter-of-fact style, 'I invite you to the Great Adventure, and on this adventure you are not to repeat spiritually what others have done before us, because our adventure begins from beyond that stage. We are now for a new creation, entirely new, carrying in it all the unforeseen, all risks, all hazards – a true adventure ... of which the way is unknown and has to be traced out step by step in the unexplored. It is something that has never been in the present universe and will never be in the same manner. If that interests you, well, embark.'

While 'The Mother' invited us to 'embark', Metatron (teacher and guide to Enoch, and creator of the *Keys*), prepares us for 'liftoff.' He relates that 'A new meridian of time will come when the foundations of the Earth will be shifted to a new magnetic foundation as the orbit of the Earth is reset within the ocean of Light.' His revelation about the future, received and recorded by James Hurtak, reminds us of what it is we most need to know. 'Eternal life exists where eternal love exists! That is why Metatron told me that I was to mention first the safety and peace one must feel "within the heart," rather than the physical security which is of temporal nature, for it is only through the Father's Grace that the soul passes through the vortexjah of the Earth and advances to higher planetary stations.'[19] The 'vortexjah' is described as a time-warp programming area for Space Brotherhoods, and is associated with major nodes of the Earth grid.

Communications with the divine force personified as Limitless Love and Truth are shared by David Spangler in his *Revelation: The Birth of a New Age*. The transmissions do not prophecy or emphasize destruction, nor do they focus attention on the negative aspects of change, or on the old. They speak directly to our inner knowingness:

I am with all. None are saved. None are lost. There is always only what I Am, but I have revealed Myself in new Life and new Light and new Truth. Those who attune to that will not be saved. They will only be attuned to what I Am in My new revelation. And those who heed Me not, but follow the downward course as human level consciousness unwinds itself and enters a new cycle, they are not lost. They only attune themselves to what I will become in a future revelation to them, but apart and separate from what I Am now ... All that will remain is of what I Am and all that is not of Me shall disappear, to follow another law and another destiny.

No man knows the time of My coming. I Am already revealed all about you, if you will look within and about yourselves and see Me. See naught but Me, and know My presence with you. There is no waiting, but for those who choose to wait for the hour of My universal revelation, they will know when it will occur. Behold! In the next second, I AM.

And, as Marion Culhane, cofounder of the international peace organization Global Family, so aptly phrased it, 'With the influx of the feminine ray (divine love) flooding the planet and merging with the existing masculine ray (divine will) we will be giving birth to the child of divine illumination – call it the awakening of the Christ consciousness, the return of Quetzalcoatl, or whatever is your most meaningful metaphor or archetype – it marks the emergence or awakening of divine beings on planet Earth.'

The wakeup call came quietly, but it echoes and awakens still. With impeccable timing, the Blue Star Supernova appeared in synchronicity with the unfolding of the Maya calendar and the Hopi revelation. In an instant, quicker than the eye could blink or the phosphene flare in the inner dimensions of the mind, the consciousness of the planet was encoded and imprinted. A superluminal transfer of extragalactic frequencies from deep space impregnated the Earth with the starseeds of neutrinos and radiation. Penetrating to the heart of Earth's magnetic core, this jump-start of cosmic energy served to accelerate the vibrational frequency of the life force, preparing us for an unprecedented evolutionary leap. Since the combined events of 1987 – when the electromagnetic bodies of the Earth and her species were fecundated with the imperceptible implant of subtle currents – something deep has been stirring.

It is Earth. The life of the Earth. Earthlife in all its forms, preparing for its emergence into springtime after its bleak progression through the cosmic Winter of the Dragon constellation. Reminding us of the dawn that follows the darkness, the Maya calendar ends with the pictographs 'Storm' followed by 'Sun', while the Aztec version ends with 'Rain' followed by 'Flower'. As surely as the Sun will stream through the clouds, and the Flower will blossom from the Earth, we should be filled with anticipation for what may happen, for that which lies in our future is awakening right now within our hearts. As the One mind of the planet becomes Self-conscious, it begins to know with the universal mind, breathe with the universal breath, resonate with the universal heartbeat ... perceive through the Eye of Light.

Significantly, we are now 'online' with radiations of increasing Light from universal consciousness – the Creator, the profound forces of the Solar and Planetary

Logi, ascended Masters, the many helpers of humanity, and Beings unknown, terrestrial and otherwise. From subtle and interdimensional sources, the transmission filters through the Great Central Sun of invisible radiance; through Hunab Ku, the luminous centre of our galaxy; through the mediation of our own Sun, the sustainer of life; and through the many invisible influences throughout the universe.

From the sleep of a million starless dreams, the pulse of the planet quickens. Restless, and deep within its being, a vision from the mists of consciousness awakes. Through myth and symbol, an externalizing force uncoils as yawning synapeses gently spark silent predawn currents of new birth. In this perfect waking moment, all life listens, holds its breath, changing focus as the void of darkness yields its shadows to the young light. The presence of the new day is all around ... permeating, invisible, throughout and within. The labour has begun ... new life awaits.

Take a deep breath ...

PART FIVE

You Can Get There From Here

17

Twelve Steps To Personal and Planetary Health

The 1990s is the decade to save our environment, and people are awakening and asking, 'What can I, personally, do to help?' These twelve steps help us to speak for the Earth, to make our contribution potent and meaningful. The following questions and resources are offered to call into action your participation as a crew member of spaceship Earth.

The journey of 1,000 miles begins with a single step.
— Lao Tsu

1. Personal Action Is Powerful

Begin making changes in your own life

As the damage to our environment increases, many of us are placing the blame on governments and corporations for allowing this destruction to continue. Yet, deep inside, we know the solutions start within each one of us. Individual responsibility is the leverage point that will guide us toward a vibrant future or to the end of our existence on planet Earth.

If you deeply desire change on the planet, start making changes in your own life. Put a check mark in each box you answer YES and tally your score throughout the Twelve Steps.

☐ I support businesses that produce products or services beneficial to the environment.

☐ I avoid products that cause pollution, exploit animals, waste energy, harm our forests, deplete our ozone layer, etc.

Resources:

How to Make the World a Better Place: A Beginner's Guide to Doing Good by Jeffrey Hollander. Wm. Morrow & Co.

New World, New Mind: A Guide to Changing the Way We Think About the Future by Paul Ehrlich and R. Ornstein. Simon & Schuster.

Inner Journeys: A Guide to Personal and Social Transformation by J. Early. Samuel Weiser Inc.

Dance of Change: An Echo-Spiritual Approach to Transformation by M. Lindfield. Penguin Classics.

Hundredth Monkey by Ken Keyes. Love Line Books.

Speaking Up & Speaking Out: A Handbook for Study, Discussion & Action by Vivienne Verdon Rowe. Video Project, 5332 College Ave. #101, Oakland, CA 94618.

The Networking Book: People Connecting with People by Jessica Lipnak & S. Stamps. Arcana Press.

Working For Peace: A Handbook of Practical Psychology and Other Tools by N. Wollman. Impact Publishers.

Vision in Action: The Art of Taking & Shaping Initiatives by C. Schaefer & T. Voors. New Society Publishers.

Manual for Group Facilitators by Center for Conflict Resolution. N.A.S.C.O. Publ.

Art of Supportive Leadership: Practical Handbook for People in Positions of Power by Donald Walters (Kriyananada). Crystal Clarity Publ.

67 Ways to Save the Animals by Anna Sequoia et al. Harper & Row.

Integral Spirituality: Resources for Community, Peace, Justice and the Earth by Donald Dorr. Orbis Books.

Year 1 (One): Global Process Work-Community Creation

from Global Problems, Tensions, and Myths by Arnie
Mindell. Penguin.
*Building a Peace System. A Book for Activists, Scholars,
Students & Concerned Citizens* by Robert A. Irwin.
Expo Press.

2. Our Diet

*Buy organic foods
Eliminate meat consumption
Plant fruit trees and start a vegetable garden*

Our choice of foods and farming practices influences the
health of our environment. Chemical pesticides and fertilizers
create hazardous waste, topsoil loss, water pollution, and
extinction of wildlife. We accumulate toxic residues in our
body. Decreased soil fertility lowers the vitamin and mineral
content of our food. We can choose sustainable organic farming, which relies on composting, nontoxic pest management,
crop rotation, planting trees and biological diversity.

A meat-based diet results in consuming vast quantities of
our resources. It is the number one cause of desertification
in North America and is responsible for more than eighty-
five percent of our topsoil loss. It destroys more wildlife
habitat and consumes more than fifty percent of America's
annual water usage.*

☐ I purchase certified organically grown food on a regular
basis.
☐ I read labels and avoid foods that contain chemical
preservatives.
☐ I purchase locally grown foods.
☐ I've reduced my consumption of red meat and fowl.
☐ I've eliminated meat from my diet.
☐ My diet includes whole grains
☐ We can rediscover the sacred foods such as amaranth
(Aztecs), blue corn (Hopi), and quinoa (Incas). I've
tasted these three foods.

Resources:

Diet for a New America, John Robbins. Stillpoint Press.
   *Hunger Action Handbook: What You Can Do & How To
   Do It,* editors of Seeds Magazine. Seeds Magazine Publ.
Shoppers' Guide to Natural Foods by East-West Journal
   Editors. Avery Publishing Group.
Goldbeck's Guide to Good Food: Supermarket Handbook
   by Nikki & David Goldbeck. New American Library.
Organically Grown Food: A Consumer's Guide by
   Theodore Wood Carlat. Wood Publ. Co.
*Animal Factories: An Inside Look at Manufacturing Food
   for Profit* by Peter Singer and Jim Mason. Concentric
   Media.
Diet for a Small Planet by Frances Moore Lappe. Ballantine
   Books.
Seeds of Change: Organic Seed Order Catalogue. 621 Old
   Santa Fe Trail, #10, Santa Fe, NM 87501. ($5.00)
*Saving Seeds: Gardener's Guide to Growing and Storing
   Vegetable and Flower Seeds* by Marc Rogers. Storey Publ.

3. Reduce, Reuse, Recycle

*Start recycling today
Simplify lifestyle
Use a canvas bag when you shop
Buy in bulk*

Recycling conserves our valuable resources. Every ton of recycled paper saves seventeen trees.

☐ I request not to have a bag whenever possible.
☐ If available, I purchase products in bulk to reduce packaging.
☐ I use mugs instead of paper cups and cloth instead of paper towels or napkins.
☐ I request paper containers instead of styrofoam for takeout food.

☐ I think of creative ways to recycle or reuse products such as glass, aluminum, plastic, and newspapers.

☐ I use both sides of paper for notes or first drafts of letters and recycle cardboard and writing paper.

☐ My city or district offers weekly kerbside recycling pick-up.

☐ If not, I will contact my local representative to start such a programme.

☐ I compost food scraps, leaves, and other materials to create healthy soil.

☐ I purchase products that contain recycled materials.

☐ I request the repair company servicing my air conditioning to recycle the CFC gases that destroy our ozone layer.

Resources:

Recycling & Waste Reduction Division, Bureau of Sanitation, (800) CITY SAN

Solid Waste Alternatives Project (202) 745-4870

Solution to Pollution: Your Personal Handbook to Recycling and Cleaning Up Your Environment by Laurence Sombke. Master Media Ltd.

Recycler's Handbook: A Simple Guide for Everyone by Earth Works Group. Earth Works Press.

Green Lifestyle Handbook: 1001 Ways to Heal the Earth by Jeremy Rifkin. Henry Holt & Co.

Earth Right: Every Citizen's Guide to What You Can Do in Your Home & Community to Save the Environment by H. Patricia Hynes. Prima Publishing.

4. Earthwise Products

Purchase environmentally sound products

☐ By purchasing products that are environmentally sound, I send a positive message to companies to produce more safe products and fewer toxic ones.

☐ I use cleaning products and detergents that are biodegradable and phosphate free.

☐ My paper coffee filters are naturally brown because the manufacturer avoided using a dioxin-producing bleach.

☐ I have a low-flow shower head.

☐ I have a 1.6-gallon toilet or I have retrofitted my existing toilet with a watersaving device.

☐ My toilet or tissue paper brand has a recycled paper content.

☐ My personal care products have not been tested on animals, contain no animal products, and more natural ingredients than chemicals.

☐ I purchase no aerosol sprays or products that contain CFCs, which destroy the ozone layer.

☐ I will purchase no tropical hardwood furniture because it causes the destruction of our rainforests. North America's hardwoods regenerate much faster and are excellent for furniture and flooring, etc.

☐ I will use natural fibre sheets, quilts, blankets or a hot water bottle instead of an electric blanket to keep warm in the winter.

☐ I purchase no products that release toxic formaldehyde gasses such as waferwood, fibreboard and certain furniture.

☐ I use rechargeable batteries versus disposable batteries to avoid poisoning our water supply with mercury.

Resources:

Shopping for a Better World: A Quick & Easy Guide to Socially Responsible Shopping by Rosalyn Will et al. Council on Economic Priorities. (800) U-CAN-HELP

Shopping for a Better Environment: A Brand Name Guide to Environmentally Responsible Shopping by Laurence Tasaday. Simon & Schuster.

Clean Environment Starts at Home: Guide to Non-Toxic & Environmentally Safe Household Cleaning by Annie Berthold-Bond. Ceres Press.

*Whole Earth Ecolog: Tools and Ideas for Earth-Conscious
    Living,* J. Baldwin, ed. Harmony Books.
Ecosource Catalogue: Products for a: Safer; Cleaner World
    (800) 688-8345.

5. Conserving Resources

*Request an energy and water audit from your utility
Insulate and weatherstrip your home*

Energy efficiency is the largest and most under utilized energy resource available. Since 1979, the US has derived one hundred times more energy from efficiency improvements than from all supply additions combined.*

Reliance on fossil fuel resources causes wars and major worldwide environmental damage to our atmosphere, forests and oceans.

☐ I've installed the new energy-saving low wattage light bulbs.
☐ When I purchase appliances, my key consideration is energy efficiency.
☐ I heat water or generate electricity with solar energy.
☐ I turn lights and appliances off when I leave the room.
☐ I have an insulating blanket for my hot-water heater.
☐ I've planted a shade tree next to my home for natural cooling.
☐ I sweep my driveway instead of washing it down with water.
☐ The plants I cultivate include native or drought-tolerant plants and/or drip irrigation.
☐ I do not use chemical fertilizers or pesticides on my plants.
☐ I will use water more than once; for instance, if I use a dishwasher, I will reuse the water for my garden, lawn, or plants.
☐ I repair all water leaks.
☐ I support education to reduce population pressures.

Resources:

*Amory Lovins, Rocky Mountain Institute, (303) 927-3851

Saving the Earth: A Citizen's Guide to Environmental Action by W. Steger and J. Bowermaster. Random House.

Spiritual Dimensions of Green Politics by Charlene Spretnak. Bear & Co.

Our Earth, Ourselves: Action-Oriented Guide to Help You Protect & Preserve Our Environment by Ruth Caplan et al. Bantam Books.

Save the Animals! 101 Easy Things You Can Do by Ingrid Newkirk. PETA, P.O. Box 42516, Washington, DC 20015.

Preserving the Environment Video Catalog, The Video Project, 5332 College Ave. #101, Oakland, CA 94618.

6. Personal Health

Balance in your life
Learn about nutrition, and exercise.
Study self-healing methods that work with the body's own healing abilities.

If we take responsibility for our own health, we will know what it means to take responsibility beyond ourselves.

☐ I will seek balance in my life.

☐ I am letting go of habitual old patterns that no longer serve me.

☐ I participate in activities that provide an outlet for releasing stress.

☐ I have received a muscle-relaxing massage in the last month.

☐ I exercise three times per week.

☐ I eat a wholefood, high-fibre vegetarian diet.

☐ I will seek holistic health choices rather than sole reliance upon treating symptoms through pharmaceutical drugs and surgery.

☐ I gather with close friends to assist in my personal development and growth.
☐ I laugh and smile more than I complain.

Resources:

Well Body, Well Earth: The Sierra Club Environmental Health Sourcebook by Mike Samuels and H. Bennett. Sierra Club.

Toward Balance: Psycho-Physical Integration & Vibrational Therapy by Rita McNamara. Samuel Weiser.

Perfect Health: Complete Mind/Body Guide by Deepak Chopra, M.D. Harmony Books.

Complete Guide to Health and Nutrition by Gary Null. Doubleday.

Survive This Day: A Doctor's Guide to These Critical Times (Magical Survival Kit III) by Bernard Jensen, N.D. Dr Bernard Jensen.

Bach Remedies: A Self-Help Guide. The Famous Drugless Therapeutic System and How to Use It by Leslie Kaslof. Keats Publishing.

It's Not What You Eat, But What Eats You: Beyond Diet – Energy Transformation for Better Health by Jack Schwarz. Celestial Arts.

How to Get Well by Paavo Airola. Health Plus.

7. Transportation

Walk or ride a bicycle
Ride the bus
Carpool

A large portion of our air pollution is generated by autos and trucks.

☐ I ride a bike as an alternative vehicle.
☐ I choose to walk when travelling a short distance.

- [ ] I ride a bus or train for longer trips.
- [ ] I carpool.
- [ ] I drive an energy-efficient car.
- [ ] I support the development of non-petroleum-based transportation vehicles.

Resources:

Bicycle Commuting Book: Using the Bike for Utility & Transportation by R. Van Der Plas. Bicycle Books.

8. Support Environmental Groups

Volunteer or join an environmental group

- [ ] I am a member of one [ ] two [ ] three or more [ ] environmental organizations.
- [ ] I volunteer for environmental projects.
- [ ] I help to raise funds for them.
- [ ] What on Earth can I do? Participate in Earth Day, April 22.

Resources:

Earth Island Institute, 300 Broadway #2B, San Francisco, CA 94133.

Environmental Defense Fund, 257 Park Ave. So., New York, NY 10010.

Greenpeace, 1436 U Street NW., Washington, DC 20009.

League of Conservation Voters, 2000 L St. NW., Washington, DC 20009.

Nature Conservancy, 1800 N. Kent St. #800, Arlington, VA 22209.

PETA (Ethical Treatment of Animals) P.O. Box 42516, Washington, DC 20015.

Sierra Club, 730 Polk Street, San Francisco, CA 94109.

World Wildlife Fund/Conserv. Fdn., 1250 24th St. NW., Washington, DC 20037.

Invest Yourself Catalogue, Commission on Voluntary
Service and Action, P.O. Box 117-34BB, New York, NY
10009.

Personal Action Guide for the Earth, Transmissions Project,
United Nations Environmental Programme, 730 Arizona
Ave. #329, Santa Monica, CA 90401.

*Environmental Vacations: Volunteer Projects to Save the
Planet* by Stephanie Ocko. John Muir Publications.

Environmental Opportunities, Box 969, Stowe, VT 05672
Tel: (802) 253-9336.

9. Trees, Trees, Trees

Plant trees
Support forestry groups

Forests clean our air, provide oxygen, moderate the
weather, make rain, filter and store water, protect our fish-
eries, refresh and restore our spirits. Forests shelter wildlife
and produce wood for our shelters. Every second, an area
the size of a football field is destroyed in our Earth's tropical
rainforests. Yet few realize that we are strip logging America's own temperate rainforests with equal speed and devastation.

☐ I have planted at least one tree in my life.
☐ I will plant a tree in the next year.
☐ I support forest conservation or tree planting organiza-
    tions.
☐ I sometimes hug a tree.

Resources:

American Forestry Association, Global Releaf (202)
    667-3300
Forests Forever (707) 462-2370
Rainforest Action Network (415) 398-4404

Tree People (818) 753-4600

The Simple Act of Planting a Tree: A Guide to Healing Your Neighborhood, Your City and Your World by Treepeople with A. and K. Lipkis. Jeremy P. Tarcher, Inc.

Dying Forests: A Crisis in Consciousness Which Means Transforming our Way of Life by J. Bochemuhl. Element Books.

Hugging Trees: The Story of the Chipco Movement by Thomas Weber. Penguin Classics.

The Rainforest Book by Natural Resources Defense Council. Living Planet Press.

Shading Our Cities: Resource Guide for Urban & Community Forests by G. Moll and S. Ebenreck, eds.

Trees: Guardians of the Earth by D. Nichol. Morningtown Press.

10. Socially Responsible Investing

Socially Responsible Investing (SRI) is investing in organizations with positive community and environmental policies. Most of us don't know how our money is used. (Teachers' pension funds presently invest in companies that are strip logging entire rainforests in Northern California and Asia.) Since business and government employee pension funds own substantial shares of the Fortune 500 corporations, they can influence policy decisions. Through pension fund coalitions like CERES,* we can exert our economic power to require that corporations not exploit life or degrade our environment.

☐ I make investment decisions based on the criteria above.
☐ I have a checking account, creditcard, and/or mutual fund with an SRI policy.
☐ I will call my bank, credit union, pension fund and/or stockbroker to determine investment policies which affect all of us.

Resources:

*Coalition for Environmentally Responsible Economics,
(617) 451-0927
Social Investment Forum, (617) 451-3252
*Investing with a Social Conscience: Everything You Need to
Know* by Elizabeth Judd. Pharos Books.
*Economics as if the Earth Really Mattered: A Catalyst
Guide to Socially Conscious Investing* by Susan
Meeker-Lowry. New Society Publishers.
The Next Economy by Paul Hawken. Ballantine Books.

11. Right Livelihood

*Choose work that is compatible with your own values and
vision*

Right livelihood means that your chosen vocation blends
with your own personal and planetary values.

- ☐ I work at an organization where ecological values are
  held in common.
- ☐ If a business or governmental organization performs
  actions which harm the quality of life on our planet, I
  seek changes in a positive way.
- ☐ If blocked in doing so, I look for other organizations
  which may offer a better opportunity.

Resources:

How Can I Help? Stories and Reflections on Service by Ram
Dass and Paul Gorman. Alfred A. Knopf.
*Do What You Love, the Money Will Follow: Discovering
Your Right Livelihood* by Marcia Sinetar. Paulist Press.
*Working From the Heart: For Those Who Hunger For
Meaning and Satisfaction in Their Work* by J. McMakin
and S. Dyer. Luramedia.

Good Works: A Guide to Careers in Social Change. Jessica Cowan, ed. Dembner.

Creative Work: Karma Yoga by E. B. Szekely. International Biogenic Soc.

Zen & the Art of Making a Living in the Post Modern World: Career Guide for Dharma Bums by Laurence G. Bolt. Lightning Press.

Holistic Health Careers by C. Grace. Grace and Goddess Unlimited.

Complete Guide to Environmental Careers by CEIP Fund. Island Press.

12. Life as Celebration

Feel free, loving, and alive

☐ Since our human personality generates the qualities of society, I am developing balance and harmony within myself so that I help to create it in the world.

☐ I participate in activities and celebrations that renew my connection with the Earth and nature's rhythms.

☐ I surround myself with art and music that inspires my spirit and creates feelings of love, inner peace, compassion and respect for all of life.

☐ I visualize the world becoming a garden planet with one people.

Resources:

Book *of Rituals* by Carol E. Parrish-Harra. International Biogenic Soc.

Feeding the Spirit: Recipes for Ritual by N. Cunningham. Resource Publications.

Four Sacred Seasons by G. de Purucker. Theosophical University Press.

New World Cycle of Celebrations Almanac & Calendar Journal. New World Celebrations.

Earthservice Datebook. Times, formats and techniques for
collective global meditations. More than twenty-five
diverse global organizations participated in this project so
that together we can realize the power of our UNITY and
generate a global spiritual awakening. (Available from:
Karuna Foundation, P.O. Box 11422, Berkeley, CA
94107. $9.95 plus $1.50 postage and handling.)

How did you score?

 01-20 It's a start.
 21-40 I can do better!
 41-60 Good work!
 61-80 Fantastic, there is hope.

If you would like a list of sources for Earthwise products
mentioned in the Twelve Steps, please send $1 and a SASE to
ECO-HOME, 4344 Russell Ave., Los Angeles, CA 90027.

Resources for Personal &
Planetary Transformation

'To know and not to act is to not yet know'

Organizations

Global Family
112 Jordan Ave
San Anselmo, CA 94960
Tel: (415) 453-7600

International peace network dedicated to supporting the shift in global consciousness from separation and fear to unity and love, so that each of us can more fully express our life purpose and join with others to co-create a world reunited as one living system. Contact them to start, or find out about connecting at the heart with a group in your area. Opportunities for personal/group empowerment, participation, networking, travel, etc.

Friends of Campaign for the Earth
or Global Connections Foundation
P.O. Box 170143
San Francisco, CA 94117

'Campaign for the Earth' is *not* an organization. *You* are it. Discover your role and take responsibility for co-creating planetary transformation and a sustainable future. Write for Campaign networking information.

The Hunger Project
P.O. Box 789
San Francisco, CA 94101

This is an international project for people committed to
ending world hunger.

It is not an organization in the usual sense. People do
not *join* the project, they *are* it. The holographic principles involved in this process are those necessary to make
the world work for everyone. There is a shift in the wind
… and an idea whose time has come. You are invited to
make it happen.

EarthNET
P.O. Box 330072
Kahului
Maui, HI 96733

A computer network to discover the most effective ways
for creative people and organizations to link up and co-
create new kinds of solutions to local and global problems. Get involved on your Apple Macintosh or IBM
compatible personal computer.

Transnational Network for
Appropriate/Alternative Technologies (Tranet)
P.O. Box 567
Rangeley, ME 04970
Tel: (202) 864-2252.

Acts as a resource centre for information and networking
on a broad range of alternative technologies. Quarterly
newsletter on holistic topics.

New Dimensions Radio
New Dimensions Foundation
P.O. Box 410510
San Francisco, CA 94141

Nationally syndicated public radio show interviews people on the leading edge of change and transformation.
One can order by mail taped interviews from their shows

with more than one thousand of the world's leading thinkers (including this author!). New Dimensions also publishes a bimonthly newsletter of inspired interviews, articles, radio listings, etc. Contact your local public radio station for times and dates of airplay in your area. For more information contact New Dimensions.

Earth Link Foundation
P.O. Box 677
Biron Bay, NSW 2481
Australia
Networks global linkage events throughout the international spiritual community via *Earth Link*, their 'journal for an awakening planet' which also contains articles of interest to those keeping up with the leading edge of change and transformation.

People for the Ethical Treatment of Animals
P.O. Box 42516
Washington, DC 20015
Tel: (301) 770-PETA
If you would like to see an end to the killing, torture, and exploitation of animals in medical experiments, product testing, and the fur, meat, and entertainment industries, you need to join PETA. Through their magazine you can become active to make a difference for the creatures. PETA educates, informs and invites participation so that when you speak up, or out, you can be honest and strong without being mean. The greatest meanness of all is what our silence does to perpetuate great evils. PETA's magazine is one of the best. Their catalogue offers products for cruelty-free living.

1% for Peace
P.O. Box 658
Ithaca, NY 14851
Tel: (607) 273-1919

Send for 'Action Kit'. A wonderful way for businesses to donate on percent of their profits for peace. Seeks to get one percent of the U.S. military budget allocated for peace promotion through understanding.

Working Assets
230 California Street
San Francisco, CA 94111

If you choose to phone long distance, travel, or access credit, a percentage of your bill is donated to environmental, human rights, peace, hunger and economic justice causes.

Long distance phone service (U.S. Sprint) – donates one percent of your net bill.

Travel – airline, rent-a-car, hotel bills – donates two percent.

Visa *or MasterCard* – donates $2 of first billing and 5¢ of each transaction.

National War Tax Resistance Coordinating Committee
P.O. Box 2236
East Patchogue, NY 11772

Your telephone tax pays for war. If you want to say 'no' to: U.S. military intervention, Euromissiles and nuclear weapons, you can refuse to pay the federal excise tax on your phone bill. Write for details.

National Housing Institute
439 Main Street
Orange, NJ 07050

Nonprofit organization dedicated to building a national network of tenant and housing groups and to providing resources and information which contribute to the creation and preservation of decent, affordable housing for all. *Shelterforce* is their magazine, a vehicle for the development of strategies for tenants and housing activists.

Eco-Home
4344 Russell Ave
Los Angeles, CA 90027
Tel: (213) 662-5207

A demonstration home for ecological living. Referral service to new home builders for ecological products and services. Educational and support network group. Networks information on: Energy-saving systems, water conservation, solar energy, recycling, Earth-friendly materials, etc. *Ecolution* newsletter. Write for membership details.

Self-Help Clearinghouse
St. Clare's-Riverside Medical Center
Denville, NJ 07834
Tel: (201) 625-7101

(They prefer that you phone rather than write.) Information/referral and consultation service. Provides current information and contacts for any self-help group that deals with your particular concern. Offers practical assistance in forming all kinds of groups. Their *Self-Help Sourcebook* ($10) also provides information and contacts for local self-help clearing houses, national toll-free numbers, ideas and resources for starting a group.

Global Cooperation for a Better World
Regional Coordinating Office
866 U.N. Plaza, Room 582
New York, NY 10017

'Global Visions' document contains input from sixty countries. Synthesizes the priorities, creative ideas, and actions of each which are deemed necessary to overcome the separations of world society and create unity and peace.

'Planetaly Connections' International Newspaper
Spiritual Growth Foundation
7 Green Oaks Road
Asheville, NC 28804

A forum for international 'good news' and new consciousness. This 'family' newspaper links up Light workers around the world who are dedicated to bringing the vision of a new era into reality. Its purpose is to create a synergistic Light Force in harmony with the Divine Plan, through new ways of communication, cooperation, consensus and balance, and working together toward planetary transformation.

Catalogues

Star Gate Awareness Resources
1374 Willamette
Eugene, OR 97401
Tel: (503) 342-8348

One of the best selections of quality 'New Age' genre videotapes available, (including subjects covered in this book: *Hopi Prayer for Peace, Moira Timms on Prophecy, Nostradamus, Sun Bear on Earth Changes, Edgar Cayce, Esoteric Egypt, Geomancy, Harmonic Convergence, Global Brain, Hundredth Monkey,* etc.) Any of the publications referenced in this Resource Section can also be ordered by mail.

The Educational Film & Video Project Catalog
Preserving the Environment Video Catalog
5332 College Ave. #101
Oakland, CA 94618
Tel: (415) 655-9050

Film and video programmes for a safe and sustainable world.

Guidebook for the '90s Catalogue
Knowledge Systems Inc.
7777 LW. Morris Street
Indianapolis, IN 46231
    Resources for effecting personal and social change.
    Books, organizations, and tapes to assist in making sense
    of the times, taking care of yourself, changing lifestyles,
    stress, learning to cooperate, etc.

Invest Yourself Catalogue
Commission on Voluntary Service and Action
P.O. Box 117-34BB
New York, NY 10009
    Listings of worldwide agencies whose areas of concern
    range from homelessness and battered women's rights to
    the rights of the disabled and environmental positions.

Choices & Connections
First Catalogue of the Global Family Human Potential
Resources ($14.95)
    Educational articles, products, services for personal, pro-
    fessional, organizational, and social development.

*Directory of Intentional Communities: A Guide to Coopera-
tive Living*
    Community listings, resources, and services. Foundation
    for Personal and Community Development, 105 Sun
    Street, Stelle, L 60919. $12

*Whole Earth Ecolog: Tools and Ideas for Earth-Conscious
    Living* . J. Baldwin, ed. Harmony Books.

*Essential Whole Earth Catalogue: Access to Tools and
Ideas* by Stewart Brand. Doubleday.

Peace Catalogue: Guidebook to a Positive Future, D.
    Sweeney, ed. Press for Peace.

Would the Buddha Wear a Walkman? Catalogue of Revolutionary Tools for Higher Consciousness by Dick Teresi and J. Hooper. Simon & Schuster.

Journal of Borderland Research
P.O. Box 429
Garberville, CA 95440
   A free-thought scientific forum of books, research files, and videos examining the living energy of the universe and probing beyond the known parameters of body, mind, and spirit.

PETA Catalogue for Cruelty-free Living
People for the Ethical Treatment of Animals
P.O. Box 42516
Washington, DC 20015
Tel: (301) 770-PETA
   The Catalogue offers products to raise consciousness about animals and their plight in our society, and helps consumers buy in ways that do not use, hurt, or exploit animals. The proceeds support PETA's innovative educational programmes.

Gifts of Service Catalog
Seva Foundation
108 Spring Lake Drive
Chelsea, MI 48118
Tel: (800) 223-SEVA
   'Seva' means 'service'. Board member Ram Dass has visited more than thirty-seven countries to raise funds, teaching service, compassion in action, and reminding us of our interconnectedness with each other as a global family. Those who love and respect Ram Dass and the service he renders will want to support his work and know about this Catalogue. Purchase of its handcrafted items is a way to support Seva's programmes of health care, eye surgery, trees, drinking water, food, shelter, and other assistance to the needy in India, Nepal and Central America.

Eco Source Catalogue
9051 Mill Station Road Bldg. #E
Sebastapol, CA 95472
Tel: (800) 688-8345

Environmentally sound products for Earth aware living:
Energy savings devices, alternative energy, recycling systems, health products, air/water purifiers, nontoxic
household supplies and building materials, recycled pa
per supplies, biodegradable pet and garden products.

Tools for Exploration
4286 Redwood Highway #C
San Rafael, CA 94903
Tel: (800) 456-9887

Emphasis on high tech devices for counteracting harmful
effects of electromagnetic energy fields and other unnatural interference with the body's systems. Also many other products, books and tapes for energy enhancement,
consciousness, and health.

Neo-Geo Playthings Catalogue
P.O. Box 66
Boulder Creek, CA 95006
Tel: (800) 372-3100

A collection of unique, handcrafted instruments that
teach us about subtle energies, the way consciousness
works, speed personal growth and increase energy. State
of the art advanced pyramid technology, crystal energy,
high tech pendulums, ionizers, energy amplifiers, etc.

Books to Build a New Society
New Society Educational Foundation
P.O. Box 582
Santa Cruz, CA 95061

Books to change the world! Worker-controlled publishing house committed to fundamental social change
through nonviolent action. They are connected to

the growing worldwide network of peace, feminist, environmental and human rights activists. These folks are founding members of Coop America, the national network of socially conscious businesses and consumers.

Books

Personal Empowerment

Nine Meditations for Personal & Planetary Peace by D. Marichild. Crossing Press.

Handbook to Higher Consciousness by Ken Keys. Love Line Books.

Love Yourself, Heal Your Life Workbook by Louise Hay. Hay House.

Love is Letting Go of Fear by Gerald Jampolsky. Celestial Arts.

Empowerment: The Art of Creating Your Life As You Want It by David Gershon and G. Straub. Dell.

Despair & Personal Power in the Nuclear Age by Joanna Macy. New Society Publishers.

Do It Yourself Psychotherapy Book by Martin Shepard. Second Chance/Permanent Press.

The Creative Problem Solver's Toolbox by Richard Fobes. Solutions Through Innovation, P.O. Box 1327, Corvallis, OR 97339. Tel. (503) 752-7264.

Earth Consciousness

Earthmind: Tuning in to Gaia Theory with New Age Methods for Saving Our Planet by Paul Devereaux and John Steele. Harper & Row.

Secrets of the Soil: New Age Resolutions for Restoring our Planet by Peter Tompkins and Christopher Bird. Harper & Row.

Sacred Places; How the Living Earth Seeks Our Friendship by James A. Swan. Bear & Co.

Connecting with Nature: Creating Moments Which Let the Earth Teach by Michael J. Cohen. World Peace University.

Gaia Peace Atlas: Survival to the Third Millennium by F. Barnaby. Doubleday.

Back to Basics

Bear Tribe's Self Reliance Book by Sun Bear & Wabun. Bear Tribe Publ.

Rural Living Handbook: An Illustrated Guide to Practical Country Skills, editors of Mother Earth News. Simon & Schuster.

The Self-Sufficient Gardener: Complete Guide to Growing & Preserving All Your Own Food by John Seymour. Doubleday.

Voluntary Simplicity by D. Elgin. William Morrow & Co.

Take Your Life Off Hold: Step by Step Guide for Simplifying Your Life by T. Dreier. Fulcrum, Inc.

Notes

Chapter 2: A Different Theory of Evolution

1. Lt. Col. Arthur E. Powell, *The Solar System* (London: Theosophical Publishing House, 1930), p. 89.

Chapter 3: Cosmic Cycles

1. Frank Waters, *The Book of the Hopi* (New York: Ballantine, 1966), p. 408.
2. H. B. Alexander, *Mythology of All Races* vol. XI: *Latin American Mythology* (Boston: Marshall Jones Co., 1932), p. 240.
3. Abé Charles Etienne Brasseur de Bourbourg, *Histoire des Nations Civilisées du Mexique et da l'Amérique Central* (Paris: A. Bertrand, 1857-1859), vol. 1, p. 53, and *Des Sources de l'Histoire Primitive du Mexique et l'Amérique Central* (Paris: A. Durand, 1864), p. 25.
4. Alexander von Humboldt, *Researches Concerning the Institutions and Monuments of the Ancient Inhabitants of America* (London: Longmans, 1814), vol. II, p. 16.
5. Roland B. Dixon, *Mythology of All Races* vol. IX: *Oceanic Mythology* (Boston: Marshall Jones Co., 1916), p. 178.
6. Foundation for the Study of Cycles, *Cycles* (January 1971).

7. Mircea Eliade, *Yoga, Immortality and Freedom*, 3rd ed., Bollingen Series LVI (Princeton: Princeton University, Press, 1973), p. 19.

Chapter 4: Astrological Cycles

1. Hans Augusto Rey, *Find the Constellations* (Boston: Houghton Mifflin, 1976); *Stars – A New Way to See Them* (Boston: Houghton Mifflin, 1967).
2. Bernard I. Pietsch, *Voices in Stone* (Santa Rosa, CA: Self-published, 1973), p. 46.
   Peter Lemesurier, *The Great Pyramid, Your Personal Guide* (Dorset, U.K.: Element Books, 1987), p. 228.
3. C. G. Jung, *Memories, Dreams, Reflections* (London: Collins and Routledge & Kegan Paul, 1969), p. 342.
4. 'A Cold Time to Switch Poles,' *New Scientist* (6 January 1972), p. 7.
5. J. J. Hurtak, *An Introduction to The Keys of Enoch* (Los Gatos, CA: Academy of Future Science, 1975), p. vii.

Chapter 5: Evolution/Involution

1. *The I Ching*, The Richard Wilhelm Translation rendered into English by Cary F. Baynes, 3rd ed., Bollingen Series XIX (Princeton: Princeton University Press, 1970), p. 97.
2. Ibid., p. 97
3. Ibid., p. 99
4. Ibid., pp. 99-100

Chapter 6: Pole Shift

1. Emil Sepic, *The Imminent Shift in the Earth's Axis* (Eureka, CA: Self-published, 1971), p. 14.
2. *New Scientist* (1 January 1972), p. 70.
3. *Nature* 253 (1975), pp. 705-6.
4. Immanuel Velikovsky, *Worlds in Collision* (New York: Dell, 1967), pp. 207-359.
5. 'Paleomagnetism,' *Science News* (July 1949).

6. 'The Mysterious Earth,' *Science Digest* (December 1960).

7. Sepic, *Imminent Shift, p. 15*

8. 'Sea Floor Spreading,' *Scientific American* (December 1968), p. 62.

9. 'Last day to be a second longer,' *Press Democrat* (31 December 1979).

10. Velikovsky, *Worlds in Collision*, pp. 207-359.

11. *Science News (5* January 1974), p. 5.

12. Patrician Barnes-Svarney, 'The Chronology of Planetary Bombardments,' *Astronomy* (July 1988), p. 28.

13. 'Tektites and Geomagnetic Reversals,' *Scientific American* (July 1967), p. 33.

14. Ibid.; and 'Magnetic Havoc,' *Time* (30 November 1970), p. 63.

15. *Science News* (3 March 1988), p. 203.

16. Watch Tower Bible & Tract Society, *Aid to Bible Understanding* (New York: Watch Tower Bible & Tract Soc., 1971), p. 1572.

17. *Scientific American* (December 1968), p. 62.

18. *Science News (14* August 1971), p. 108.

19. *Journal of the Philosophical Society of Great Britain XII (1910), p. 49.*

20. Archibald Geikie, *Textbook of Geology* (1882), p. 869. Quoted by Immanuel Velikovsky in *Earth in Upheavel* (New York: Dell, 1969) p. 51.

21. James Geikie, *Prehistoric Europe* (1881), p. 137. Quoted by Immanuel Velikovsky in *Earth in Upheavel* (New York: Dell, 1969) p. 27.

22. 'Archeological Investigation in Central Alaska,' *American Antiquity V* (1940), p. 305.

23. C. O. Dunbar, *Historical Geology* (New York: J. Wiley, 1969) p. 453.
    Also J. D. Dana, *Manual of Geology,* 4th ed. (New Haven: Connecticut Academy of Arts & Sciences, 1984), p. 983.

24. Herodotus, *The Histories* (Harmondsworth, U.K.: Penguin, 1985), Book Two, p. 186.

25. A. Pogo, *The Astronomical Ceiling Decoration in the Tomb of Senmut (XVIIth Dynasty)* (New York: Isis Press, 1930), p. 306.

26. Adolf Erman, *The Literature of the Ancient Egyptians* (London: Methuen, 1927), p. 309.
    H. O. Lange, *Magical Papyrus Harris* (Copenhagen: Det. Kgl. Danske Viden skabernes Selskab, 1927), p. 58.

27. Leket Midrash 2A, Perek 8, quoted from Rabbi Elieser, a contributor to the Talmud, quoted by Louis Ginzburg, *Legends of the Jews* VI (Philadelphia: Jewish Publication Society, 1925) p. 24.

28. Dunbar, *Historical Geology.*

29. 'The Earth's Magnetic Hiccup,' *Science News* (5 October 1985), p. 218.

30. Pietsch, *Voices in Stone*, p. 44.

31. Louis C. Kervran, *Biological Transmutations* (Binghamton, NY: Swan House, 1972).

32. Stephen Langdon, *Tammuz and Ishtar* (New York: A.M.S. Press, 1914), p. 97.

33. Franz Cumont, *Les Mysteres de Mithra,* 3rd ed. (1913), p. 111. (Reprinted as *The Mysteries of Mithra* (New York: Dover, 1956).

34. Velikovsky, *Worlds in Collision.*

35. Hurtak, *Introduction to Keys of Enoch, p.* 25.

36. Bruce Cathie, *The Energy Grid: Harmonic 695* (Albuquerque: America West Publications, 1990)

37. Gene Savoy, *The Child Christ Codex* (Reno, Nevada: International Community of Christ, 1973).

38. Sister Thedra, *The Sibors Portions,* Part 1 (Mt. Shasta, CA. Assn. of Samanda and Sanat Kumaran, 1972).

Chapter 8: The Great Pyramid

1. E. A. Wallis Budge, *The Egyptian Book of the Dead* (New York: Dover, 1967), p. 26.

2. John Greaves, *Pyramidographia* (London: J. Brindley, 1736).

3. Pietsch, *Voices in Stone,* p. 62.

4. Dave Davidson and H. Aldersmith, *The Great Pyramid, Its Divine Message* Vol. 1, (London: Williams & Northgate, 1925); and *The Judgment of the Nations in the Great Pyramid's Prophecy* (London: Covenant, 1940).

5. Lemesurier, *The Great Pyramid, Your Personal Guide*, p. 119.

6. Alain Danielon, *While the Gods Play* (Rochester: Inner Traditions, 1987), p. 266.

7. Eklal Kueshana, *The Ultimate Frontier* (Chicago: Stelle Group, 1963).
   Tom Valentine, 'The Pyramid Mystique,' *Newsreal* 5, September 1977, p. 53.

8. Pietsch, *Voices in Stone*, p. 36.

9. *C. G. Jung Speaking*, William McGuire and R. F. C. Hull, eds. (Princeton: Princeton University Press, 1977), p. 232.

10. Trevor Ravenscroft, *The Spear of Destiny* (New York: Putnam, 1973).

11. *The Christian Science Monitor* (6 July 1987).

12. Brad Steiger, A *Roadmap of Time* (New York: Prentice-Hall, 1975).

13. José Argüelles, *The Mayan Factor* (Santa Fe: Bear & Co., 1987), p. 143.

14. Earlyne Chaney, *Initiation in the Great Pyramid* (*Up*land, CA: Astara Library, 1987), pp. 42-47.
    Dean Hardy, Mary Hardy, Marjorie Killick, Kenneth Killick, *Pyramid Energy: The Philosophy of God, the Science of Man* (Clayton, GA: Cadake Industries & Copple House, 1987), p. 288.

15. William Kingsland, *The Great Pyramid in Fact and in Theory* (London: Rider, 1932).

16. Hardy and Killick, *Pyramid Energy*, p. x.

17. Louis Pauells and Jaques Bergier, *The Morning of the Magicians* (New York: Stein & Day, 1964).

18. Ibid.

19. Lawrence Blair, *Rhythms of Vision* (New York: Warner, 1975), p. 161.

20. Bill Schul and Ed Pettit, *The Secret of Pyramid Power* (New York: Fawcett, 1975), p. 209.
21. Alice Bailey, *The Externalization of the Hierarchy*, vol. IV: *Esoteric Healing* (New York: Lucis Publishing, 1980).
22. David Spangler, *Revelation: Birth of a New Age* (Elgin, IL: Lorian Press, 1981), p. 74.

Chapter 9: Meishu Sama and Johrei

1. Meishu Sama, *The Door of the Mystery Opened* (Los Angeles: World Messianity, 1963).
2. *Organic Gardening and Farming* (March 1973).
3. U.S. Dept. of Agriculture, *Report & Recommendations on Organic Farming* (Washington, D.C.: U.S. Dept. of Agriculture, 1 982).
   U.S. Dept. of State, *Global 2000/Global Futures* (Washington, D.C.: U.S. Dept. of State, 1981).
4. Moira Timms, *Natural Sources* (Millbrae, CA: Celestial Arts, 1978), p. 16.
5. Johrei Fellowship, 'Fragments From Teachings of Meishu-Sama', *Johrei Newsletter 16* (Los Angeles: Johrei Fellowship, 1990).

Chapter 10: The Hopi

1. Could there be a connection between the Hopi Fire clan and the ancient 'Sons of Fire'? In the commentary to the hermetic text 'The Virgin of the World' [G. R. S. Mead, *Thrice Greatest Hermes* vol. III (London: John M. Watkins, 1964), p. 81] we are told that in the original Golden Age the 'Sons of Fire' (of the race of Hermes) left the record of their wisdom engraved as symbols on 'stone,' in charge of others of the same race (but less evolved than themselves) before they ascended to heaven. Could this be why the Fire clan inherited the stone tablets of the life plan?
2. *Science News* (3 July 1970).
3. Indian Law Resource Center, *Report to the Hopi*

Kikmongwis and Other Traditional Hopi Leaders on the Continuing Threat to Hopi Land and Sovereignty vols. I and II (Washington, D.C.: Indian Law Resource Center, 1979).

4. Hardy and Killick, *Pyramid Energy, p.* 176.

Chapter 11: Edgar Cayce

1. Node 45 of the Becker-Hagens grid schematic. *Pursuit* Vol. 17: No. 2 (Little Silver, NJ: Journal of the Society for the Investigation of the Unexplained, 1984), p. 72.
2. *Geotimes* (October 1979), p. 24.
3. St. *Louis Globe-Democrat (5* June 1959).
4. Mr Scallion's publication, *The Earth Changes Report, is* available from Matrix Institute, RR1, Box 391, Westmoreland, NH 03467.
   A newsletter also monitoring prophecy is *Coming Changes,* 937 St. Mary's Street, De Pere, WI 54115.

Chapter 12: The Bible

1. Michael Baigent et al. *The Dead Sea Scrolls Deception* (New York: Summit Books, 1990).
2. Adolf Erman, *The Literature of the Ancient Egyptians* (London: Methuen, 1927), p. 309.
   H. O. Lange, *Magical Papyrus Harris, p. 58.*
3. Franz Xavier Kugler, 'Babylonische Zeitordnung,' *Sternkunde und Sterndienst in Bable* vol. 11 (Munster, Germany: Aschendorff, 1909), p. 114.
4. Editorial, *San Francisco Chronicle (22* February 1976).
5. *Press Democrat (14* November 1976).
6. Examples of such electrically charged winds are the khamsin, sirocco, sharav, zonda, foehn, chinook, mistral, Santa Ana, etc.

Chapter 13: Babylonian Prophecy

1. Mircea Eliade, *The Myth of the Eternal Return,* Bollingen Series XLVI (New York: Pantheon Books, 1954), p. 122.
2. G. R. S. Mead, *Thrice Great Hermes* vol. II, (London: John M. Watkins,1964), p. 200.
3. Eliade, *Myth of the Eternal Return,* p. 14.
4. Stephen Herbert Langdon, *The Mythology of All Races* vol V, (New York: Archaeological Institute of America, 1931).
5. William Safire, 'Desecration Just Another Crime by Hussein in World War 2.5,' *Eugene Register Guard* (12 October 1990).
6. *Newsweek* (8 January 1991), p. 21.
7. 'Happy Birthday to Me,' *Time* (21 May 1990).
8. Nostradamus wrote his prophecies around 1550 A.D. – thirty years before Shakespeare set pen to paper. Understanding Elizabethan English can be tedious and difficult. Therefore, the reader should be aware of the difficulties in translating archaic French axioms and idioms as well as the language mutations that have occurred over the centuries. Translations used were primarily from:

   Edgar Leoni, *Nostradamus and His Prophecies* (New York: Bell Publ. Col, 1982);
   Henry C. Roberts, *Complete Prophecies of Nostradamus* (New York: Nostradamus Inc., 1969).

9. Newsweek (8 January 1991), p. 21.
10. Richard Hinckley Allen, *Star Names and Their Meanings* (New York: G. E. Stechert Publ., 1899), p. 303.
11. Eliade, *Myth,* p. 15.
12. The Islamic exclamation 'Allaho Akbar' is usually understood as 'God is Great'. According to Sufi Ahmed Murad Christi, Samuel L. Lewis, its true meaning is 'Peace is Power'. The Murshid, whom I knew briefly before his passing, was recognized by eight different

Sufi brotherhoods; he was confirmed as a Zen Master, a Hasidic rabbi, a Yoga master, and a teacher of Christian scriptures. The following words about 'Allaho Akbar' are from his work *The Jerusalem Trilogy: Song of the Prophets* (Novato, CA: Prophecy Pressworks, 1975), p. 283:

'The greatest teaching I have ever learned was that 'Allaho Akbar' means 'peace is power', not 'God is great' (great in relation to what?), but PEACE IS POWER. Not force, but peace. Not 'peace with justice'. Not peace with, but Peace ... Peace is the removal of all things that disturb ... You see the whole Oneness, you don't have any ill-feeling about another because you see essentially the other as also from God.'

Chapter 14: Astrological Predictions

1. Christopher Hedlund, 'The Pursuit of Possibilities – the 1990s & the Uranus-Neptune Conjunction,' *Magical Blend* 23 (July 1989), p. 22ff.

Chapter 15: Maya Prophecy

1. Michael D. Coe, *The Maya* (New York: Praeger, 1966), p. 18.
2. Carolyn Hutt, *The Maya* (Virginia Beach, VA: ARE Press, 1972), p. 19.
3. José Argüelles, *The Mayan Factor* (Santa Fe: Bear & Co., 1987); *Surfers of the Zuvuya* (Santa Fe: Bear & Co., 1989).
   Barbara Hand Clow, *Heart of the Christos* (Santa Fe: Bear & Co., 1989).
   Hunbatz Men, *Secrets of Mayan Science/Religion* (Santa Fe: Bear & Co., 1990).
   Tony Shearer, *Lord of the Dawn* (Happy Camp, CA: Naturegraph, 1971).

Frank Waters, *Mexico Mystique* (Chicago: Swallow Press, 1975).

4. Argüelles, *Mayan Factor, p. 206.*

5. 'The Chronology of Planetary Bombardments,' *Astronomy (July 1988),* p. 27

6. Peter Tompkins, *Mysteries of the Mexican Pyramids* (New York: Harper & Row, 1975), pp. 301-302. 7. Tompkins, op. cit., p. 303, attributes this quote to FrankWaters. The quote is found in Waters's *Mexico Mystique,* p. 302, but is by Roberta S. Sklower, who contributed the Appendix.

8. Shearer, *Lord of the Dawn,* p. 71.

9. C. A. Burland and Werner Forman, *Feathered serpent) Smoking Mirror* (New York: Putnam, 1975), p. 45.

10. Herbert J. Spinden, *A Study of Maya Art* (New York: Dover, 1975), p. 221.

11. *Anales de Cuauhtitlan,* trans. Robert Bierholst, in *Four Masterworks of American Indian Literature* (New York: Farrar, Strauss & Giroux, 1974), pp. 24-26.

12. Nigel Davis, *The Toltecs* (Norman, OK: University of Oklahoma Press, 1977), pp. 24-51, describes the various meanings of this name. Cited in David Carrasco, *Quetzalcoatl and the Irony of Empire* (Chicago: University of Chicago Press, 1982).

13. Carrasco, *Quetzalcoatl,* p. 65.

14. Oral E. Scott, *The Stars in Myth and Fact* (Caldwell, ID: Caxton Printing Ltd., 1942), p. 322.

15. Men, *Secrets, p. 89* (I have not been able to verify that Berossus said the fish men he described [in several *Fragments of Berossus]* were actually Maya.)

16. Charles Gallenkamp, *Maya* (New York: Pyramid Books, 1962), p. 110.

17. Burland and Forman, *Feathered Serpent, p. 43.*

18. Carrasco, *Quetzalcoatl.*

19. Gallenkamp, *Maya, p. 20.*

20. Ibid., p. 150.

21. Octavio Paz, *Conjunctions and Dysfunctions* (New York: Viking, 1974), p. 10.

22. Men, *Secrets, p.* 29.
23. Hurtak, *Keys of Enoch, p.* 210.
24. R. O. Becker, MD, *Cross Currents: The Promise of Electromedicine, the Perils of Electro Pollution* (Los Angeles: Tarcher, St. Martin's, 1990), p. 238.
25. Mircea Eliade, *Yoga, Immortality and Freedom* (Princeton: Princeton University Press, 1969), p. 271.
26. Moira Timms, *The Raising of the Djed* (book in progress).

Chapter 16: 'Our' Prophecy

1. 'Interview,' Welcome *to Planet Earth* (Spring 1987), p. 31.
2. Hunbatz Men, *Secrets of Maya Science/Religion,* p. 84.
3. Robert P. Kirshner, 'Supernova, Death of a Star,' *National Geographic* May, 1988, p. 647.
4. Donald Goldsmith, *Supernova!* (New York: St. Martin's Press, 1989), p. 135.
5. Kirshner, 'Supernova, Death of a Star,' p. 635.
6. Ibid., p. 635, and Goldsmith, *Supernova!*
7. Heinrich Conrad Khunrath, *Amphitheatrum sapientia aeternae solius verae, Christiano-Kabalisticum, divino-magicum … Tertriunum,* Catholicon (Germany, Hanau: 1604), p. 197.
8. Violet Staub de Laszlo, ed., *Basic Writings of C. G. Jung* (New York: Modern Library, 1959), p. 65.
9. Ibid., p. 66.
10. Stan Woolsey and Tom Weaver, 'The Great Supernova of 1987,' *Scientific American* (August, 1989), p. 32.
11. Jose Arguelles, *Mayan Factor, p.* 115.
12. Staub de Laszlo, *Jung, p.* 61.
13. Richard H. Allen, *Star Names and Their Meanings* (New York: G. E. Stechert, 1899), p. 300.
14. Staub de Laszlo, *Jung,* pp. 65-66.
15. Raymond Mardyks, 'Starchart,' *Meditation* (Summer 1987), p. 14.
16. Available from The Planting Stick Project, Route 9, Box 78, Santa Fe, NM 87505.

17. Matrix Software, 315 Marion Avenue, Big Rapids, MI 49307.
18. C. G. Jung, *Collected Works* Bollingen Series (Princeton. Princeton University Press, 1956-72), vol. VI, ch. V, p. 3.
19. Hurtak, *Keys of Enoch*, p. 556.

Illustration and Photo Credits

p.13 Reprinted by permission: Chicago Tribune Media Services.
p.17 Moira Timms
p.23 University of Chicago Press
p.76 Reprinted with permission from *Nature* (5/3/60), Macmillan Magazines Limited
p.85 Moira Timms
p.87 Public domain – printed in cooperation with the National Oceanic and Atmospheric Administration
p.111 Moira Timms
p.116 Copyright British Museum
p.122 Moira Timms
p.123 Moira Timms – adapted from 1800's archeological graphic
p.125 M. Duke Lanfre, Pyramid Products, Manhattan Beach, California
p.130 Dean Price
p.139 Reprinted by permission of Ray Tobe
p.144 Moira Timms
p.151 Hopi Shield Symbol – Moira Timms
Petroglyph – Public domain
p.170 Moira Timms
p.184 Moira Timms
p.186 Moira Timms
p.202 Joel Brodsky
p.204 Reprinted by permission of American Friends Service Committee, Pacific Mountain Region
p.246 Copyright 1993 by Hansen Planetarium, Salt Lake City, Utah, with all rights reserved, printed by permission.
p.270 Moira Timms
p.283 Moira Timms

All other illustrations are in the public domain.

Index